CW01308198

The Handy Half-Hour

John Beresford

ISBN: 9798361407583

CONTENTS

Background

In the summer of 2012 I was in a bind. My first novel, War of Nutrition, had been published in February and here I was four months further on with no more idea of what I wanted to write next than I'd had on the day I wrote the final word of that story. Then, out of a clear blue sky, inspiration struck. That summer day had turned out to be the most glorious of the year so far in Manchester. Determined to make the most of it, my daughter Natalie & I took a lunchtime walk in the park, during which she gave me a progress update on her art challenge: Paint 100 pictures in 100 days. For inspiration, she'd been using a set of short prompts, garnered from online sources. The rule was she could spend only 30 minutes on each piece of art.

The more we talked about how important it is to "keep your hand in" with artistic endeavour, flex the creative muscles, and not worry too much about the quality of the output (at least initially) but instead concentrate on getting it done and trying new things, the more the parallels with writing became obvious.

Despite noodling around with an idea for a new novel over the previous few months, I hadn't done anything that could be called Serious Writing since finishing War. With time taken up chasing an agent, looking for a traditional publication route, rewriting, repeating the search for an agent, deciding to self-publish, and finally following through on that, I'd lost a scary total of four years. Even at my less-than-snail's writing pace I could have had half a novel done in that time (or so I thought back then).

We're always being told to "write every day" and "write the first draft from the heart" and so on. I knew that with a little discipline, I could easily use those couple of hours every day in front of a computer that belonged totally to me. It's an ideal time to write.

Most days, I'm up before 5.30am. I know, I know, it's crazy, but it's been happening for so long now it feels normal. I think it was sometime in 2010 when we first began waking up stupidly early. We decided we may as well get up and enjoy a pot of coffee before going to work. Two mugs each, sat in front of our computers catching up with the previous 12 hours emails, facebook updates, tweets (for Nikki – I've never been able to "do" Twitter for longer than five minutes at a stretch, and have no interest in actually posting anything there) and news feeds. I can't remember when this flipped, from something we did because we happened to be awake early into The Daily Routine, but it wasn't long. It's a self-fulfilling routine too, because getting up at stupid o'clock also means you're ready for bed at stupid o'clock. And going to bed at stupid o'clock means you've had enough sleep so that you wake up at stupid o'clock. And so it goes.

But emails and facebook don't take two hours. Even when you add in the washing up (usually while the coffee is grinding and brewing); still not two hours. So what am I doing between the last email and going to work? I just know you're way ahead of me. Spider Solitaire. What can I say, it's an addiction.

A writing challenge was just what I needed to fill that early morning hour, and "reboot" my writing. First cup of coffee to wake up while I'm emailing and facebooking, and then SECOND cup of coffee to accompany the new writing. That was the plan. Pick the next prompt from the list, and off we go. So my next task was to find those prompts.

As Nat predicted, it didn't take much searching to come up with a set of themes. To this day I still don't know whether it was the best list, or even a good list. I'm not even sure I'd be able to recognise a "good" list. But it is A list, and perhaps more importantly it became THE list, because the point of the exercise was to try new things, not spend hours searching for a list I felt comfortable with. A degree of discomfort is probably a Good Thing. I didn't know either, at that stage, if I'd be able to come up with anything remotely interesting for each theme. It was a shot in the dark, but all the more exciting for that.

Method

In Nat's case, she allowed herself 30 minutes painting time. I didn't ask her how much thought went into each piece, or if that thinking time was included in the 30 minutes, but for the writing challenge I decided I would allow myself up to 10 minutes to think about the topic, but without writing anything down in terms of notes, plot, etc. Then once I had an idea how I intended to interpret the theme, I'd set a 30-minute reminder and write until it went off. I expected there to be a high proportion of unfinished pieces, but hoped I'd also craft some good ones – maybe even the odd scene I could use in a novel, or the germ of an idea for a short story. I decided also not to restrict myself to narrative fiction. If the theme suggests a poem then I would rhyme for 30 minutes; if I was inspired to write an opinion piece or a memoir, I'd do that instead.

Rules

- No editing.
  The pieces are presented exactly as they were when finished, with no editing or polishing. This goes against the grain for me, big time, but I think it's important both for me and for you, dear reader, to see what can be achieved with a first draft, and, at the same time, how it could be improved with a few changes to word choice or a little less repetition.
- Max 30 minutes
- … but I allowed myself to stop earlier than that, if

> I thought the piece had reached a sensible conclusion (or, even better, a decent cliffhanger – *evil laugh*).

Themes

The list of topics I used is basically the Table of Contents. In this anthology I've given each piece its own chapter, to make them easier to find. To be entirely accurate the list is represented by those chapters beginning "Day n…" – there's a few "wash-up" chapters at the end.

Each piece is followed with some short "biographical" notes explaining where/how I got my inspiration, and offering any other background information I think may be of interest. In some cases I've also added editorial notes to explore where I think the piece could be improved, and how.

Beyond saying where she found them, the owner of the site where I found them didn't link the source, so I haven't. The list is not copyright, but it has been used for inspiration by many people. In my case, the posts inspired by these themes are whatever I came up with on the day – poems, short stories, random thoughts or just regular blog entries if, for example, the topic triggered a memory. My source mentioned that she had used the themes to create a novel outline for NaNoWriMo, and reckoned it was surprisingly easy to do so, using each as the basis for a scene. OK, I'm not THAT ambitious! Besides, I already have more novel ideas than I'll ever be able to write!

The one hundred days began on July 28, 2012 with an appropriately named theme…

Day 1: Introductions

"Hello. I'm Nigel."

"Steven."

"Good to meet you."

"Is it?"

"I'm sorry?"

"Is it? Is it good to meet me?"

"Well... yes. It's always good to meet new people. Isn't it."

"Not in my experience. Not always."

"Well no, I suppose not. But you can't go around introducing yourself with 'Hi, I'm Steven. Dreadful to meet you' – can you?"

"More's the pity."

"And anyway, you don't know, do you, at the beginning, whether it's going to be good or not–"

"I'm beginning to get an idea."

"–so it's better to err on the side of expecting it to be good and then revising your opinion down later–"

"In the light of evidence."

"Exactly – rather than starting off thinking the worst, by which time it'll be too late to feel better about the encounter."

"Because you'll have pissed the person off so much they'll have left?"

"Well, I, I don't know about that. I don't usually give up that easily."

"So I've noticed."

“I like to give everyone a fair chance–”

“Big of you.”

“–often people are a bit uptight meeting someone new. It’s a British thing. Supposed to be. Although I’m British, and–”

“You’re not.”

“No, I am. My parents–”

“No, I mean, you’re not uptight. Obviously.”

“Oh! No. I mean yes. I’m not.”

“So, how do you know her. Are you a writer too?”

“Me? No! Well, not professionally. I dabble. The odd poem for someone who’s leaving from the office, that kind of thing.”

“What do you do? In that office?”

“Sales. Telephone sales.”

“Ah.”

“Don’t get the wrong idea! We don’t do cold calling.”

“Glad to hear it. I might have had to kill you.”

“Ha! No. No, we met when she was just starting out. Well, I say met. We were both writing for the same firm, but it was all online. This is the first time I’ve actually seen her in the flesh.”

“So you are a writer? The sales is just a day job.”

“Yes, but–”

“No buts. Do you write?”

“Well, yes. But–”

“No buts! If you write, you’re a writer.”

“You must be a writer too then. Only other writers talk

like that. Or..."

"Or?"

"You could be a coach. Tutor. Mentor. That kind of thing. Woo-woo happiness guru, helping people get in touch with their inner genius."

"Woo-woo?"

"You know. Mystical magical shit. Meaningless meanderings to mess with your mentality."

"Alliteration's bad form for a writer."

"I'm not writing at the moment."

"Had a bad experience with mentors?"

"Not especially."

"But not good."

"No."

"Probably haven't found the right one."

"You're sounding more like a writing coach every minute. What do you do?"

"I attend a lot of book launches."

"No, come on. Seriously."

"I'm her agent."

"Aaah!"

"Don't."

"Don't what?"

"Don't say what you were going to say. Ask what you were going to ask."

"How do you know what I was going to say."

"I'm psychic."

"Rubbish!"

"Well, OK. Not psychic. But I may as well be. You get enough experience–"

"So what was I going to say?"

"You were going to ask if I could take a look at your manuscript. You've been writing it for years. No-one has ever read it, not even your wife. Not even your closest friend. It's a masterpiece. It's what the publishing world has been waiting for. You're a genius. All it takes is for someone – some ONE person – to believe in you. Give you the break you've always dreamed of. Everything else will follow. Chat shows. Movie rights. You'll be set up for life and the whole world will buy your book and wonder at the awesome prose, the deep insights, the almost biblical

[These two characters meet again at the very end of the writing challenge – on Day 100 in "Endings"]

Author's Notes

Firstly, and obviously, this is the first piece, the first time I'd written "to a timer", and so the story had not reached any kind of natural break-point when that timer went off. As you'll discover, I got better at this as the challenge progressed, and fairly quickly too though I say so myself.

One of the great joys of writing is having the freedom to write characters who say and do exactly what you would like to say or do in the same situation, if only you could free yourself from the shackles of propriety and good manners. Or to explore the darker side of human emotions. I take a small step in that direction here, with an agent who doesn't care what his companion thinks. He just goes ahead and says what's on his mind in the shortest, most succinct, and most direct way. Some readers will find him objectionable – he could be the basis of a character you love to hate, and the possibilities for dark humour are endless – others will think it's refreshing. But I did enjoy the opportunity to take my more acerbic side out for a spin.

Finally, we're always being told to "write what you know", and one aspect of this is drawing on any and all past experiences when writing. I do know a writer who fits this tale, we did work together (or at least, concurrently) for an online writing site, and I did attend one of her book launches. That's where the similarities with real life end though. The launch event simply provided the inspiration for the story. I didn't meet anyone like this there (actually don't remember speaking with anyone apart from her the whole time I was there – I don't do well in large groups of strangers), and I certainly didn't behave like either of these characters! No, honestly.

Day 2: Complicated

Now don't you go gettin' the wrong idea. I ain't tryin' to make it complicated. Heck if it wuz complicated I couldn't tell ya nothin' about it. Fact is I'm just sittin' out here on ma stoop tryin' to get ma head around it maself.

Mr. Murphy always used to say "Kid, it don't take no genius to complicate things. The genius is in keepin' it simple. So you're about as close as a body can git round here to fuckin' Einstein."

Well that made me colour up to the top of ma head. I could feel it, heatin' right on up there. I mean, far as I know, Einstein was a guy. I ain't gonna fuck no guy. But Mr Murphy was right about one thing. I AM good at keepin' it simple. The boys down at the store tried to tell me one time there ain't no black or white, only shades of grey. I just laughed at 'em. I mean there wuz a black stallion sat right outside in the street for starters. And what about them black folk? They's black all right. And we's white. And you never see no-one any shade of grey. Well, 'cept Mrs Hardcastle some times, when she can't get her breath, but she ain't always grey. Far as I can see, there's a lot of things that are black or white. Them boys just don't know what the heck they're talking about.

I know they wuz probably only tryin' to trick me. I don't mind. I just ignored 'em. It's simpler that way. I like things when they's simple.

Which is why I'm in a bit of a pickle right now. I mean, it's not exactly complicated – you know? But it sure as heck ain't simple neither. I wish Mr Murphy was still here. He could do that thing where he just sat down and got on with his whittlin' while I talked it through and you know what? Half the time he never had to say nothing. I wouldn't be much more'n half way through the telling about... well... whatever it was, and the answer would just pop right into ma head. All by itself! How do you like that? Nothing complicated about that.

I tried it with Ma once, but it weren't no good. She jes wouldn't keep still. And talk! Lord sakes. She's ma Ma an' all but I sure wish she'd hush up now and then. Seems like every word I said she'd come out with a question. Now THAT was complicated. I never had no time to think at all. I'd no sooner answered one question and then picked up ma threads and got the next word out, and there she'd be with another dang question. I said "Ma. Hush your mouth and jes listen to whut I'm sayin'." But she wouldn't. That wuz the first time I ever realised what the boys at the store mean when they say "Yadda Yadda Yadda." Fact I should call Ma that, I reckon. Yadda.

Anyways where was I? Yeah, so I ain't got no Mr Murphy to sit quiet, and Ma ain't no good for the job, so who'm'a gonna ask? An' I wuz thinkin' and thinkin' when little Martha May came walking by, smiles at me from under them pretty yeller curls of hers and sez "Hey there Joe, watcha doin'?"

Well THAT made me colour up too, same as when Mr Murphy said that about, you know, doin' it with Einstein. Only this time I sure wasn't thinkin' about doin' it with Einstein. No sir. But you can guess I WAS thinkin' about doin' it. An' then I got to thinkin' about talkin' it through with Martha May and that made me colour up some more.

And Martha May's sayin' "Jesus Joseph, what did I say? You're as red as a beet!" and I'm jes startin' to realise that this ain't the kind of thing I can talk out loud about... with a girl.

Author's Notes

Second piece, and already I've succeeded in giving this piece a more natural conclusion. Well, no, I agree it doesn't really qualify as a "conclusion" – the story hasn't ended. It's barely even begun. We still don't know what Joseph is talking or thinking about. I didn't know, when I wrote it. I set off with the idea of a slightly simple "country bumpkin" who was easily confused and embarrassed, and let the story take me wherever it wanted to go. But at least it doesn't end mid-sentence.

He has a distinct accent, or "voice." Accents are tricky, in writing. The most common comment about their use is "a little goes a long way." Setting up the accent in a reader's mind can be done with minimal use of accented words, and since it's way harder to read than regular prose, overdoing it risks turning the reader off, or exhausting their reading muscle. I probably overdid it here, even though I tried to restrict myself to a few words and phrases. Ma, instead of my. Jes, instead of just. And a smattering of contractions, especially those dropped gs from "-ing" words. Remember, none of these pieces are edited, so if this appeared in any "real" work, I would've read over it several times and probably cut some of the accent parts. Once Joe's voice is established, there's no need to flog that (there) horse, you hear?

Day 3: Making History

If anything, the heat was even more oppressive than usual as Joan rode the elevator to the 11th floor. The acrid stench of the morning rush assailed her nostrils, made even more pungent by the welcome waft of fresh air as she joined the flood of grey-suited humanity jostling through the halls. By contrast the hushed sighing of moving paper from one desk to another in Room 1101 calmed her flailing heartbeat as she took her place in the parade of identical desks.

She took a sip of coffee and turned to her screen.

"I don't know how you can drink that stuff."

Her coworker, Stanley Brown, gave a disgusted grimace from his desk facing hers.

"When you remember what it should be like."

"I'm not sure I can remember."

"Damned sure I do. And I wouldn't touch that crap."

"Don't let the supervisor hear you. That's a definite demerit and loss of privileges for a week. At best."

"Privileges? Ha! That's a joke."

"Don't start. I have way too much to do to get into another 'bash the party' argument with you."

Stanley shrugged and turned back to his screen, his expression unreadable. Joan flipped over to a long list of documents, the top five of which flashed urgently. She opened the first: "Letters from a Wounded Hero", and scanned the first few pages, taking regular sips from her coffee and scribbling notes on a yellow pad in front of her in a neat, rounded hand. After a few minutes, she dropped her pen and sat back, blowing out the breath she had been holding and running her hands through her hair.

"Problem?"

"I can't see what's wrong with this but there has to be something. It was at the top of my list."

"What is it?"

"Letters from a Wounded Hero."

"Who's the hero?"

"Edward MacArthur."

"Hmm. Pretty sure it was his nephew who was recently charged with Conduct Unbecoming. My guess? MacArthur isn't a hero any more."

"I should check with Winston."

Stanley shuffled uncomfortably in his seat and looked quickly at the nearest workers. All appeared engrossed in their screens.

"Winston... isn't here today."

"Well I can't leave this until tomorrow. It's at the top of my freakin' list!"

"He won't be in tomorrow either."

Author's Notes

Reading the topic "prompt" for this day instantly made me think about the most famous fictional work in which history is literally "made" – recreated and rewritten in the everyday work at the Ministry of Truth.

Armed with this idea, I had a lot of fun dropping hints of Nineteen Eighty-Four into the piece: Room 1101 in place of Room 101, mention of "the party," and finally and most obviously referring to the protagonist's colleague "Winston" who is inexplicably now absent.

Notes from an Editor's perspective

This piece includes the first example I've so far noticed, of the repeated use of words in close proximity. It's something that happens to me a lot while drafting, but which I make every effort to cut during editing. I even went as far as to write a macro for MS Word that would highlight words, other than common ones like conjunctions, if they'd been used close together.

The sections I'm talking about here are "…she took her place…" and shortly after "She took a sip…" In the first editing pass, I would have removed one or other "took".

Day 4: Rivalry

The sun ached brightly from a sky of smudged aquamarine. Under its hazy canopy, a panoply of village dwellers gathered excitedly on the green, jostling for the best view. A buzz of expectation hovered above the crowd, drowning out the buzz of local bees who bumbled away at several flowers, industriously gathering their nectar and pollen. Toddlers sucked on silencing lollipops and ice creams, while mothers wiped up drips or tried unsuccessfully to keep two eyes on their three children. The men, those not involved in the contest, gathered at each side of the green, pints or bottles in one hand, cameras or mobile phones in the other. Some loudly exchanged memories of previous encounters, others gesticulated at the opposition, laughing.

In the centre of the green two small groups assembled – one to the North end; the other to the South. In a nod to traditional stereotypes, those standing at the North were dressed in flannel trousers, white open-necked shirts and flat caps, while those on the opposite side wore top hats and tails, or bowlers with pin-striped jackets.

But although the top half of their garb may have been frivolous, their bottom halves meant business. To a man they wore heavy walking boots, or steel toe-capped safety boots with deep treads. There was not a pair of trainers to be seen.

As the village clock began to chime the hour, the adjudicator stepped from the throng carrying a white cloth.

"Take your positions," he intoned.

North and South picked up their ends of a rope which had been lying unremarked across the green. The teams adjusted their relative positions, testing their grips and their footings as the centre marker swayed back and forth above the grass.

"Take the strain!"

The teams pulled slowly, taking up the tension of the rope. The adjudicator eyed the centre marker and turned to South.

"Give way, six inches," he shouted, raising his voice above the increased hubbub from the audience and lifting his white flag. As the marker approached centre a hush fell over the crowd.

"PULL!"

Boots bit deep into turf and muscles bulged as the teams tugged hard on the rope. North took an early advantage, leaning back strongly and with each team member having secured a solid stance. South, by contrast, having had to swap their anchor at the last moment for a relatively new member of the team, were initially caught off-guard. The centre marker swayed dangerously close to the line before the others recovered their balance and gained a holding position.

Beads of sweat stood out on the faces and arms of every man; sinews taut with effort and each face gurning with determination that the marker should, or should not, move any further.

Author's Notes

Once again my reaction to the "prompt" was near-instantaneous. This was written on the last day of July. I can't remember if we had visited the local festival that year, or if this was simply drawn from memories of earlier years, but back then the "tug-of-war" was still a traditional part of midsummer on the local green, and formed an obvious focus for a piece about rivalry.

Another of the huge joys of writing for me is the chance for observation, and to translate those mental notes into prose that is hopefully both entertaining and recognisable, in an original way. Writers never really "switch off" their writerly eye. It's a well-known axiom that you should never tell a writer something you don't want to appear in one of their stories.

Day 5: Unbreakable

Every action has an equal and opposite reaction. Newton's Third Law of Motion has been embedded in the zeitgeist for almost as long as it has been codified. If you give a push, the world pushes back, only in most cases it's not as poetic as that.

Investigations and theorising at the quantum level have revealed a fascinating possibility that the Third Law has an echo right down at the lowest level humans can, at the moment, conceive. The level of subatomic particles, where infinitesimally small lumps of matter "carry" waves of force and where intuition must be left at the door. Because these particles behave in ways that sound crazy, and you almost have to make yourself crazy to think about them, or to undertake research into them.

One such craziness is the Heisenberg Uncertainty Principle, whereby an experimenter can never be certain of the position and momentum of a particle until it is measured, but the act of measuring it changes its state.

However crazy the lay person might believe the theories of quantum mechanics to be, the fact of their correctness is proved every day by people all over the world. People who use computers. Because computers rely on microprocessors and at their most fundamental level microprocessors are just enormous collections of microminiaturised transistors, and transistors were conceived on the back of quantum theory. A real-life creation based on some extremely counter-intuitive physics, that works perfectly everywhere, every day.

But quantum physics isn't done messing with our heads yet. Not by a long way. In recent times physicists have begun expounding the theory of quantum entanglement and have had some success proving this theory both mathematically and in the real world. This is the echo of

Newton I referred to earlier. A condition where an action on one subatomic particle (for instance, inducing it to spin clockwise) will cause an equal and opposite reaction in a particle with which it has been "entangled" (it will begin to spin anticlockwise).

Thus the rudimentary building blocks of a communication mechanism are established at the quantum level. If you can introduce a signal at one end (clockwise spin) and measure the result of that signal at the other end (anticlockwise spin) then you have effectively transmitted one "bit" of information from one particle to the next. And where you have bits, you can have bytes and thenceforth characters, music and high definition video streams.

But the theory doesn't stop at merely transmitted the information. Quantum entangled particles will interact over any distance. A particle in the next room will still be affected by the spinning of its partner. So will a particle in the next galaxy. They are bound by an unbreakable bond that transcends distance. This has staggering implications for communication in space and brings to life the Star Trek concept of "sub-space communication". Life imitating art, once again.

As if it were possible, recently the theory has developed in an even more bizarre direction. Mathematically it appears the particles remain entangled even after they cease to exist. And before they existed in the first place. I warned you this stuff was counter-intuitive. But these early theories begin to shine the first faint light on the potential for real-life time travel. That's a huge leap from where we are today. But transistors were a huge leap in their day, yet here I am typing this on a computer, just as you are reading it on one. Truth, it seems, really is stranger than fiction.

Author's Notes

My first opportunity to switch from a work of fiction to one of opinion. A blog entry, effectively.

I spent an entire career (38 years, in case you were wondering) in the computing industry. The science of that has always fascinated me, but as with many sciences you don't have to entirely understand it to be able to use it. That's never really been enough for me though. I crave the "understanding" part. And I don't restrict myself to computing science. Physics, especially the very small (quantum mechanics) and the very large (cosmology), holds me firmly in its spell, though my paltry intellect has often failed to achieve anything approaching "understanding" at either end of that compelling spectrum.

Nevertheless, my first thought when I read the topic was a recollection of an article I had recently read on the strange – unbreakable – bond between entangled particles, so the stage, as they say, was easily set for that day's attempt at writing.

Day 6: Obsession

My obsession is brown. It is cold, crisp and brittle. It emerges from the frigid dark, enveloped in purple and gold, and lies heavy in my hand, filled with possibilities. It is versatile, my obsession. Almost limitless in its ambition, from unremarkable beginnings it has stretched and grown into its power until it spans the globe. It is not only my obsession but that of countless millions of others. A popular obsession. An addiction.

It sweats, my obsession. Slicked with greasy exudation it threatens to slip through my fingers and be lost. My attempts to hold it tighter only risk more rapid and certain loss. I'm reminded of the old saying: if you love something, let it go. If it comes back to you, it's yours. If it doesn't, then it never was. So I let go, and my obsession stays, even though I am not holding it. They knew what they were talking about, those old soothsayers.

My obsession is white, too. A rainbow obsession. As many colours as there are races of human beings, and like those races each wears its tribal costume. Gaudy in their splendour. Eye catching. Irresistible. From childish designs – broad strokes of garish colour – to mature and sophisticated black and gold, or silver, the costumes are as varied as an individual's taste and yet at the same time familiar. Instantly recognisable. Comforting.

It softens, my obsession. Lying there where I have released it. Its previous brittleness forgotten, its coldness discarded. As if it has forgiven me my possessiveness. As if it has decided to love me in return; to yield to my most secret desire. I might even be its obsession as it is mine. I catch the merest hint of its delicate perfume as it lies there, softening further in the early evening sun. I decide to undress it.

My obsession is uncovered. Its costume lies discarded on

the floor. Partly unfolded, partly ripped off in my haste to enjoy the sight of it naked. Now defenceless, I can melt its heart. The heavenly smell of its body fills my senses as I move closer. My tongue caresses its smooth skin, tasting the first sweetness, feeling the silky surface slip beneath me as my mouth closes on its flesh. Nibbling. Biting.

It melts, my obsession. Its fluid slips into my mouth, its flavour filling my mind with longing. It slides down my throat, coating my taste buds and tonsils with warm, languid waves of liquid satisfaction. With superhuman self-control I resist the urge to bite down on the last dwindling lump as it dissolves into a whispered sweet nothing.

Author's Notes

I've been a chocoholic for as long as I can remember. My Dad worked Saturdays and one of my earliest, and strongest childhood memories is how he would always bring home bars of chocolate for all of us. They were consumed almost as soon as they were handed over (or snatched from his briefcase while he was hanging up his coat). There was no concept of "saving some for later" in our house. If you hadn't scoffed the lot before the end of whatever TV show we were watching, someone would inevitably say "don't you want yours?" Little wonder I have a weight problem with that kind of exposure to the wrong kind of neuro-linguistic programming from an early age.

So my choice of "obsession" was almost a knee-jerk reaction. More of a challenge was the question of how to present it in an interesting and original way. I'm familiar with the comedic trope "I'd rather give up sex than chocolate", so I decided to make the sensual, almost sexual nature of the indulgence the focus for the piece.

Day 7: Eternity

There's a trick to eternity. It has to do with elephants. Elephants and sand.

"How do you eat an elephant?" management trainees are sometimes asked. You can't, they say (unless they've ever, at any time in their lives, been on the Internet); it's too big. Well, says the tutor smugly, with your puny management trainee brains, YOU might think it's impossible. It's not impossible. It's just big. And big things are easy to cope with – if you break them down. So the traditional answer to the question "how do you eat an elephant?" is: one bite at a time.

So with unassailable logic, I submit that eternity is not impossibly big to deal with either. You just have to consider it one moment at a time. You might not know that a moment does, in fact, have a defined length. It's a medieval time unit approximately equal to one and one-half minutes. 90 seconds.

There's a lot of 90 secondses in eternity. Work it out. If eternity goes on forever, then how many moments – how many chunks of 90 seconds – are then in it? Well, as Aleksandr might say: Simples! An infinite number. Aha! you're thinking. Your logic is not as unassailable as you think. If there's an infinite number of moments in eternity then no matter how quickly you consider each one, you'll never get to the end. You could spend an eternity considering eternity's moments, and you'd still have an eternity left to go.

That's the thing with infinite numbers. They're not finite.

OK so maybe the elephant approach was a bad start. How about the sand thing? I'm guessing William Blake wasn't as much of a physicist as Lewis Carroll was a mathematician, but even so he may have been onto something when he wrote

To see a world in a grain of sand,
And a heaven in a wild flower,
Hold infinity in the palm of your hand,
And eternity in an hour.

Easy. All we have to do is find that world in a grain of sand and we'll not only have compressed eternity into an hour, but we might even have regained our lost innocence. The poetry of innocents may be dashed by the literal interpretations of physicists, but there is also poetry to be found in physics. Not to mention beauty. Don't believe me? Take a look at some fractal pictures. Consider the movements of planets, and the unexpected behaviours of subatomic particles (see "Unbreakable" – Day 5's challenge entry).

So is there a world in a grain of sand? Since that grain is the result of millennia of erosion by the sea, wind and ice, you could say it's undergone a world of change. If it were then to find itself on the seabed, compressed by millions of tons of similar grains resting on top of it, and subjected to the elevated temperatures closer to the Earth's core, it may very well find itself transmuted into sandstone. Yet more millennia later, after being erupted from the seabed through tectonic action, that same sandstone may well be mined and quarried, possibly built into a drystone wall; a church; a crofter's cottage, or even transported through prehistoric means and carved into one of the sarsens of Stonehenge. There may not be a world in the sandstone, but there is a world of possibility.

Each of these writing challenges only lasts half an hour. That's (*calculates*) 20 moments. If, by any stretch of the imagination, I've managed to emulate Blake, then I may have succeeded in holding half of eternity in that half-hour. Unfortunately, according to the mathematics of infinite numbers, that means I still have all of it left to deal with.

Author's Notes

As any writer will tell you, drafting and editing are two different activities. They use different "brains". So when you're writing, it's important – for speed, flow, narrative voice, and such considerations – to resist the urge to edit what you're writing as you go. Come back and do that later. Plus, the whole point of this challenge was to discover how much I could write in those 30 minutes, and experiment with a variety of styles and topics.

So I'll admit I broke, or at least bent, those rules for this piece. I'm familiar with Blake's poem, naturally, but not so confident of my recall that I could drop it into the piece without checking its accuracy. I used a bit of my "allowed research" time to investigate the strict definition of "a moment", because the idea to use it in this way occurred to me before I started, but the use of Blake only popped into my mind while writing, so…

In the interests of full disclosure I should add that – for this anthology – I've also subjected it to a minor edit, to explain the use of "Aleksandr" for audiences unfamiliar with the Meerkat commercials.

Day 8: Gateway

Like a floodtide of human flotsam, sunlight winking off their bright costumes and beribboned staffs and instruments like the sparkling shimmer of a white-water gully, the inhabitants of Berikatanya moved slowly across the valley floor.

Dotted over the hillside, a few shepherds, children, and those too old to partake in the ceremony watched the colourful parade as it approached Stanring – the sacred circle – and formed itself slowly into a larger circle around the standing stones of the ancient ceremonial site.

To the East of the circle a small group of hooded figures, obviously more plainly dressed than the rest of the throng, took up position atop an outcrop of black rock. As the bowl of the Stanring filled, they began chanting quietly. At first their voices seemed to vie with each other, but as they settled into their rhythm it became clear that there were three distinct chants, each different and yet each designed to complement and augment the others so that the whole acquired a cadence that echoed across the valley, reaching even the furthest shepherd on the most distant hilltop.

To the West, where the late afternoon sun was about to fall below the craggy top of the nearest bluff, stood four individuals whose costume outdid even the most garish of the company. Red, blue, ochre and white, each of the four wore robes of a single colour, yet which flashed and glimmered in the last rays of sunlight as if arcane patterns of many complementary hues were woven into the cloth. Each carried a staff fully twice as long as they were tall, and the staffs were topped by enormous gemstones mirroring the colours of their garb.

These four took positions in front of four great stones on the West side and as they moved into place an expectant hush fell over the rest of the congregation. The music of the hooded chanters appeared to swell as the hubbub of conversation died away, and the four mages raised their staffs. Each began to intone song of his or her own, threading their incantations amid the three continuing melodies of the chantsmen while the reddening orb of the sun fell ever closer to the bare rock surrounding the valley.

As the lower edge of the sun crossed the boundary and the light around the circle began to fade, the mages' singing took on a more urgent note, increasing in pace and acquiring a more complex rhythm. In the centre of the circle, a faint mist began to gather, slowly resolving itself into a spinning disc of greyness through which those standing on the hillside could clearly see stars.

Author's Notes

This is probably one of my first attempts – if not the first attempt – at fleshing out my ideas for my fantasy series The Berikatanyan Chronicles. At this stage, even the series name was not settled, although the name of the planet where most of the action takes place clearly was. Originally this scene, or its eventual successor, was intended to form part of the prologue. I eventually abandoned the idea of a prologue and moved the full description of this ceremony onto a piece of parchment that the hero discovers later in the story.

Notes from an Editor's perspective

As you know, apart from minor contextual changes to make these pieces work in this format, all of the text is first draft, without any editing. Even a cursory glance (or attention paid to Word's, or GoogleDocs', grammar checker) will reveal a missing "a" from the penultimate paragraph, which should be "...began to intone a song…" I've been told I write a pretty clean draft, but slips like this still… slip through.

Day 9: Death

Of all the things Not Spoken Of In Polite Company – I'm sure you can think of your own list – death will probably come at or close to the top of most people's. It's often been remarked that, despite it being one of the only certainties in life, one of the few things that everyone will experience, it's also one of the least discussed. And, in most cases, one of the least prepared for.

At least 50% of people die without making a will. They leave it up to the laws of whichever country they die in, to decide how to distribute their worldly goods when they're gone. True, there are those who may think they don't have a lot to leave, but at a time when home ownership – and the value of those homes – remains high, it's not unusual even for ordinary people to leave at least one item worth around a quarter of a million pounds. I don't know about you, but I don't want incompetent jobsworths in whatever government department deals with inheritance to decide on my behalf where that kind of money goes. It's even more complicated for those who don't have children, or for those who have more than one and one or more of them don't get on. Why would anyone want to saddle their offspring or near relatives with potentially years of bitter feuding, arguing and recrimination, for the sake of not taking an hour out to write down a simple will?

I guess it's looked upon as one of those things you'll get around to at some stage. But death doesn't always wait on your convenience. It doesn't sit there waiting for you to sign on the bottom line before swinging its scythe of doom. Without wanting to sound morbid (and there I go, veering off in the direction of the apology for even daring to consider it), death can come at any time. It'll surprise you. We don't all get to enjoy the "luxury" of a ripe old age, dying in our own beds surrounded by family and friends.

The various manners and means of alternative death (by which I mean the alternatives to that "ideal" death referred to above) are each in their own right awkward to even think about let alone talk about. Death through short- or long-term illness (cancer, heart disease, lung disease) is familiar to everyone, and a fairly high proportion of people will also know someone (or know someone who knows someone) who has died through sudden means of one sort or another. A fall, a car accident, or drowning for instance. And yet the single most often uttered comment, when faced with another's grief is: "I just didn't know what to say."

If death itself is rarely spoken of, its companion topic – Life After Death – is an even more unwelcome subject for polite after-dinner conversation. We generally steer clear of this. Perhaps because we think it's a foregone conclusion that it either does, or does not, exist, or through imagined embarrassment at admitting to either of those views. True, some people hold their view so closely to their hearts that no debate is possible, and any attempt is met with frosty disdain or heated argument, either of which is more than enough excuse to avoid the subject altogether. There are some opinions, it seems, that it is uncomfortable to air in the aforementioned polite company.

Which probably explains why those with strongly held beliefs tend to seek out like-minded individuals and even invent societies, closed clubs, cliques and organisations, along with their attendant rules, regulations and rituals. Some of these are so successful that they "enjoy" over a billion members and find themselves among the richest organisations the world has ever seen. But even then death is rarely discussed until it happens.

Another unwanted side effect of discussing the afterlife is ridicule. Even a slight misjudgement of audience on those rare occasions where one might feel moved to – for example – explain that one has proof of life after death will be met with ridicule more often than with interest, in a proportion of roughly 20 to 1. Little wonder the subject is avoided most of the time. Ridicule is, of course, often a smoke screen for embarrassment on the part of those doing the ridiculing. Are they embarrassed by their own beliefs – or lack of them? Or simply embarrassed to be associated with, or even listen to, someone who holds such beliefs. Does believing in life after death make you "other?" Or does the line become stepped over only when you decide to voice your beliefs. Or, indeed, write about them? Are such things so personal, so intimate, that they fall into the category of things that it is forbidden to speak of, along with what kind of sex you had last night and how often, or whether you secretly enjoy listening to Jimmy Carr.

Author's Notes

Not a lot more to say about what is essentially an opinion piece, except for the technicals:

Notes from an Editor's perspective

Another common "drafting tic", as I mentioned earlier, is the repetition of words in close proximity. It's as if an echo of the word sticks in your brain while drafting, tapping you on the shoulder and saying "hey, buddy, you've used me once, why not go for the double?" What leaps out at me now, with my editor's brain engaged, is the proximity of "...one of the least prepared for." with "At least 50%..." It grates on my senses. It would be one of the first casualties of an early editing pass, to rephrase one or other of those and avoid the repetition of "least".

Day 10: Opportunities

Opportunity is a master of disguise. Sometimes it is so good that you don't see it at all. At other times you might see it, but believe it to be a threat, to be avoided at all costs. Often its disguise is polarised so that from the present it doesn't look anything like an opportunity but once you've sailed past it and are looking at it from the future (so that the opportunity is in the past) you can see that it really was an opportunity after all.

Many years ago my father was offered a dream job in another city. I was around 9 at the time and I remember my parents going for a long walk to discuss whether or not he should take it. Because I had no alternative child care they took me along with them. I didn't understand much of the conversation and in any case a lot of it was spoken in hushed voices, but I heard enough to know that if the decision went in favour of this new job it would involve moving. At that age, it was an uncomfortable prospect for me. I've never really been one to embrace change wholeheartedly. My instinct is more usually to avoid it in case it turns out badly rather than welcome it on the chance that it will be great. I'm like that now, with all my adult armour and skills. At age 9 I was just a bundle of no.

As the conversation came to a conclusion I remember them asking my opinion. It's only really come home to me now, at this point of writing about it and with both of them now dead, what a wonderful gesture that was. To give a 9-year-old a vote on such a momentous family decision. I do hope my opinion wasn't the only thing that swayed them because I voted no, and the decision in the end was no, so my father continued in his unsatisfying job working for a boss who rarely showed his appreciation for the diamond he had working for him.

For years my recollection of this incident was that the city in question was Birmingham. However in conversation with my Mum many years ago it turned out I had misremembered. The opportunity was to move to Manchester. Thinking about that now still gives me a small tingle. How I – effectively – turned down the chance to move to Manchester at age 9, but that fate had very definitely inked Manchester into my future and was determined to get me here one way or another. I didn't get the grades I needed for my first choice of University course, but the college who had the best offer of an alternative place was in... Manchester. So I moved here anyway when I was 18, and moved back again permanently when I was 44. What would have been different had I come when I first had the chance? Who knows. That's the thing with opportunity: it's often a one-time, one-way offer.

In 1984 or 85, when I was enjoying one of the most successful points of my career – responsible for 19 people all engaged in the world-wide 3rd line support of what was widely regarded as one of the best (if not the best) operating systems in the world – I was offered a job working as a full-time contracted employee for a major government department, doing a similar role but with a much larger team, and on "the other side of the fence" – working for a customer. The job would have entailed moving to Lytham St Annes (or commuting from Staffordshire – not THAT much of a stretch). Once again my aversion to change kicked in. I'd just bought a house that I was very pleased with, felt on top of my game in my job – I knew everyone; how to get the job done quickly and efficiently; I was good at it and yet it still challenged me daily – so as far as I could see the only incentive to move was the offer of more money.

That wasn't enough to persuade me. I turned them down.

A colleague of mine, who ran the support team for a different part of the OS, took up the offer in my stead. Months later it was reported that she had been spotted as a rising star and had quickly been promoted into a much more senior role with an even more advanced salary. Moreover she was working 14 hour days, 6 days a week, and even at that senior level the job still paid overtime. We huddled round our calculators and worked out that she must have been pulling in around a quarter of a million pounds a year – back in 1985!!

I think it would be true to say she made the most of her opportunity. I think it may also be true to say she made the most of MY opportunity. Would I have been able to follow it up to the same degree? Who knows. We had similar skills, but if I'm honest where we differed was in outlook. I've never been driven by money (even though I've been fortunate to only rarely be "short" of it), but I don't think I'd have been prepared to put in those kind of hours no matter what the remuneration.

So in conclusion – opportunities come and go. Sometimes – as in the example of moving to Manchester – they will revisit you at a later date, wearing a different disguise. But in the same way that opportunities can appear to be threats, their dark siblings threats are also able to dress themselves up as opportunities. Knowing how to tell them apart is a clever trick that no-one can pull off 100% of the time. But while you're trying desperately to avoid jumping from the frying pan into the fire, it's worth bearing in mind that what looks like a fire may in fact be the magic alchemist's forge that can transform you from base metal into gold.

Author's Notes

In a comment on the original piece, I reflected on how surprising and rewarding it was when these daily prompts dredged up memories in the way this one did. There's a lot of "memoir" in this piece sitting, I hope comfortably, alongside the op ed bits giving my take on opportunity and threat. If I were to comment now on the "writerly" aspect of both this and the previous entry, I'd be tempted to observe how much easier it is to write a longer piece filled with opinion compared with a piece of fiction where, by definition, there has to be more "invention." Maybe I should have been a journalist ;o)

Day 11: 33%

I was a zero. For the longest time I expected to stay that way forever. Oh, no, don't get me wrong. I wasn't comfortable like that. It's just... well... that's how it was. I wasn't part of anything. Or anyone. I had a routine, same as anyone I suppose. Sometimes I used to feel as if I was sitting outside of my life watching it going on around me but not really being a part of it, you know? When Ben came along I thought for the briefest instant that I had suddenly shot up to being a 50%. Then it dawned on me: I was really only 33%. There was another. A third. And it wouldn't be just the two of us any time soon. And, you know, I'm OK with that, really. I mean, 33% is better than 0%. Isn't it. Much better. Looking back, I didn't really like being a zero. I never let on, hardly even to myself, but it was lonely. The flat was cold when I got home (even in summer) and there never seemed much point cooking a proper meal just for me. Now I can really push the boat out. Three courses, wine, candles, the posh crockery. Everything. I mean, OK, there have been times when I've done all that and it's still been only me. Ben's had a last minute crisis or something, and hasn't been able to make it. But that's OK. I've learned to make things that will keep. Or that I can take for lunch the next day.

*

I was part of something, once. More than part. Half. I was half of something. I was 50% of a wonderful partnership that I thought would last forever. Wine and roses. Ha. Makes me heave now, just thinking about it. I found out, you see. Found out that my percentage isn't as big as I'd thought. Like a partner in some seedy deal where the pot is salami-sliced thinner than you'd been expecting. Wouldn't you feel cheated? Huh! Cheated. Now there's a word. A fitting word. I'm sure you can guess why, but I'm going to tell you anyway. I'm going to tell everybody. Why should he get away with it? Taking my lovely, expensive, safe, eternal 50% and replacing it with a tawdry, second-rate, tarnished 33%. I might as well have been left with nothing, because that's what I feel like. Nothing. And you know what makes me sick? Somewhere, out there, in some dirty little skank's cheap, stinking apartment, there's another 33%. And I don't want to know. I don't want to know what it looks like or where it lives or even that it EXISTS, but I can't UN-know it. That bastard did this to me. We can't go back. We can't ever go back to that warm place where there were two of us and we were equal. Now all I can think of is one of those ghastly pie-charts that he's always drawing for work, like some kind of God-awful Ban-the-Bomb sign or something, only it's my happiness that's been banished. Now I'll only ever be a third. The rest of it's been cut off and given to HER.

*

Dude! How's it hangin'? Me? Fine! On top of the world. Why wouldn't I be, with Jill at home and Chantelle on the side? Got my hands full there alright. I guess some folk would say I was part of a three-way – just one third of the piece – but you know what? I don't think like that. I like to look at the bigger picture, if you know what I mean. When I'm with Jill, I give it 100%. When I'm with Chantelle, she gets 100% of me too. So you see I'm a lucky guy. I don't have 33% – I have TWO HUNDRED PERCENT when you take it all into consideration. Yessir. Lookin' good. I mean sure, there's times when I have to let Chantelle down, and I feel bad about that, you know? She's done me meals three or four times now that I've had to duck out of. But she's cool with it. That's one thing I like about her – no histrionics. She never kicks off. Dude that chick is so laid back she can hardly stand up, if you know what I mean. No, sometimes I just have to be around for Jill. Now there's a woman who knows how to throw a tantrum. But listen, I've been keeping her sweet for years.

This time's no different. She'll calm down eventually. She's knows when she's onto a good thing: me! Anyway listen, I gotta go. Got my eye on that new piece over at Tawnee Miller's Bar & Grill. Whooo boy! She's one hot momma, and she's been givin' me the eye for the last coupla weeks. Some girls can just spot a good thing from a mile away, know what I mean?

Author's Notes

The leap from today's prompt of "33%" to the idea of a menage-a-trois was virtually instantaneous for me. What that says about the way my mind works it's probably best not to contemplate.

Writing that tangle from the perspectives of the three people involved – the grateful mistress who isn't really happy with the situation but knows it's better than what she had before; the damaged wife who really wants to (and ought to) leave, but probably won't; the annoying lothario who believes he deserves every good thing that comes his way, and still wants more – was a blast. I've met every one of those characters in real life, and I'm sure you have too. This set-up is so familiar from so many works of fiction (and with a wealth of real-life anecdotal evidence) that it almost wrote itself. The characters emerged fully realised as soon as I began writing them, but also gave great scope to dust them over with a salt-shaker full of originality.

Final note on the name of the Bar & Grill. It's funny what memories pop up while writing against the clock. When I reached that part of the narrative I needed a name for the place, and jumped at the chance to give a loving nod to one of my favourite places to eat in all the world: Jawny Baker's in Toronto.

Day 12: Dead Wrong

I've heard people talk about things "going round and round" in their head. I wish that was me. At least if something was going round and round there'd be some movement. I'd have chance to see it from other angles. Or at least watch its precession. As it is I'm stuck with just one thought. It's there all the time. Right there. In front of my mind. Wherever I look, it hangs there in the air in front of me. Whatever sounds I'm hearing, it's like they're just background noise. In my head is only my voice, saying that one thought over and over: It should have been me.

Warren wasn't supposed to be going into the office that morning. It was his turn to look after Dylan and Brigit. I was going in – different office; same building. In fact I had a bitch of a deadline and I'd already been up half the night preparing the presentation. We had clients lined up, the board, everything. I don't know what made me check my email before I set off. Normally I wouldn't have bothered. I didn't get to bed until almost 3am, and nothing much ever comes in after that, even in our business. But something told me I should give it one last check and sure enough, there's this new message, marked urgent, sent at 5:35am from Roger – our MD.

Presentation postponed – urgent family illness for one of our client's team – will advise new date soonest.

And that was it. I felt a bit let down to tell you the truth. I'd got myself all worked up for it. All psyched up and nowhere to go, that was how I put it to Warren when I walked back into the bedroom where he was engaging in a game of Voyage to the Bottom of The Bed with Dylan.

"Huh?" he mumbled from under the covers.

He poked his head out from the bottom left hand corner of the duvet, face all red from exerting himself under 15 togs.

"Nowhere to go?"

"Presentation's off."

He looked thoughtful.

"So you've nothing on today?"

"Well, no. No I guess not. Roger isn't gonna want me to get distracted with anything else, and there's nothing more to do on this account until we can get it in front of the customer."

"Would you mind if I went in then?"

"It's supposed to be your home day."

"I know, but there's a couple of things I could get on top of if I went in. I wouldn't have bothered if..."

"No, it's OK. You go. It'd be great to have an unexpected day with the kids. What do you say kids?"

Brigit had just appeared at the door, dragging her threadbare Snoopy.

"French Toast?"

Her sleepy crumpled face lit up.

"Yayy"

"Yayy," echoed Dylan from under our duvet.

Warren was already in the shower.

Later we all kissed him goodbye just like it was any other working day. I guess 3,000 or so other partners and children did the same. Those who were up so early.

I was putting the French toast pan in the sink when the phone rang. It was Michelle.

"Put the TV on. The news. Oh God."

I could hear her TV on in the background. It seemed

much louder than usual. I flipped our kitchen TV to the news channel. At first I couldn't make sense of what I was seeing. It was just a cloud of dust. I thought one of those terrorist mobs had gone through with their threat of exploding an Anthrax bomb or something. Then they reran the footage of the planes. The towers. Warren. I dropped the phone. And then I must have gone onto autopilot because suddenly I was scrabbling to pick it up again. To hang up from Michelle and call Warren's office. And I couldn't get through and couldn't get through and then I thought 'what if he's trying to call me?' and I hung up and waited.

And at that very moment, the second I hung up, the second tower came down and I knew. I knew he was in there. In his office on the 72nd floor, when it should have been me. I should have been there. But I was here and he was there. And he would never have been able to get out. Not from that. He was dead and it should have been me.

That's when it started. I don't know when it's going to end. If it ever ends. Even after so long. It's faded a little, but it's still there. It still feels wrong. Dead wrong.

Author's Notes

I don't know if there's much more to say about this. There are as many tales to tell about that day as there are people who died, or watched them die. One of those horrifying, historical landmark days on which everyone can remember what they were doing, and where they were doing it, when they first saw that news footage.

I visited Ground Zero in early 2006 when it was still just a hole in the ground surrounded by high wire fencing; photos and tributes to the dead pinned to every inch. Another memory that will always remain with me.

Day 13: Running Away

Moonlight poked a sharp silver lance between Doug's curtains as he lay, fully clothed, beneath his duvet. He checked the clock for the fourth time in the last five minutes. 1:23am. One of those special times that he often saw. Often wondered whether they had any hidden meaning. 1-2-3 was definitely the start of something. It was a sign.

Yet still he hesitated. The house wasn't entirely silent. The central heating, which had gone off more than an hour earlier, was still cooling down. Pipes clicking and clanking as they shrank back infinitesimally to their cold size, rubbing against flooring joists and skirting boards. Through his open door he could hear his father snoring from his parents' bedroom across the landing. Definitely asleep – but what about his mother? No light shone in, so she wasn't reading in bed, but was she asleep too? Or was his Dad's snoring keeping her awake like it often did?

He sat up and swung his legs over the edge of his bed, cringing at the old bedsprings as they complained at the movement. He reached under his bed to retrieve the backpack he'd been filling over the past few months. Socks added one by one so it looked as though the washing machine had eaten them. An old pair of jeans that his Mum had told him to throw out. T-shirts from the bottom of his drawer that he hadn't worn for ages and which wouldn't be missed. At least, not quickly enough for his plan to be discovered.

An owl hooted from the copse. Doug jumped at the sound, his bedsprings moaning again, loud in the quiet of the sleeping house. "Come on!" he told himself. "DO it!" He stood up slowly and crept to his door. With one last backward glance around the darkened room to check he hadn't forgotten anything important, he stepped onto the landing, remembering to avoid the loose floorboard right outside his bedroom door.

Hardly daring to breathe, Doug inched his way to the stairs. From the other room his father gave a loud snort, coughed, and turned over. Doug froze. Waited. In a few moments the snoring resumed, gentler this time. Doug started down into the hallway, the bright cold light of the full moon flooded through the staircase window, lighting his path. He shivered nervously. Despite months of planning and longing for the moment he could get away, now the time was really here he felt unexpectedly uncertain. Was he doing the right thing? What if he'd forgotten something really obvious? Could he have persuaded his parents if he'd tried harder? Argued more coherently?

No. He gripped the backpack harder, tightening his mental grip on his resolve at the same time. There was no other way. He'd debated it endlessly with himself and this was his only option. They would never really understand him. They never supported any of his choices – friends; hobbies; books. Especially books.

His mother:

"Got your head in a book again? You should be out in the sunshine."

His father:

"What are you reading NOW? You only just finished one yesterday. Why don't you go and kick a ball about with Jeff and Iswar like a normal kid?"

It was hopeless. Doug reached into his pocket, pulled out his keys. They jangled loudly. Why was everything so damn noisy? He turned the mortice lock slowly, letting the tumblers fall one at a time. He smiled at the memory of oiling the lock last weekend. His Dad, for once, had offered a word of praise.

"Oh, thanks for that Doug. I've been meaning to oil that lock for ages."

He slid the bunch of keys back into his jeans' pocket and slowly released the catch. A sudden gust of wind blew up a flurry of autumn leaves from the front garden, causing Doug to squint against the dust. A leaf fluttered unnoticed through the door and landed on the hall carpet. Doug stepped out into the chill night.

Author's Notes

Even knowing each of these pieces would only be 30 minutes long, there were many occasions where I still couldn't resist leaving a trail of seedcorn for where the story might go, were I to pick it up at a later date and run further with it. That's why the leaf flutters in. It will be a beacon of incongruity the next day, when Doug's parents wake up.

I have reused many of these pieces in my fantasy series. In the case of "Running Away", I put it to work in a collection of horror stories I'm working on, taking the idea of runaways in general, and Doug in particular, and giving it a chilling twist.

Day 14: Judgement

It was a perfect afternoon for walking. Sunny, but not too bright. Warm, but not too hot. A light breeze to freshen up a brow damp with exertion. The sky such a solid crystal blue that Reg thought if he reached up and struck it with his stick it would ring like an expensive wine glass.

Birdsong echoed from a nearby copse, filling the air with the sound Reg always associated with summer. With his boyhood spent walking in the woods and fields. A happy sound. He knew, vaguely, that it wasn't really happy. The birds sang aggressively, declaring their territories and defending them against all-comers. Reg understood that, deep down. Understood it, and was intimately familiar it. He'd spent most of his adult life defending territory of one sort or another. Had served time for it, in fact.

He never expected to get out of prison so soon, yet here he was out in the country air once more, his polished old oak staff in his hand, a stalk of long grass between his teeth, and a clear path before him. He smiled and stopped for a moment to take in the view. To his right, a meadow stretched gently down a slight incline to a large copse which nestled at the bottom of the valley. Beyond that the rest of the valley's secrets were hidden behind a curtain of summer haze. To his left a high stone wall curved away both in front and behind until it too disappeared from sight. The path on which he walked, dried by the sun, consisted of nothing more than dirt and small stones. It was edged with neatly cropped grasses and occasional wild flowers. Reg noticed with almost imperceptible surprise that none of the dust from the path had settled on his boots or trouser bottoms.

He exchanged his chewed grass stalk for a fresh one, adjusted his grip on the smooth wood of his walking staff, and resumed his trek beside the curve of the wall. He had just begun to wonder what, in this beautiful out-of-the-way place, would need such impenetrable protection as a twelve-foot wall, when a gate came into view around the bend. Fully half again as tall as the wall in which it was set, the gate was more ornate than anything Reg had ever seen. Filigree threads wrought of the finest gold and copper patterned the uprights and cross-pieces of the gate, which appeared themselves to be of gold. Each of its two halves vaulted up to an enormous golden crown set atop them both and which, although it must have been in two pieces to allow the gate to open, appeared to Reg to be whole.

The gate was closed. Beside it, an old man sat on a wooden arbour seat, his eyes closed and face turned to the sky, enjoying the warm afternoon sun. As Reg approached the man turned toward him and regarded him with piercing blue eyes.

Author's Notes

Shorter than average, in hindsight this piece contains a wealth of detailed description that I wouldn't normally expect in a "first draft". I would never have broken my rule and returned to edit the piece, so the only explanation is that I wrote with an editor's brain to start with, pausing to consider each word and phrase before committing it to the document and therefore achieving a much slower pace than usual.

The tale is informed by two memories. The more recent one is of a watercolour painting I used to have in my home, which I loved but no longer own (either the home or the painting). A simple rural scene of a path beside a stone wall, stretching down a rolling hillside with an idyllic view in the distance. I often stared at that painting, wondering where the path led, what was on the other side of the wall, and what the air smelt like on a balmy day in late summer.

The earlier memory is a cautionary horror story I read in my youth, of a soul who didn't yet realise he was dead, walking beside a wall that appeared heavenly but actually was only the devil's artifice, designed to trick the person into entering hell. This is pretty obviously the direction I intended to take this piece had I ever completed it, my first interpretation of the topic being a kind of Judgement Day rather than any other kind of judgement, and also hinting that the walker's eventual destination would depend on his own personal judgement of whether the walled, gated, and guarded place was where he should spend eternity.

Day 15: Seeking Solace

Sid shivered. Not from the cold. No. Even though it was late November and the night air was chilly right enough, his shiver came from the chill he felt inside. It was the kind of discomfort a man of conscience might experience when embarking on something... questionable.

Even so, the need drove him. The loneliness. He stood alone at the edge of the anonymous suburban car park staring up at the anonymous green door at the top of a rusting fire escape and shivered again, this time with resolve. He waited for a car to pass, briefly speared by its headlights like the archetypal rabbit, turned his raincoat collar up against the damp November mist, and crossed the road.

As he started up the steel stairs the driver of that car pushed past him, climbing quickly and confidently. Over his shoulder the man remarked snidely, "ey-up Granpa! You sure you're in the right place?" He reached the green door before Sid had attained the first landing, knocked, and was admitted.

Slightly short of breath after the climb, Sid stood in front of the door a few moments later. He hesitated, looking nervously around. Below him the almost-empty car park sat silent, cones of illuminated mist shining down from the sodium lamps. A dog barked in a nearby house. Sid knocked. A previously unremarked panel in the door opened to reveal a pair of heavily made-up deep blue eyes.

"Yes?"

"Is Winston in?"

The door opened, warmth washed over Sid's face, carrying the heavy scent of cheap perfume.

"Come in then dear, don't let all the heat out!"

He stepped slowly over the threshold, the blue-eyed woman closing the door behind him. Sid clutched his raincoat around his chest.

"Not been before, have you dear?" Blue Eyes asked. She smiled, revealing yellow teeth, but her eyes glistened like wet flint. "Can I take your coat?"

She held out her hand. Waited.

"Er... yes. Thank you," Sid mumbled, reluctantly undoing his raincoat and handing it over.

He looked furtively around the room. It was decorated simply, with a pale yellow blown-vinyl wallpaper which matched the deep gold of the shades on table- and standard-lamps set around the room, far enough apart to create pools of soft light. In the shadier spaces between the lights, overstuffed sofas and chairs had been laid out in niches and booths. In one corner three men sat together in arm chairs, sharing glasses of whisky and conversing in hushed tones, laughing occasionally. Two sofas facing each other held five other women whose make-up matched Blue Eyes'. In contrast to the men, the women were not talking. They looked bored. One of them flicked slowly through a copy of Heat magazine. One filed her nails. The others appeared each to be fascinated by separate areas of pattern in the vinyl wallpaper.

Along the short wall opposite the door a small bar had been installed. It was tended by a thin, balding man wearing thick glasses. He was reading a book. There was no sign of the car driver.

"See anything you like, dear?" asked Blue Eyes.

"I th-think I'd like a drink first," Sid whispered. He cleared his throat. "A relaxer."

Blue Eyes smiled again, the flintiness never leaving her eyes. "Of course dear. You can see where the bar is. Just let me know when you've made your mind up, or if there's anything... special... you need." She flashed him a knowing look and walked round behind the heavy mahogany desk that sat next to the door.

Author's Notes

I've never visited a brothel – no, that's not entirely accurate: I visited one, briefly, during a business trip to Athens (for my American readers I should probably make that "Athens, Greece") in the mid-90s with a colleague. One of the most uncomfortable experiences of my life and a tale for another time. Suffice to say we beat a hasty retreat without "enjoying" anything more than a small glass of the most expensive Coca-Cola in the world – so this piece is entirely a work of fiction and imagination. No judgement here – I understand why someone would choose to go (today's prompt was, after all, "seeking solace"), or why someone else might choose to work there – but it's definitely not my thing.

It is, however, informed by memories of conversations I've had over the years on the subject of brothels, and where they might be located. I have, allegedly, lived fairly close to two brothels in my life, albeit unwittingly. The description of this one, with its first floor location, rickety fire-escape access, and nearby car park, is based on one of those.

Day 16: Excuses

"So I hope you've all remembered that your homework assignments were due this morning?"

Miss Angela Demeanour regarded the class with a look that somehow managed to mix expectation with incipient and utter lack of hope. Silence remained unbroken across the jumble of desks. The thought crossed her mind that her career-defining experiment in reducing the regimentation of neat ranks of desks in order to free her students' creativity was proving less successful than she had hoped.

"Because I haven't had any in so far?"

Her gaze flicked from pupil to pupil until eventually she caught the eye of one.

"Tommy?"

"The dog ate it miss."

A fit of snorts and giggles twitched around the room. Miss Demeanour gave Tommy a hard stare.

"No, really Miss. He's only a puppy and–"

"Alison?"

Alison Grainger flushed beet red to the roots of her dyed blonde hair. Angela felt a pang of regret for picking on the girl so soon, but of all her students she had expected Alison to finish the assignment. She waited, determined not to cut short the painful pause.

"P-please Miss, I had to look after Rory last night and I didn't have time to finish it."

"Couldn't you have started it the day before?"

"I had to look after Rory then too."

"Or submitted an unfinished piece? You would have

earned some marks...?"

Alison's colour turned from beet to that of a sun-ripened tomato.

"I didn't really have time to start it, either."

"Uma?"

"Tommy's dog ate mine too Miss. I was working round at his house."

"Neil?"

"I left it in the pocket of my jeans miss, and my mum put it in the laundry."

"Adrienne?"

"I finished it, miss, but I left it on the bus."

"Casper?"

"Tommy's dog–"

"Oh please!" Angela interrupted. "You can't all have been working round at Tommy's."

"I wasn't miss!" Casper added quickly. "I called round for him this morning to walk to school and I had it in my hand. Steptoe ran out into the garden and snatched it. He'd chewed it all up before I could get it off him."

Miss Demeanour turned back to Tommy.

"You really ought to start feeding Steptoe something other than homework, Tommy." The class laughed. "It's not good for a growing puppy."

"Before we go on," she said, raising her voice and turning to face the whole class, "has anyone else's homework come to grief in the mouth of Tommy's dog?"

No-one answered. A few of the class shook their heads.

"Good. So. Catherine?"

"I left mine in the library miss."

"Well, go and get it now."

"Not the school library, miss. Central Library. I was looking something up."

"Germaine?"

"I lost the question miss, so I couldn't remember what to do."

"Andrew?"

"I finished it miss, but I left it in the kitchen and my baby sister threw up all over it."

"Morris?"

"Please miss, Tommy's dog–"

"Oh no! No, no, no! We've only just agreed that no-one – no-one ELSE's homework – was eaten by Tommy's puppy."

"But Miss he didn't eat it. He... um... poohed on it."

The class erupted with laughter.

"Quiet! Alright. Tommy, please make sure that from now on your puppy is shut away from any contact – ANY contact – with your, or your friends', homework, or from any contact whatever with paper-based material. And the rest of you, any of you that think you can get away with blaming Steptoe in ANY way for the demise of this week's homework, you'd better start thinking of a different excuse. Because we're not going to start anything new until I've had an explanation from all of you. Starting with you, Stephen."

"Well miss, I'd heard about how dangerous Tommy's dog was when it came to homework, so when I'd finished mine I put it on the window sill where it would be safe. We've got a dog too Miss and I thought–"

"Yes, yes, we get the picture Stephen. So why haven't you brought it in?"

"It rained in through the window Miss, and the ink all ran together."

Author's Notes

Perhaps it's a cultural thing, but the first thing I think of whenever the subject of "excuses" comes up is: the dog ate my homework. So that was the immediate and easy starting point for this piece. I had a blast thinking up enough ways to put a twist on that one excuse, and also to come up with enough other more original excuses, to fill half an hour.

Incidentally it's also my habit, when drafting, to give characters amusing names. These are usually temporary – there would have to be special circumstances indeed to even try to get away with calling someone misdemeanour – but obviously with my rule forbidding any post-hoc editing, this one has survived.

Day 17: Vengeance

"You sure this is the right road?"

"Yes! A34, south of Alderley Edge the message said. It was quite clear."

"Well where is he then?"

"I don't know! Keep looking!"

Their blues illuminated the hedgerows on either side of the narrow, winding 'A' road to the south of Manchester as Foxtrot Uniform 32 sped through the failing evening light. Jed Evans, driver, watched the far side while keeping one eye on the unruly road. His fellow paramedic Trixie Mbantu stared fixedly at the nearside hedge, waiting for any sign of the crashed vehicle they were looking for. Jed had killed the siren once they'd left the main street of Alderley, and the traffic, behind.

"It's getting harder to tell which of these are gates and which might be crash damage," Trixie yelled over the noise of the engine as Jed changed down into a tight left-hander. "Wait! There!"

The ambulance had entered a short straight section of road. Trixie pointed ahead at a collapsed section of hedge. Their headlights revealed fish-tailing skid marks leading to the hole in the foliage.

"Looks like he lost it on that last bend," Jed said, braking the vehicle to a stop. "No sign of the car though," he added, peering through the gloom.

They left the ambulance with its blues still flashing a warning to oncoming vehicles, and started across the verge. Trixie picked up a mangled lump of metal from the side of the road.

"What's this?"

"Give it here?"

Jed turned the debris over and examined the surface.

"Looks like part of a motorcycle fender."

"I thought you said this was a car crash."

"It is. Supposed to be. But there's bike tracks here look, in the mud."

Single tyre tracks were clearly visible in the soft verge, deeply bitten into the mud. Trixie had already reached the hole in the fence. She shone her powerful halogen torch into the field beyond. A few yards away a silver Mercedes had been stopped catastrophically quickly by a large oak tree. Steam hissed from its wrecked bonnet and dissipated quickly into the cooling air of the evening.

"Over here! I've found it!" she called, starting through the fence without waiting for Jed, her paramedic's bag catching on the spines of the blackthorn.

The driver had attempted to free himself from the crumpled cabin. He had fallen through the opened door leaving his legs at an unnatural angle under the displaced steering column. He gave a soft moan as Trixie approached.

"Hello? Can you hear me? I'm a paramedic. Can you tell me your name?"

"Did... did I get him?"

Author's Notes

I love movies. The subject of road rage, often including a driver's "revenge" is one that has been well covered in film over a number of years. The classic, and original, "Duel" is an obvious example, and more recently I've enjoyed "Unhinged". So it's not surprising that a road-based theme was uppermost in my mind when I came to today's prompt.

I chose the location for the tale because I'm familiar with that road, having driven it to work hundreds of times when I was based in an office to the south of Manchester. Moreover, I was involved, peripherally, in an RTA there one morning when I noticed a vehicle had left the road and ploughed through a fence. Mobile phones were still a rarity back then (early 90s) but I had one provided by my company, and used it to call the emergency services.

So this piece draws on several sources, and also ends on a kind of cliffhanger, which I think gives it a nice twist.

Day 18: Love

wow love i mean such an overused word i love you like in the song those three words they're said too much and not enough i love it where it could be anything you vaguely like or you're trying to impress the person who has it whatever it is and you don't really like it all that much but you're all oh yeah i love it baby i love it you love your friends that's a different kind of love to the love you have for your mum or your dog or your favourite pencil and then there's those weird kinds of love that some people have but other people that's most of us think are icky or embarrassing or just plain wrong those kinds of love have to be hidden away in special words with philia in them like necrophilia or coprophilia look it up or paedophilia not the kind of love i really want to talk about but then there's the usual kind and that comes in all different flavours too like love of your life and unrequited love usually love for the girl next door i used to think i loved the girl next door but it was just an adolescent thing really i only wanted to see her tits and she just thought it was kinda handy to have someone her own age living next door who she could play silly games with she never really loved me and in the end she moved away anyway and i never even heard from her again but i think about her from time to time but even that wasn't my first experience of love oh no i was only six years old when i fell in love the first time and my parents were all oh don't be so silly boys of your age don't fall in love but it sure felt like it to me when i was feeling all sick in my stomach and thinking about her all the time and making sure my fingernails were clean when i went to school and deliberately putting my tie on crooked so she could straighten it for me because she was a proper little girl who wanted to grow up to be a wife and mother and she'd seen her mother straighten her dad's tie so obviously that's the kind of thing you did when you loved somebody so she used to do it for me too made my head tingle anyway we only ever kissed a few times and then it all kinda blew over i never did really find out why she went off me for that other guy he even had dirty fingernails and she always told me she couldn't stand that i guess that's the thing about love you can have all these rules about the kind of person who's ideal and all that but when the right one comes along all those rules go out the window i used to ask my mum how will i know when i'm really in love and she used to say you'll just know that didn't really help me very much cos every time it happened to me i thought i knew but then it turned out i didn't know after all especially with that helen i used to let her do all sorts of stupid stuff to me just to try and spend time around her but then it turned out she was just making fun of me and talking about me behind my back saying how dumb i was to let her do all that stuff i used to get that sick feeling in my stomach when i was with her too but later on it turned into a different kind of sick anyway that was all a long time ago when i was only a little kid things got even worse when i was an older kid and i started getting all these urges i never realised it was so easy to mix up love and lust i spent a long time trying to sort that one out and it got me in one whole heap of a heck of a lot of trouble i can tell you i don't know what it was but when a girl kissed me i went kinda mad i think i remember reading once that love is a kind of madness or at least that hormonal buzz that comes with it you can get addicted to that a lot of people stay that way their whole life like rock stars and film stars and other folk with a lot of money they always say they're looking for love in their songs and films but really they're just addicted to hormones or the thrill of the chase or something i don't think that's real love at all but then when you get to thinking about real love and comparing it to that flirty kind of young love and chasing about all over the place it can seem kinda boring from the outside you know when two people have been together a long time like them old folk you see walking along holding hands and people will say oh look at that old couple isn't that wonderful and all the young people start to feel a bit sick not the kind of sick that i mentioned earlier but you know kind of embarrassed and ewww and like that because all they can think about the young people that is all they can think about is the old people doing it and i think it's universally recognised that the thought of old people doing it is kinda yucky until you're an old person that is and then i guess it's perfect natural even though you don't do it as often as you used to but that's because by the time you're that old you've discovered that love really isn't about doing it at all that's only one very small part of it and all the rest the stuff that sounds boring to the youngsters well that's the stuff that love is really about caring and sharing and understanding and being gentle and kind and doing stuff for each other because you want to make their lives easier and taking pleasure from simple things like a warm sunny morning or a kitten playing or your grandchildren bringing you a daisy chain so all in all i reckon love means different things to different people at different times of their lives but it always means something to somebody at every time of their life and that's why they say it makes the world go round.

Author's Notes

A couple of years after I started running a book club, we read "A Million Little Pieces."

It became infamous for initially claiming to be memoir before being called out as fake and subsequently remarketed as "semi-fictional", but what makes it stick in my mind is Frey's "stream of consciousness" writing style.

To be honest if it hadn't been chosen as a "book club read" I would probably have given up on it, but back then if a book was chosen I thought I should at least make an effort. So I stuck with it, and once I got past the weirdness of unpunctuated dialogue and the lack of differentiation between external and internal dialogue, I started to really enjoy it.

That was four years before I undertook this challenge, but once I arrived at the theme of "Love" – which is so central to, and ubiquitous in, human experience – even starting to think about what to write on the topic was quite overwhelming. And then it dawned on me. Why not take that "overwhelm" and just present it as a stream of consciousness? Every passing thought and twist and turn and blind alley that my mind threw up as I considered the topic is represented here, insofar as my flying typing fingers could keep up with my unfettered imagination.

Day 19: Tears

I was glad to step out of the heat into the unremarkable, almost invisible, pawnbroker's that afternoon. The dust of the market had already formed a pale crust on my skin. I felt as though another moment in the crowded streets would be enough to petrify me like a wrongdoer in an ancient tale from the Arabian Nights.

The small brass bell sounded unnaturally loud in the quiet crepuscular interior of the shop. Traffic noise rudely disturbed the calm, which I restored by fastening the door closed behind me. An old man sat beside a makeshift counter at the back of the shop, examining a tooled silver dress knife with a jeweller's eyeglass.

The knife's owner stood a few respectful steps away from the shopkeeper, impatiently moving from foot to foot. At the sound of the door he had turned quickly to see who might be entering. Since I was no-one he recognised and I looked harmless enough, his attention had been recaptured by the ongoing valuation of his heirloom. At length the shopkeeper let out a breath he seemed to have been holding since long before I arrived.

"It is not the best workmanship. And there is some damage to the hilt. I offer two hundred dinar."

"It is an insult!" the man cried, snatching the knife from the hand of the merchant. "This has been in my family for three generations! It is worth at least ten times that amount!"

"Then I wish you good fortune in finding someone willing to pay it," said the trader with a shrug. He turned back to his counter, ignoring me completely.

"A thousand then!" said the owner loudly. "May my ancestors forgive me."

"I told you. It is worth no more than two hundred."

"You are trying to rob me!"

"I am merely being honest. Take it somewhere else. The tale will be the same."

"Can you at least give me five hundred?" the man asked, a note of desperation beginning to colour both his voice and his posture. "I have bills. Debts."

"Don't we all?"

"Look, four hundred. It must be worth at least that much for the metal."

"My friend I don't think you can be aware how much the price of silver has fallen. But I can see you are in dire straits. Two hundred and fifty dinars. It is my final offer."

The man hesitated. For one moment I thought he was going to bite. Barely better than ten percent of what he had thought the object was worth. But the weight of his ancestors' expectations overwhelmed him. He turned on his heel and walked out into the heat of the afternoon.

The merchant regarded me with a belligerent stare.

"Can I help you?"

"My master has cried rivers of tears in his quest for a special gift."

The merchant's demeanour changed instantly from confrontational barterer to supplicant. He edged past me to lock the shop door and pull down the shutters.

"Come with me, effendi."

He led the way past the counter, through a curtained entrance to the dingy living quarters at the back of the shop. Taking a huge bunch of keys from the folds of his robe he unlocked a small door, flicked a switch and started down a rickety old flight of stairs without another word or even a glance in my direction. I followed.

The basement was illuminated by a single bare bulb. The merchant had knocked it on his way past and now it swung rapidly to and fro, casting eerily moving shadows on the filing cabinets, old cast-off furniture and anonymously sheeted objects that filled the mould stained cellar. Incongruously, one wall held a bright, clean, polished steel safe. The merchant stopped, turning to look at me.

"Please."

I looked away. The buzz and click of the combination wheel's spinning filled the small chamber. The merchant swung the handle and, reaching inside, retrieved a small dark blue velvet bag. He closed the safe again and span the wheels.

In one corner of the room sat a large partner's desk covered in a clean white sheet. The merchant switched on a large desk lamp, flooding the desk with an achingly bright arc light. He loosened the ties on the bag and slid out the contents.

Flashing blue and silver in the harsh white light the largest single diamond I had ever seen slipped into his hand.

"Your master will be pleased, effendi, no? This is the stone known as the Tears of Munra."

Author's Notes

One of the days where I could've kept going for much longer than thirty minutes. Even in that short time what I ended up with is a strong piece that could certainly be turned into a short story, or even a novella depending on the provenance of, and possibly supernatural powers associated with, the Tears of Munra. The beginning of the story lends itself to being taken down any one of several avenues.

Staring back down the ten years since I wrote this, I can't be certain, but it's at least possible that I wrote the last line first. Knowing where I wanted the story to end, that would have been a sensible approach, leaving me free to use the remaining minutes to fill in as much detail as the time allowed.

Notes from an Editor's perspective

The debate about whether to use first person, third person, or any of the other alternative points of view (POVs) never ends. I know people who won't read first person, finding it uncomfortably intimate and difficult to follow. From a writer's perspective it is harder, since it restricts what the narrator can "know" or see. Alternatively I also know those who find third person boring to read, being somewhat divorced from the action, often told in retrospect and therefore (possibly) lacking in pace or urgency.

I have no empirical evidence to support this view, but I believe the younger a reader is, the more likely they are to prefer first person. I think it's become more common in recent years, and I think the influence of the Internet, social media, etc, has meant that attention spans have shortened, the need for instant gratification has increased, and all of these influences conspire to make first person more attractive, or more digestible, to the modern reader.

Personally, I prefer to choose whatever POV feels more natural to me for the piece in question, and in this case I went with first.

I'm pretty happy with it overall. I think it establishes a good sense of "place" and has some strong descriptions. Re-reading it with an editor's eye reveals several parts that need "work." A touch of passive voice creeps in near the end ("The basement was illuminated by…" which I would have gone back and switched up to "A single bare bulb illuminated the basement"); the combination safe breaks continuity by switching from having a single numbered wheel to more than one (so my editor's pen would redraft the line as "He closed the safe again and span the wheel."); and there's repetition between "large partner's desk" and "large desk lamp" that would be lost during the editing pass, with one or other of the larges replaced by an alternative adjective.

Day 20: My Inspiration

For a long time I thought I got my inspiration from others.

When you work in the kind of high-tech, leading edge company that I did back in the 80s and early 90s (it's still the same company now, but I no longer think of it as leading edge. Even though it is still in the business of high tech), you become so familiar with being surrounded by people of enormous intellect that it's easy to feel almost less than normal. Or at least, below average.

Over the years I've heard anecdotes from ex-colleagues who left. They all shared a theme: no-one within the company really knows how good they are until, voluntarily or otherwise, they step outside it. Only when given the chance to compare oneself with regular people outside can one begin to appreciate the amazing talent that exists inside.

Without wishing to blow my own trumpet overmuch, it's true that in all the 34 years I've been there I have never been asked to do something that I couldn't, eventually, succeed at. And before the cynics among you start, I have been asked to do some pretty off-the-wall, technically challenging stuff. But even allowing for the fact that the staff in general were above average for "the marketplace" there were still some particular outstanding individuals that I looked up to, wanted to emulate, and who I thought of as a source of inspiration.

Outside the workplace, in common with a lot of people (at least those who don't allow their work life to grow so that it consumes their entire life) I got busy with private endeavours. More artistic endeavours. Here too I was lucky to meet people who I looked to for inspiration.

But in thinking of how I would approach this theme, it came to me that these people, almost to a man person, did not inspire me. I was confusing inspiration with aspiration.

I aspired to emulate them in some way, either to be as clever, as resourceful, as knowledgeable, as inventive, as dedicated, whatever. But my inspiration – my source of ideas, or commitment – was not them.

It was me.

When I seek an idea for a story, or a poem, or a song, I don't go to people I respect or admire. I sit quietly, possibly listening to music (yes, also possibly, just possibly, playing Spider Solitaire) and I run ideas through my head. Or, more often, I wait for them to come to me. I open myself up to what ancient scholars would have called my Muse. And I've learned, more so in the last few years than at any time in my life, to trust it. If I let my mind free wheel, ideas come. It might only be a line of dialogue or it might be an entire conversation. My memory is so poor, and the ideas often so fleeting, that I have to write them down as quickly as I can. The trick there is not to start writing too soon. To let the idea ripen and develop until it feels "done." You could liken it to letting dough "prove" before baking. Only then can I write it down without losing it, and so that I don't lose it. Getting the timing of that right is quite a delicate balance, and I still miss regularly (mostly on the side of waiting too long and forgetting the important bits, unfortunately).

Of course when it's a song I'm writing I have the source of inspiration right there on my computer. The music. I can just let it play over and over on repeat until the words begin to suggest themselves. I've often referred to this as "letting the music tell me its story," and that's exactly how it feels.

The example I most commonly use to explain how this inspiration works when at its best, is the time I wrote Tumbleweed (one of the poems in my first collection: Well of Love). It was a quiet weekend afternoon and I simply sat at my keyboard, opened up my mind and started writing. To my astonishment the words poured onto the screen, my thoughts flying so fast I could hardly type quickly enough to keep up with them. So fast, indeed, that I was hardly conscious of what they were saying. It was an exhilarating experience. At the end of that brief period of frantic typing I had well over 90% of a completed poem. The only missing parts were where I had felt my mind groping for a word or a phrase that was missing from the stream of consciousness I was recording. When that happened – only three or four places in what is quite a long poem – I simply skipped over the word or line, leaving a dash to mark the place.

Going back over the piece and replacing the dashes with real content was a matter of only half an hour or so. The words were there, it just felt as though they had somehow "got stuck" in the frenzied flow.

I can't explain it and it's probably silly to try. It has only happened once since, although on that occasion it was a deliberate experiment to see if I could repeat the experience – this time with a song rather than a poem. Contrarily perhaps, the fact that it worked a second time has made me reluctant to try again until and unless I reach a point in my writing where I absolutely need it. It's like a pure wellspring that I don't want to drink from too often for fear of tainting it. That probably sounds crazy, but

Author's Notes

With a topic like "my inspiration" it was a no-brainer to write about what… er… inspires me. So what we got was an opinion piece on creativity, and – to an extent – about the difference between inspiration and aspiration. One-fifth of the way through the challenge and the first time for several days where I ran out of time and stopped mid-sentence. Not really a surprise, since there is no "story" or structure to the piece. I had no cliffhanger in mind; no eventual destination for the narrative, it is simply the documentation of my thoughts on my creative process.

Notes from an Editor's perspective

As usual it suffers from my personal drafting tics – the punctuation is a bit clunky (overuse of commas!), and it's overlong in parts – but I think it still works as a "blog piece".

Day 21: Never Again

You might think you've left it behind you
That chapter is over and done
You'll wake up one day
And hear yourself say
That really the book's just begun

The story you're actually reading
Is the one that you wrote on your own
Though you stayed up all night
It's still not quite right
But my! How the hours have flown

Not only the hours are flying
The days and the weeks have gone too
And all of those years
Still slippery with tears
So what are you going to do?

With the time that remains on your candle
The wick burning bright at both ends
Shining back through the haze
Of those warm splendid days
And nights that you spent with your friends

There should be many more of those coming
Exactly how many's unclear
It's time to get real
Explain how you feel
To the one you hold dearest of dear

Take hold of her hand one fine morning
Explain all the what, why and when
Look into her eyes
Take off your disguise
And never say never again

Author's Notes

I've written a total of 45 poems over the years (including this one, but not counting the lyrics on Beresford & Wallace's two albums of folky pop, or poppy folk). Perhaps not surprisingly my most prolific RhymeTime™ was during, and shortly after, going through a long drawn-out and acrimonious divorce. Times of strong emotions drive the creative engine in ways, and to heights, that are often not achievable once the emotional tide has ebbed and you find yourself in calmer waters. Right enough, once those turbulent times were past, I pretty much stopped writing poetry altogether, other than occasional flashes of inspiration.

After living through those painful years, I always told myself I'd never marry again (having at that stage failed at it twice). So that was much on my mind when the prompt "never again" came up, but by that time my personal pledge had been overtaken by events. Something like six weeks before Day 21 of the challenge, I had in fact married for the third time.

So with these two, apparently conflicting thoughts in my mind, I found the opening words of a poem coming once again almost unbidden – the first time I'd experienced this aspect of creativity in almost six years. These six verses of doggerel – again, as per the rules, all first draft – are the result.

Day 22: Online

A pair of honey bees hummed lazily from blossom to blossom among the weeds and wild flowers decorating the disused sidings. The day was still and hot, the afternoon sun a coruscating furnace in a cornflower sky.

Niall rested momentarily against the hot wood of the old cattle pens, watching the bees and soaking up the ambience of the old station. The trains, still regular users of the branch line, no longer stopped here. The local farmers sent their livestock by road now. The commuters had to make their way the four miles to the next nearest station.

From a nearby suburban garden, the sound of a child playing happily in the summer afternoon disturbed his reverie. He plucked a stem of grass from the path and set off toward the old stone footbridge further down the track. As a boy he had stood on that bridge and watched the trains, passengers and traders as they bustled and jostled around the busy station, making careful notes in his spotters' book. He wanted to relive that memory even if the only elements left to it were himself and the occasional speeding train.

The path started its slow incline to the shoulder of the bridge. He could hear the child's voice more plainly now, even though he was walking closer to the rural side of the station, leaving the housing estate behind. He could even start to make out the odd word. It sounded... surely not... it sounded like someone crying for help.

He broke into a run, heading for the low wall at the side of the bridge, and looked along the track, shading his eyes from the glare. Two hundred metres or so from the other side of the bridge, a young woman was lying across the track, waving frantically.

Guessing she must have been walking on the track side and twisted her ankle, Niall vaulted the wall and slid awkwardly down the bank onto the gravel. He checked his watch as he began to run toward the woman, ruefully remembering that he had no idea of the train timetable.

As he approached the woman he saw that she was not simply lying on the track. She was tied to it.

"Oh God," she yelled as he ran, "thank God! Please help me!"

Niall slid to a halt on the loose gravel and knelt down.

"What the hell?" he began. "Who did this? Why...?"

"Please," she gasped. "The train is due any minute. I'll explain later. Please get me out of here!"

Niall examined the knots. Although no expert, he was pretty sure he'd never seen anything like them before. Thick nylon climbing rope had been wrapped around the woman's waist and leg. Looped around both the steel rails of the track and the heavy sleepers, it had been tied in a complex weave that Niall struggled to comprehend.

Half-remembered scenes from silent movies and Wile E. Coyote cartoons flashed through his racing mind.

"I'll never get this undone in time," he panted, still breathless from his short run. "I'll have to cut it."

He pulled a pocket knife from his jeans and began sawing at the rope.

"It's no use," the woman yelled. "You'll never cut through all this – there isn't time."

A thousand metres away, around the bend in the track, a train whistle sounded urgently.

[this story is continued later in the writing challenge – on Day 39 in "Out of Time"]

Author's Notes

Only the second time I'd linked a prompt with another later in the challenge. Some of these were planned, having occurred to me when I first found the topic list. Others revealed themselves on reaching the later prompt and recalling a story I had already started earlier in the challenge. Linking stories in this way became one of the most satisfying aspects of the exercise for me.

The location for this story comes from a childhood memory. I grew up during the "Beeching" years in the UK, when the railway network was being hacked apart and many branch lines closed; stations abandoned. One such station, an early casualty of the cuts, was located close to my childhood home. As in this story, its cattle pens survived, as did the station building although slowly decaying, with its windows smashed by local vandals, and more and more weather damage appearing over the years. It was a popular place to play for me and my friends, no doubt quite dangerous in hindsight.

Unlike the story, trains had long since stopped running on the line, though the balmy summer days, wildflowers, and stone bridge over the track all existed, as vivid in my memory now as if I were still walking there.

Notes from an Editor's perspective

With ten years' writing experience under my belt since this piece was penned, some of the MC's documented thoughts read a little clunky to me now. Using phrases like "he thought" is bad form, and were I to edit this piece now I'd certainly replace "ruefully remembering that he had no idea of the train timetable" with something snappier and less removed from his POV, such as "...a pointless exercise, since he had no idea…"

Day 23: Failure

I'm a few days ahead of myself with this challenge (always good to have a few posts in hand with something like this, in case of unforeseen eventualities) so by the time you read this a week will have passed since the closing ceremony of the Olympics and I expect by now, in the way of these things, it's all just a rapidly fading memory. Normal service has been resumed on all channels and maybe even the interminable post-mortems will have become terminable, or terminated.

But for me, it was just last night. A madcap three hours of social networking as friends from as far afield as the other side of the world and literally as close as next door came together in our living room while I sat with iPad in hand both reading and writing a staccato running commentary.

So as the glow of what has been heralded as the best Olympics ever fades, I wanted to say a word about failure. And it's a good job I did, because that's the theme for today!

In among the many superb golds, world and Olympic records, and personal bests that have been clocked up over the last 17 days, I've been struck by the number of athletes who didn't win, and having had a microphone shoved under their noses before they've even had chance to catch their breath, felt compelled to say how sorry they were that they'd failed and "let everybody down."

Dear Athlete, Gymnast, Swimmer, Competitor: In what sense can you be said to have failed? Have you stopped trying? OK, maybe this was your last chance at an Olympic medal. Coming round so rarely, in many sports competitors only have two or three attempts to "medal" (one of the many dire "new verbs" we've been introduced to recently). You may have set yourself the goal of gold, but not achieving your goal is not the same thing as failure.

Your attempt at the gold medal depended on so much more than your own efforts. How can you allow for others' training, skill, talent and preparation? Wind conditions (a particular bugbear in the pole vault, and some throwing events)? The last minute sore throat or dodgy stomach? None of these things are under your control. All of them can prevent you winning a medal.

Did you do your best, perhaps even achieving a personal best? You haven't failed.

Did you even make the attempt in the first place, when most of us can only lift ourselves off the sofa long enough to fetch another beer? You haven't failed.

Did you inspire even one young person to visit their local sports club this week, who wouldn't have otherwise gone? You haven't failed.

Did you make one person shout out in support, make one heart skip a beat, make one tear fall for joy or hope or pride? You haven't failed.

Did you turn one person, even for only a moment, from the weary path of the cynic to the sunny broad track of the committed competitor? You haven't failed. And on that basis alone I can tell you that none of you failed, because I was that cynic. And I was turned. If not into a believer then certainly, and perhaps only briefly, into an enthusiastic supporter.

Failure is a big word. And it is also, similar to opportunities and threats on which I wrote a few days ago, one of those things that can disguise itself very well. What might appear at first to be a failure could turn out to be nothing more than a stepping stone. A doorway to another future. A fork in the road. Or a bump.

Many people think fear of failure is a barrier to success, and it can be. What isn't often realised (except among coaches ;o)) is that an even bigger barrier is fear of success.

At least that's one problem our Olympians don't have to worry about.

Author's Notes

For once, I don't have any. Ten years later, and with two further Olympics under our global belt, I think what I wrote back then stands the test of time quite robustly. I still believe everything up there.

Day 24: Rebirth

The smell of formaldehyde was overpowering, evoking long-buried memories of my ham-fisted attempts at dissection as an 'A' Level Biology student. Bunsen burners didn't appear to have evolved much in the last 30 years either. One rasped its curling yellow tongue of flame at the ceiling from a bench on one wall of Professor Manneheim's laboratory.

The Professor himself, his face hidden by a shock of wild grey hair in true stereotypical mad scientist style, gave his rapt attention to a series of dials on a control device at the far side of the lab. He remained outwardly undistracted by my entrance, but called out as I started across the polished tile floor.

"Have you disinfected?"

The anti-bacterial regimen was posted on every wall of the approach corridors. They were impossible to miss. The laboratory doors would not unlock unless the automated hand gel dispensers had been activated during the previous minute. The professor's question was redundant. I humoured him.

"Disinfected, masked and gloved," I informed him from behind my surgical mask.

He beckoned me over to his console.

"The final stage is almost complete," he said, snapping a toggle switch on his console. It was the first time I had ever seen him show even the faintest excitement, or apprehension. "Do you have a recording device?"

I showed him my digital camcorder.

"Does it have enough capacity?"

"Unless the experiment is going to take longer than a day," I laughed.

The professor offered me a withering stare. He was a famous man, but not for his sense of humour.

"Turn it on," he snapped. I turned it on, and set it on the bench beside the console, adjusting the viewfinder so I could check the professor was in shot. A few feet in front of the bench, a large glass panel provided a view into the sterilised room beyond. Several arc lights flared into life as Manneheim flicked another switch, revealing a hospital gurney surrounded by several large canisters, each of which was topped with a motorised valve. From the valves, surgical tubing snaked across to the gurney on which lay the pale naked body of a man.

"Rebirth Experiment #665," intoned the professor for the benefit of the recording. "Twentieth August Twenty Twelve, six twenty-one a.m. Professor Otto Manneheim conducting, James Reilly observing. Preliminary stages one through eighteen complete, subject has been dormant for twenty-four hours according to protocol, cell function nominal."

The professor proceeded through his experimental protocol, reading off measurements from his dials even though the computerised telemetry recorded everything. It was impossible to tell whether he did it from a sense of occasion, importance, or because he thought it was what later observers would expect – to provide a sense of theatre.

Finally, he fell silent. For one moment I thought he was hesitating on the brink of history. The full weight of the implications of his experiment bent his shoulders. He seemed to shrink, crumpled by the responsibility. The possibility of failure. The moment passed. He shrugged off his fleeting doubts, flipped the cover of a red switch at the right of the console, and threw it.

Bright blue liquid oozed along the tube leading from the canister marked "A", shortly followed by a thin yellow liquid from “B”.

Author’s Notes

Several vivid memories informed this piece. I was indeed once an ‘A’ Level Biology student, and attempted several dissections – a frog, a rabbit, a catfish – all of which needed to be preserved from one lesson to the next (often a week apart); hence the formaldehyde.

In these days of “health and safety” I have no idea whether Bunsen burners are even allowed in school laboratories now, but they were a distinctive feature of my old labs back in the mid-1970s, one per workstation (shared between two students) and more often than not left burning in their “safety flame” state. I bet they don’t do that now, with the price of gas! ;o)

Having been a fan of horror and SF from an early age, and seen more than a few Frankenstein films, the interior of the lab and the processes that the mad professor undertakes were easily brought to mind, playing like a showreel in my mind during the writing. With my traditional “numerology” fixation, the experiment number of 665 was a deliberate choice – one less than 666; the biblical “Number of the Beast”. My intention was to imply the experiment wouldn’t work this time, but might next time, had the story ever reached that point. In the end I appreciated the chance to end on another cliffhanger.

Finally the merging of the two liquids was prompted by a memory of a very old joke in which another mad scientist performs an experiment with two beakers, one containing blue and the other yellow. He pours them into an empty third beaker, saying “Yellow Stuff… Blue Stuff… Aha! Just as I expected! Green Stuff!”

Day 25: Breaking Away

Silence reigned. Silence, and frost. A frost so ancient that nothing alive remembered its falling. So deep that it could swallow a mountain. Yet all it chose to swallow was more frost, the new joining the old. Compacting under ever newer layers, crushed by the years, the centuries, the millennia, until no single flake or shard was distinguishable from the rest. Only a solid mass of frigid blue. It stood, apparently motionless, over the land. Guarding the bedrock like a shield, the frost was absolute. Impenetrable.

But only apparently motionless. To the casual observer. On another scale of time the frost flowed. Like a crystal river it coursed across the land so ponderously that it had its own word: glacial. As close as anything can come to stationary and still be moving.

The frost was absolute in its solidity; resolute in its movement. The silence was neither absolute nor resolute. Its reign was temporary. More of a regency, really. Disturbed at a visceral level by the gargantuan creaking of the lethargic ice, the silence gave way to the voice of the glacier. A gut-wrenching moan of deliberate agony. A slothful yawn. An occasional crack, like the bones of a leviathan, stretching through a valley hidden deep beneath its glassy flesh.

Yet though the frost appeared infinite, the land beneath it was finite. And though the frost crept infinitely slowly towards land's end, still eventually was that end attained. At which point the frost stood at the brink, peering out over the chill sea as if searching for lost brethren on the horizon, or deciding how to continue its journey on such comparatively uncertain footing.

That decision, ultimately, was not one for the frost to make. It was one for physics. For gravity. Overhanging the edge of the land like a gelid curtain, the glacier knew stresses and strains previously undreamt of. The torment called fresh moans from the frost, until with cold inevitability the land-locked mother ice bid a noisy farewell to its new-born daughter as a quarter-million-ton chunk broke free and crashed majestically into the calm waters below.

Author's Notes

I decided long ago not to question the way my mind works. We're all individuals and think in individual ways. Sometimes the ideas that pop up work, other times not so much. So the first idea that came to me when I saw the prompt for today was of an iceberg breaking away from its ice shelf, and I set about trying to describe that in a "literary" way.

It was my desire for literariness that led to the piece being considerably shorter than usual. Rather than steam ahead writing the first thing that came to mind, I extracted every word individually, sorting and discarding, comparing, rewriting, carving out a sentence almost as glacially slowly as my subject matter.

I also allowed myself a single piece of research. I didn't know how much an average iceberg weighs. Not for the first time I wondered how on Earth anyone wrote anything before Google. If I'd had to walk down to the local library (I guess I should think myself lucky that's still an option) to research the weight I wouldn't have bothered, or would have guessed at a figure. As it is, Google tells me an average "Grand Banks area" iceberg weighs in at between 100,000 and 200,000 tonnes, so I think with dramatic licence a quarter of a million tonnes adds a little – cough – weight to the description.

Day 26: Forever and a day

Try as I might I cannot get past the hyperbole of this topic. "Forever and a day" might only be "one of those sayings" to most people, but to a dyed-in-the-wool pedant like me it's an irritating reminder of how meaning is lost through overuse, or how casually words are thrown around without, it seems, conscious thought.

Forever is, by definition, infinite. It means the same as eternity. The whole of time. And, as with all infinite numbers, adding one to them doesn't make any difference. Forever and a day is, literally, no longer than forever. So while the massed populace thinks they're expressing something that means they're going the extra mile, doing something more, making a special effort, actually all they're communicating is their paucity of imagination or understanding.

Here's another: 110%.

I gave it 110%. No you didn't. You can't. If you've somehow managed to do more than you did last time, all that means is you gave less than 100% last time. Or alternatively, that your capacity to give was smaller back then, and you gave 100% at that time, and THIS time you have an increased output and you're giving 100% of that. In the same way that eternity, or forever, means the whole of time, 100% means the sum total of whatever it is you're talking about.

Imagine eating 110% of a cake. It's impossible, right? Once you've eaten 100% of the cake there is no more cake. Unless you've hidden a second cake somewhere and you've stuffed 10% of that down your gullet as well. But that's a different cake. It's not an extra 10% of the first cake. That would be like having your cake and eating it too. Which if I was feeling like writing another diatribe on physics might lead me on to a debate about the impossibility of creating (or destroying) matter (or energy). But I won't stray down that path.

In fact since I've been sitting here staring at the screen for the last two minutes with not even an extra 1% of an idea of where to take this argument next, it appears I'm not going to be straying down any path. Even the one I thought I was on. Maybe I should just call it a day. Since I've been arguing against ever saying "forever and a day" we could agree that the "day" we're going to call it is the day we've just subtracted from "forever and a day."

Makes no difference to me. Or you for that matter. Because in the same way you can't add a day to forever, you can't take one away either. Infinite numbers, eh? I could write about them forever...

Author's Notes

Wow, I gave full rein to my pedantic side there, didn't I? What a rant. Still, it seems pretty obvious that the subject stood solidly in the way of any chance I might be able to imagine an alternative treatment. I do, normally, keep that side of my psyche on a tight leash, so it was… a relief to have the opportunity to let it out for a run around the park for once.

Still one of the weakest pieces of the whole Challenge though, I reckon. Which I guess confirms what I wrote in the comments for the previous piece: sometimes my ideas work, and other times…

Day 27: Lost and Found

The city shivered. And with it, Carl. Sat on his favourite corner of Mason, leaning against the cold marble of a high-rise office block, his hat on the sidewalk in front of him. A dog-eared cardboard sign was propped at a dangerous angle behind the hat.

VIETNAM VET. PLEASE HELP.

He watched the people. They ignored him. Intent on their Christmas shopping, wallets and purses bulging with cash, or gold credit cards, they rushed from one retail opportunity to the next with scarcely time to draw breath. Their attention was nailed to the sales signs, bright window dressing and 2-for-1 offers. They had none to spare for him. Thirty years on from his last trip to 'Nam and he was still flying beneath the radar.

"Woof!"

A dog's bark jolted him from his war memories. Between the criss-crossing legs of the Yuletide shoppers, Carl caught a brief glimpse of a black-and-tan collie nervously checking out the faces of the rapidly passing throng. The dog ran first one way, then the other, its head permanently held at an upward angle, its eyes flicking from face to face. Occasionally the collie's tail would wag tentatively before curling back down between its hind legs in fear.

"Here, boy!" Carl called, uncertain whether the dog was in fact male but figuring it wouldn't be offended. "Come on! Come here!"

Attracted by the sound of a friendly voice directed toward it, the collie stopped, staring across the few yards of pavement that separated them. Trying to decide if this was a friend, or a trick.

Carl rummaged in his filthy knapsack for the remains of his meagre breakfast. The last inch of a cereal bar was all he had left. He held it out to the still waiting dog.

"Here y'are fella! Come and get it!"

The dog cocked its head to one side, considering. A kindred lost spirit, thought Carl. He could understand its reluctance to trust a stranger. He set the crumb of comfort down on the sidewalk beside his hat and sat back, regarding the dog with what he hoped was a friendly expression in canine terms.

After a moment's further hesitation the collie approached, sniffed the cereal bar, and snapped it up in a single bite. Carl held out his hand for the dog to sniff. It wagged its tail and came closer. Carl ruffled the nape of its neck gently.

"There boy. See? You can find a friend in the strangest places. Lost, are ya? Lost your folks?"

The dog whined and lay down on the sidewalk beside Carl. He had just begun to consider the benefits of having a dog to attract greater sympathy from the passing crowd when an excited voice cut through the street noise.

"Roger! He's here!"

A young woman in expensive looking jeans and a cut-off top that reminded Carl of his Vietnam lifesaver vest struggled to push her way towards him through the mass of people who all seemed to be rushing in the opposite direction.

"Vince! Vince! Mummy's here boy!" she called. Carl noticed a man a few yards behind the woman, an empty leash trailing from one hand. Roger, he guessed. The woman had successfully negotiated the crowd and crouched down beside the dog. Vince looked at her, panting. Carl would've sworn the dog was smiling.

"Ruff!" the dog exclaimed quietly, starting to lick the woman's hand.

"Thank God you found him," the woman exclaimed. "We thought we'd never get him back in all this mad crowd."

"Actually, he found me," Carl began to say as Roger breached the last of the shoppers and joined his wife and dog by the wall.

"Hey fella!" Roger said. Carl was unsure if he was addressing the dog, or him. The dog, still intent on washing his mistress's hand, ignored Roger. Roger reached into his pocket, pulled out his wallet and fished for a bill.

"Here, buddy. Thanks for looking after Vince. We thought–"

"You'd lost him. Yeah, your wife said. It was nothing, really. He found–"

"No, take this," Roger said, holding out a hundred-dollar bill.

Carl's eyes widened. More money than he'd seen in a month. He hesitated.

"Come on, take it. Look as if you could use it, and we might never have found Vince if he hadn't stayed with you. He doesn't normally take to strangers."

Carl took the bill. He turned it over in his hand.

"Vietnam eh?" Roger went on. "Did two tours in Iraq myself. Tough times. No worse than what you went through, I guess."

"I guess."

"Listen, do you have a place to stay, friend?"

[this story is continued later in the writing challenge – on Day 81 in "A Place to Belong"]

Author's Notes

Comfortably in the upper 50% of these pieces in terms of length, this was a stand-out for such an early day in the Challenge. As you'll see in the "Lessons" section at the end, on average I wrote more as the Challenge progressed. Back on Day 27 the average was only around 620 words, which makes this 20% longer.

But it's not really about the word count, it's more about the story, and in this case it almost wrote itself. It proved a rich vein of material too, since the tale of Carl and his meeting with the dog owners continues in not one more entry, but three.

Notes from an Editor's perspective

The first thing that lights up like a beacon to my ten-year-more-experienced eye is the line "A kindred lost spirit, thought Carl." As previously mentioned, I no longer document thoughts, as in "he thought" "she thought" etc. I've learned that it raises a barrier between the writer and the reader. The piece is written from Carl's POV, so everything we're reading is his thoughts. Were I drafting this now, or going back to edit this now, this is one of the changes I'd make. The line works much better as simply "A kindred lost spirit."

Day 28: Light

He's out there. Sitting in the dark. Why does he do that? How can he? Always leaves it to me to shoo our guests home, collect their unfinished glasses of wine and stack the dishwasher. While he steps out into the night. Sits on the deck with his bloody pipe and his glass of single malt. Cogitating.

Why doesn't he put a light on? I've given up asking. Never get a straight answer. I don't know how he can sit in the dark like that. I hate it. The dark. Too many awful memories. Don't ask. I probably couldn't even explain half of them. Buried, they are. Or cremated. With candles, tea-lights, open fires. Anything that banishes the darkness. But mostly the blessed, bright, searing light of a decent 100-watt bulb. That'll banish the dark from even the most intransigent corner. I felt uneasy when they stopped making 200-watt ones, but you can still find the 100-watts if you know where to look.

Don't know how they managed in the old days. Gas lamps and such. Nightmare. All those shadows that seemed empty but could have been filled with God knows what. Carrying a candle up to bed and trying not to let it blow out. Its wispy yellow flicker trying to light your way. And failing. Here comes a candle to light you to bed, here comes a chopper... Ugh! I always said we wouldn't play those mind games with any children of ours, though of course we never had the chance. One way or the other.

No, I have to have a light on. Even if I get up in the night. Bedside light. Landing light. Bathroom light. If it was up to me I'd probably have them all on all night. He won't have it though. Can't sleep with the light on, he always says. What about us who can hardly sleep with it off? If it wasn't for the street lights I'd never get any sleep at all. Sometimes I crack the curtains to let more of it in. He thinks the track needs adjusting. But it's OK. He won't even get round to looking at it for another six months, and anyway I don't do it every night. So he forgets.

I could never live in the country. We went on holiday to Cornwall, once. Stayed in a country cottage. It was pitch black at night. Absolutely pitch black. You couldn't see your hand in front of your face. I had to sleep downstairs.

Things always look jollier when it's bright, don't you think? It's not just darkness that gets obliterated. Other bad things go too. Moods. Tempers. Even dark thoughts turn brighter with a decent light on. And it's easier to get things done. Better than sitting dwelling on... No, you need to be able to see what you're doing, I always say.

I saw a film once. The Unbearable Lightness of Being it was called. If I'd made it I'd have called it the Bearable Lightness. Or the Wonderful Lightness. There's already too much darkness in this world. What we need is more light. They say that eventually, in a few million years, the world will stop spinning and one side will be permanent day, the other always night. I know which side I'd live on!

He wouldn't be able to sit out on his damned dark deck on my side of the world! Anyway, everything is tidy now. Dishwasher's on. Leftovers are in the fridge, all covered up. I quite fancy one last drink on the deck myself.

"Don't you want a light on out here?"

[this is a companion piece to "Dark" which appears next in the writing challenge – on Day 29]

Author's Notes

I'll cover these together, so skip swiftly on to "Dark" below.

Day 29: Dark

[this is a companion piece to "Light" which immediately precedes it in the writing challenge – on Day 28]

She's in there. Bustling around in the light. Light in every room. Why does she do that? Always leaves it to me to turn the lights off everywhere. We'd have a bill like Blackpool illuminations if it was left to her. Can't bear it unless it's incandescent. Like everywhere needs to be under noonday sun, even in the middle of the night. Most of the time, the light from the next room is enough for me. Or even from outside. I prefer it dark, me. You can think in the dark. Cogitate.

In the light, everything is right there. Visible. Open. There's no hiding in the light. No mystery. And no room for rational, careful thought when all of life is crashing in on you at 100 watts. Most folk make do with 60 watts. Or even 11, if it's an energy saver. Not her. It's 100 watts or nothing with her. How can you even start to think straight when there's so much... stuff... to look at. It doesn't help to close your eyes. Not with 100 watts. All you can see is the pattern of veins on your eyelids. Can't think when you're wondering where each little pathway leads, or thinking about how many blood cells are racing through the network.

Must have been wonderful back in the days of gas lamps and candles. Must have been a dream. All those soft, flickering shadows. No hard edges. Nothing demanding your attention the whole time. Time to think. It's no wonder we don't come up with as many inventions now as they did back then. It's not that everything's already been discovered or invented. It's that people could think by gas light. They didn't have highly polished surfaces winking at them or glinting chrome and glass yelling into their eyes and brains. I would have told our children that, if I'd had the chance. If you want to think, I'd have said, really think, turn the light off. Nothing to be afraid of in the dark. Course, I never did get the chance, what with one thing or another.

No, I have to have the light off. Especially to sleep. Can't stand it when she gets up in the night. Bedside light? Click. Landing light? Click. Bathroom light? Click. I'd rather grope about with just the light from the street. We get plenty from there as it is, especially with those broken curtains. They won't shut properly, see? Some nights, if the moon's up and the street lights haven't gone out yet, it might as well be daytime in our bedroom. Easily enough light to get any normal person to the bathroom and back without burning out the retinas of those poor souls still trying to sleep. I'm going to have a look at that track one of these days. There must be something wrong with it.

See, the thing about the dark is, it's cool. So much easier to keep calm in the dark. Things always look clearer, you know? Easier to work out. It's funny that – that things are easier to see when you can't see very much. It's all a question of focus. Concentrating on what's important. And there's another thing, too. You can lose yourself in the dark. Don't need any other kind of disguise. My face takes on a kind of scowl when I'm thinking. People are always telling me. Well, I don't need that kind of aggro do I? When I'm thinking in the dark, I don't need to worry what I look like. Or who's watching.

She'll be out here soon. I can hear the dishwasher. That's always the last thing. That, and a glass of wine. No more thinking for me tonight, I'm guessing. Talking, maybe. Thinking, no.

"Don't you want a light on out here?"

"If you like."

Author's Notes

The link between these topics was clear as soon as I first scanned the topic list. The only question left was: how?

In common with most couples, there are areas (many!) where my wife and I "gel", and other areas (few!) where we don't. Coincidentally, one of these is exactly the difference between the couple in these two pieces. I will always avoid switching a light on if possible; she will always switch it on if there's the slightest excuse.

Real life creeps into these pieces in several other ways too. I honestly think this helps your writing to come alive. If you can give it a grounding in real life, and illuminate it with real memories. Not only does this give it added depth and realism – even in a fantasy world – it also makes it unique. As unique as your own personal experience and understanding. The caveat in a fantasy world is, obviously, other rules of physics etc may apply, but even there you can make the most exotic world seem familiar using real-life experience.

We do have a deck, and I do like to sit out there after an evening's entertaining with a glass of whisky, although I've never smoked, so the pipe is fictional, and I almost certainly don't sit out there as often as I should. It's a great "space", very quiet and still even though we live in the heart of suburbia, and on a balmy evening at twilight we're often visited by bats.

Anyway, I enjoyed the chance to get inside the heads of this couple, and consider their various reasons for looking at light and dark the way they do. It was also amusing to give the two perspectives on "household jobs" (the curtain rail), resonating with the old T-shirt legend "If a man says he'll do something, he'll do it. He doesn't need reminding every six months"; to offer a poignant nod from each of them to their childlessness; and to end on a note of detente; the husband acceding to the request for light from his wife.

Day 30: Faith

Early morning sun filtered through the intricately-patterned windows, stretching gentle fingers of blue, red and gold into the dust laden air. Individual motes sparked and glinted, moving at the insistence of unseen currents and draughts. Despite these small movements, the atmosphere inside the chapel felt still and calm as Moira closed the heavy wooden door behind her. It moved silently and smoothly on ancient, worn, but well-oiled hinges. The latch clicked into place, unnaturally loud in the quiet of the nave.

The building was deserted. Although services were still held regularly, Moira had come in the middle of the working day, when worship was the last thing on most people's mind. She had chosen the time deliberately, craving the silence and solitude. She started up the aisle towards the altar, wondering briefly how the gleaming woodwork and worn leather pews stayed so clean in the midst of so much dust. The air was heavy with it. The smell of age, tinged with the slight damp of decay, was everywhere. Yet the stalls looked newly polished, and the gold design on the pulpit was as bright as if it had been wrought that very morning.

She sat down in the front pew, stroking the woodwork unconsciously with her hands. She dropped her head, chin resting on her thin cream blouse, eyes staring unfocussed at the old corded hassock in front of her. She had come here to pray, but now that she came to it, the question she had meant to ask of her God eluded her. She was certain He knew what it was already, of course, but He still needed to be asked, although Moira wasn't entirely sure why.

She hadn't forgotten her problem. Problems, in fact, since they were many. But earlier it had seemed to her that all her troubles had come together, forged themselves into one burning question. If only she had the answer to that question, everything else would be alright. Or, if not alright, then somehow it wouldn't matter so much. Gripped by her need of an answer, she had hurried here to pray. But now, surrounded – no enveloped – by the serenity of the chapel, all urgency had deserted her. And so, it seemed, had the question.

The anguish welled up inside Moira again. Stronger now. Coloured by frustration and anger. Those problems – those agonising quandaries and life-sapping convoluted complexities – were still out there waiting for her. Outside the church, where all was not serene and old and quiet. Why wasn't God out there, where he was needed, instead of keeping himself shut away in here surrounded by gold and stained glass and polished oak? And why didn't he answer her question straight out? When he must know what it was, even if she couldn't remember it?

She stared up at the face of the plaster Jesus, hanging from his cross behind the pulpit. His blind white eyes stared at the floor in front of the altar. That did look dusty, Moira noticed. The stone flags, worn into hollows by hundreds of years of faithful feet, looked as if they had been covered with all the dust left over from the woodwork and leather, marble and gold.

Moira began to sob quietly.

Author's Notes

A difficult topic for me, this, as I don't personally believe the answers to our questions can be found in church, and I've always had a problem with how the behaviour of many religious fundamentalists never really matches up with the written "word" of the God they purport to believe in so strongly.

So once again I drew heavily on my childhood experiences of churches (I don't think we ever visited a village in our many UK-based family holidays without poking around its dusty, deserted church for half an hour) for the imagined chapel in this piece, and then purposely left unresolved both Moira's question and its potential answer. You might say I had "faith" that the reader would draw their own conclusion.

Day 31: Colours

"Samdip! Another juice?"

The bar was unusually crowded, even for a Friday, and I could see he was uncomfortable, but I hoped he'd stay for at least one more. It was hard enough to get him to come with us after work as it was, without the added disincentive of a loud, rebellious crowd. He looked over to me, then at his glass, then back to me, the turmoil clear on his face.

"Go on then. One more."

I smiled as I turned back to the bartender and added Sam's drink to my order. As I waited I became aware of a small group of tattooed men in grubby work clothes further down the bar.

"Samdip?" one said to his mates. "Kind of a name is that?"

"He'll be sam deep in the shit if I get my hands on him," a second one added as the others laughed.

I risked a glance in their direction. They had clearly been drinking for a while. Probably knocked off early and spent the afternoon in the pub. Several of them swayed gently where they stood and all were red-faced despite the day having a distinct autumn chill. The one who had spoken last caught my eye as I turned away. Too late.

"tchoo looking at?" he challenged in the universally recognised prelude to thuggish confrontation. I ignored him, hoping he would lose interest as rapidly as he had reacted to my stare. No such luck.

"You. I'm talking to you. Friend of Samdip."

His mates let rip with a chorus of mixed laughter, jeers and taunting repeats of "friend of Samdip." They were still in fairly good humour, but their notional leader was just getting into his provoked stride. He swaggered over and leaned on the bar beside me, his pudgy, red, sweaty face inches from mine as he repeated menacingly, "I'm talking to you."

His breath smelt like the bottom of a fish tank. I backed away.

"I'm not looking for any trouble," I murmured.

"I think you brought some with you," he sneered, jerking his thumb towards the window. "Ol' Samdip there. Friend of yours, is he?"

"I work with him, yes."

"Did I ask what you do for a living?" Fish Tank Breath leered, following me as I tried to avoid death by halitosis. "I said: is he a friend of yours?"

"I guess, yeah. He's a good bloke."

By now FTB's hangers-on had sensed the beginning of what they probably thought of as entertainment and began to gather round. The barman set a glass of orange juice down beside the rest of my order.

"That's twenty pounds and forty-nine pence altogether, please."

I looked over at my group. All were still deep in conversation, none of them looking my way. I guessed the crush in the bar would make it hard to tell the difference between regular punters and those just about to embark on halitocide, but even so I'd hoped at least one of them would have offered a hand with the drinks. I realised Fish Tank Breath was talking again.

"... pie on his head?"

"Sorry?"

"God. Are you deaf as well as ignorant? I said why does your best mate Sandip wear that pork pie on his head?"

"It's a turban. He's a Sikh."

"What's he seeking?" asked the man who had spoken first, earlier. This clearly qualified as the height of humour among his fellows as they all made a big deal of falling about laughing and holding their splitting sides. Fish Tank Breath ignored his mate's question. He changed the subject.

"That Samdip's drink, is it?" he asked, indicating the orange juice.

I handed a twenty and a five to the barman. "Keep the change. Yes, that's right. Sikh's don't drink alcohol."

"We'll see abaht that," Fish Tank Breath muttered, turning to the barman. "Put a double voddie in there mate, willya? My shout."

The barman reached for Samdip's glass. I covered it with my hand. "No, it's OK. Leave it."

"S'matter?" Fish Tank Breath asked, moving even closer to me and exhaling aromatically. "My drinks not good enough for ya?"

Author's Notes

From a distance of ten years I'm struggling to remember the connection I saw between "Colours" and the text that follows. "Nailing your colours to the mast", possibly? Or maybe I intended it to mean the "tribal colours" of two sides engaged in conflict – in this case, racists vs normal people.

We've all seen this scenario played out, both in fiction – especially in the bar room brawls and shootouts common to Westerns of all kinds – and in real life. No-one lives in a city for very long without at least witnessing an event like this or, worse, becoming embroiled in it. Thankfully I've never been directly involved in one, although I've come close a couple of times.

So once again I had some real-life experience to draw on, alongside those dozens of Westerns I've watched over the years. Fish Tank Breath is a real person, drawn larger than the man I knew but with the same intense odour of rot. And I have known several Sikhs over the years, uniformly gentle, kind, and unassuming people who have gone some way to restoring my faith in organised religion, which has been badly eroded as described in the piece on "Faith".

The question about where this story might go is a good one. A commenter on the original piece asked whether it would be the start of a short story. I don't know. It was uncomfortable to write (not necessarily a bad thing, at least in terms of dramatic tension), and it could "go either way." But it would fit perfectly into the collection of short stories based in and around Manchester that I thought at one time I might write.

Notes from an Editor's perspective

Although the characters in this story are reasonably well realised given the time constraints, one of the hardest parts of drafting, for me, is maintaining a character's voice. When I'm doing a full edit, I dedicated an entire pass (read-through) to focusing on this. Making sure every aspect is consistent: verbal tics, vocabulary, cadence, whether the character is verbose, laconic, or anything in between, etc.

So with this in mind, it occurs to me on re-reading this piece, that FTB would not use the word "ignorant" in his speech "God. Are you deaf as well as ignorant?" Characters like him speak in simple monosyllables, occasionally reaching the dizzy heights of two. Words of three syllables? That's a stretch too far. He'd be more likely to say "Are you deaf as well as stupid?"

Day 32: Exploration

"Three minutes to ion ignition."

Yevgeny Orlov stared through the observation window beside him. At this distance Mars was still a small red blob, but the ion engines required a much longer burn than the old chemical rockets. He checked his velocity and attitude readouts again to confirm the captain's burn countdown.

Still many thousands of kilometres distant, there was no visible sign of Curiosity. The old Mars rover that had paved the way for the first manned exploration had long since stopped broadcasting, although WSA technologists, some of whom were old enough to have worked on the Curiosity project, still kept alive a flicker of hope that the craft would have some small reserves of energy remaining. It was programmed to continue monitoring operations even if transmission was interrupted, cycling its buffers until contact was re-established. Remotely, or manually.

The thought of manually retrieving Curiosity's records – making actual physical contact with the rover after all these years – sent a thrill down Yevgeny's spine. A thrill that was interrupted by Captain Hu's announcement.

"Ion burn initiated. Commence orbital insertion procedures."

*

The dull red arc of Mars filled Yevgeny's observation window as the Red Rider completed orbital insertion. The operations cabin was filled with muted voices calling out readings and the click and beep of switches being thrown and computers responding, signalling, or calling for attention. At this stage of the journey, Yevgeny had little to do except support the others. As the mission's planetary scientist his work wouldn't really start until they achieved planetfall.

Just about every other station on the Rider was occupied by crew members whose fierce concentration on this critical phase was almost tangible. Richards, the astrogator, monitored her course by the second. Doctor Singh kept tabs on all the physiological telemetry readouts for the crew. Several of his outputs glowed amber, indicating high stress levels which were only to be expected, but thankfully none of them had yet strayed into the red. The only red in the cabin of the Rider was the glow from beyond the windows. Mars rotated slowly beneath them, beautiful and – despite the masses of information transmitted by Curiosity over the previous twenty-seven years – mysterious.

A low bell-like chime sounded, indicating successful orbit had been achieved. The crew cheered, high-fived and exchanged relieved smiles. Time for a brief but well-earned rest before moving on to the next phase of the mission: preparing their lander for launch. Once again Yevgeny thrilled at the thought that the culmination of his life's ambitions – actually setting foot on an alien world, seeing first-hand the strange and unique landscape, and investigating the seismology, geomorphology and mineralogy without any interstitial robots or radio links – was now only hours away.

[this is a companion piece to "Seeing Red" which appears next in the writing challenge – on Day 33]

Author's Notes

Having been a fan of Star Trek in all its incarnations since it was first broadcast in the UK, I'm well aware of Roddenberry's desire to represent the future of the human race as one of equality, camaraderie and cooperation. So the appearance of Russian, Chinese, and female crew in this piece is deliberate.

I'm especially keen to include dynamic, strong, independent women in my fiction. As someone with two daughters and many female friends, I'm acutely aware of the trap a lot of male authors fall into – of making their protags and MCs white, male, and heterosexual. It's a trap I always try to avoid, although I won't pretend that I always succeed.

I don't write much "hard" SF and this piece (and any others like it) is about as close as I come. It's hard work to make the best job of representing futuristic tech in a believable way. It's something else Star Trek is immensely good at, but we're all familiar with work where the tech isn't quite so well realised, and how dreadfully laughable that can be. I'd prefer to avoid that too!

Notes from an Editor's perspective

Lots of passive voice in this piece, I notice. "The operations cabin was filled…", "every other station on the Rider was occupied by…" etc. And some instances of close repetition of terms and phrases too. "Orbital insertion" and "manually" leap out at me. Both of these are common artefacts of my first drafts and I would pick them up on the first editing pass.

Day 33: Seeing Red

[this is a companion piece to "Exploration" which immediately precedes it in the writing challenge – on Day 32]

Yevgeny Orlov stopped, unable to move, at the last rung. Twenty centimetres above the rust-red dust of the Martian surface, on the very brink of achieving his lifelong dream, Yevgeny froze. Inside his environment suit, a miracle of modern engineering designed to protect him from external extremes far beyond what he was likely to experience on Mars, a fan whirred into life, spurred to action by the suit's sensors which detected a considerable increase in humidity from the sweat which now stood out on Yevgeny's brow. The biomonitors reported his condition to the lander.

Doctor Singh's voice crackled into his ears. "Problem, Yev? Your stress levels just spiked like I have never seen."

He cleared his throat, which seemed to be reacting to the still-settling dust cloud the lander had thrown up, even though none of it could possibly have breached his seals.

"Give me moment," he managed. "This big event for me."

"For all of us, Orlov," Captain Hu broke in. "But Richards and Kowalski still need to get down here, so if you would be so kind as to get a move on, we can get on with our tasks."

He passed a gloved hand over his visor, wiping away the thin layer of dust that static had attracted, and looked out again at the dimly lit landscape. The sun, close to its zenith, shone pale and tiny in the ochre sky. Forcing his hands to unclamp themselves from the ladder, Yevgeny stepped at last onto his first new world.

He took a tentative step away from the lander, remembering to compensate for the less-than-half gravity compared with Earth that they had practised under during the months of training for this mission. Jan Kowalski appeared at the rim of the hatch above him.

"Look out below!" he yelled, launching himself out into the thin atmosphere, catching the ladder with one hand and sliding down it like a clown entering the ring. "Wheeee!" he shouted, causing Yevgeny to reach for his intercom volume adjuster. The engineer had no sense of occasion. He behaved like he'd just arrived on a day trip to the solar system's biggest playground.

Yevgeny turned his back on Kowalski's childish antics and set off in the direction of Curiosity, which they had overflown during landing. He intended to retrieve the rover's data set before too much was overwritten, duplicating what their lander and the Red River still in orbit above them were already recording. If their last reports were accurate, there had been considerable seismic activity recently, completely at odds with everything they thought they knew about Mars' geology.

Captain Hu said something unintelligible. Yevgeny increased the gain on his intercom.

"Say again, Captain?"

"Don't waste too much time on your pet rover," Hu repeated. "We have a full schedule of tasks as it is, without wasting energy on an almost-dead probe."

Wasting energy? Didn't the man realise they wouldn't be here if it wasn't for the trailblazing, plucky little rover? The least Yevgeny could do was grab its data. By now he had emerged from the artificial dust cloud. He had a clearer view across the plain towards Mount Sharp, where the rover had completed its mission. Flicking controls on his arm console, he deployed the telephoto lenses mounted on his visor and panned the horizon.

After ten minutes scanning the entire crater wall in this quadrant, and checking back with Richards that this was definitely the direction from which they had made their final approach, Yevgeny had to admit: there was absolutely no sign of Curiosity.

Author's Notes

I can never resist a cliffhanger. A strong beginning for a short story, this, and I'd love to know where Curiosity has gone. They flew over it, so it's only just disappeared. No doubt connected with the seismic activity. Suggestions to me on an e-postcard at the usual address :o)

Day 34: Shades of Grey

How many shades of grey do you think there are? I'm guessing that, unless you've been entirely out of touch with the zeitgeist over the last few months, the first and possibly only answer that's popped into your head is: 50.

I haven't read it. I don't intend to read it. Not my kind of thing at all. But I have read reviews of it, and while I'm the first to admit that one should never judge anything solely on the basis of reviews of that thing, the reviews I've read of 50 Shades of Grey have been universally condemnatory. Sometimes exceedingly eloquently so. And other times side-splittingly amusingly so.

So, armed with my Shield of Smug, I will continue to protect myself from being sullied by any and all exposure to the actual text of the document in question. Unfortunately my shield is of little use against other works of similar "quality," many of which regularly crop up as book club choices. I can't remember how old I was when I began to think, while reading, "God. I could write better than this," but I was almost certainly still in short trousers.

In the intervening (*counts on fingers*) 46 years, things haven't got much better. Of course, I've read some good stuff during those years. Many, many examples of excellent writing that have thrilled, captivated, engaged and transported me to their writers' worlds. But there's an almost equal number of appalling turkeys in the mix, and the question that comes back to me, time after time, is: how on Earth does this drivel ever get published?

As a writer myself (if you hadn't noticed) I'm all too painfully familiar with the concept of a publishing gatekeeper. Enough of them have slammed their blimmin' gates shut in my face over the years, so I should be. They have SUCH little time, and SO many submissions, and they can ONLY take on ONE new writer this year. So I'm sorry, your manuscript is not what we're looking for, or we're not actually looking for anything at all, or we're too busy with our existing client base, yadda yadda yadda.

So if all that's true, wouldn't you think that they would expend their oh-so-precious time and resources actually sifting out the nuggets from the endless piles of dross that fly across their desks every day? Is it just that they become so exposed to utter crap that when they eventually bother to read a piece that's just this side of crap, they think they've uncovered the next Virginia Woolf? A woeful lack of perspective brought on by living too close to worthless rubbish.

A little while ago I read an interesting bit of speculative insight into what might be going on. It debated the success of books that are really quite badly written, versus the opposite story, often told, of the well-written book that doesn't do well with sales. There's an example of this latter category in the side bar over there on your right . Cough. It's a common theme with self- or e-publishing that the gatekeeper I referred to above – agents and traditional publishers, editors, etc – has been removed from the process and hence (potentially) the floodgates have been opened to (yet more) half-arsed dross. But through all this, the interesting point of the article was that really successful books have a compelling story AND are well-written, but books will also generally do reasonably well if they have the former but not the latter.

That is to say, a poorly written book that has a compelling story will still be read. A well-written bore will not. This is an unpalatable truth for those of us writers who take utmost pride in the craft of writing. Grammar, spelling, punctuation, tone, vocabulary – selecting EXACTLY the right word to replace the ALMOST right one – this takes a lot of effort. It took me, for War of Nutrition, years. Literally. Although admittedly part-time. To the majority of readers? It doesn't matter. They absolutely do not care if I chose one word or the other. Whether I keep to the point-of-view rules or not.

Whether they can't tell the difference, or they don't notice, or they DO notice but they don't care because the story is SUCH a page-turner… I don't know. But even quite a few 1-star reviews complaining about grammar and spelling will not slow the sales of a book that also has a good smattering of 5-star reviews saying "I couldn't put it down." It's galling, and I would never lower my standards to get a book out faster based on that truth, but that doesn't make it any less of a truth.

In the case of 50 Shades of Grey, many many reviewers bemoan the awful English. The poor sentence structure and grammar. The parroting of hackneyed phrases. The bad word choice. But the sad fact is the subject matter had a popular launch point (as Twilight fan fic) and has an even more popular, naughty, faux shocking, main subject. And it sells by the million.

So have I told you how good my book is? It's got chases and setbacks and world-wide sickness and a hero who... [spoiler deleted]. And it's got a bit of risqué sex. And some regular sex. And every single person who has read it has told me how much they enjoyed it, and what a page turner it is, and some of them have even gone into print on t'Interweb to say so. Publically. For which I'm sincerely grateful. But as of now, it's not selling millions. Unfortunately.

I live in hope.

Author's Notes

When I wrote this, Fifty Shades of Grey had been out a little over four months, and was still a hot topic of conversation. You may say it's an easy target. I might agree. I would also add that it's not a good look for a writer to berate another writer's work. I don't do it often. I stopped writing reviews on Goodreads (after 3) for that very reason. But occasionally it's cathartic to have a good rant, which is what this is.

Ten years on, and the book I refer to – no, the other book: mine – still isn't selling millions. And now it's fallen below Amazon's radar. It is widely accepted that Amazon doesn't like "old things." So they won't show it to you, and they don't even particularly like showing the (few) ads I run to it, even though I pay for them. No, when you're still building a readership, the only way to move copies of older work is to find people who like your newer work (which Amazon will treat more kindly) and hope they're sufficiently engaged to try out the rest of your back catalogue.

You might think that sounds like a challenge. Like a gauntlet thrown down. I couldn't possibly comment.

Day 35: Forgotten

The memories of those warm summer days were all that was left to it now. Day trips to the river with the man and his son. Sunlight flashing and sparkling on the slow-moving water. Early morning mist and the distant muted sound of weekend traffic on the bridge, making its way into the city. Back then the phrase "retail therapy" hadn't been invented, but that's what they would call it now.

It felt useful, on those days. The man's work-roughened hands were warm and strong as he fitted it into place. Into its well-worn groove. It liked that. Being in the groove. It sounded modern. Which for an antique piece was an exciting thing. Slotting into the groove had been part of its experience for countless years. It had belonged to the man's father. And before that, to his father. During those most recently remembered summer mornings by the river, there was no hint that the family tradition wouldn't be continued with the son. The boy who accompanied them on these frequent trips to the water's edge and sat disconsolately munching on a chocolate bar to keep him from fidgeting and disturbing the prey.

On such working days, there would be time to think. Out in the fresh air, tainted with the damp green smell of the river, the faint oily scent of the traffic fumes from the bridge, there were long periods of inactivity. Of gentle contemplation and relaxation. Occasionally there would be conversation between the man and his son. Quiet words, so as not to scare off the timid prey, but deep too. The kind of subject matter that a father would share with his son. The wisdom of ages. The reminiscences. The juvenile, innocent questions. A bonding experience it felt privileged to be a part of, even if only a supporting role.

Then, on good days, there would occasionally be a burst of excited activity when the prey took the bait and its full abilities would be tested to their limits as the battle raged, sometimes short, others long, until the prey was secured and the bait cast out again.

Distant memories, long gone. Now it occupied a lonely corner of a window sill in the old shed. The sill too high to catch sight of anything outside. Gardening activities had stopped soon after the outings to the river, and the shed was rarely opened up any more. Whole seasons, entire years went by with no visitors except the woodworm that rasped at its dull mahogany surface and the spiders who covered it in gossamer.

Soon, even the spiders left. Died out through lack of food in the closed-up shed, or left to seek their fortunes in more well-stocked larders. Their ancient cobwebs slowly gathered dust, hiding it further from sight, and from memory, one mote at a time. Its handsome varnish had long been worn away by the hands of erstwhile owners, and the exposed woodwork decayed gradually under the influence of the damp air of the shed. Brass ferrules and chasings had long lost their shine and become tarnished and pitted.

The shed door opened. A remembered voice disturbed its reverie.

"God. All this too."

"Ugh! I can't go in there. Too spidery. What's that round thing on the sill?"

"What, this?"

"Yeah."

"Oh, wow! My Dad's old reel! Haven't seen this for years."

Author's Notes

A real memory ("reel" memory hahaha), written from the

point of view of the remembered object. My Dad died in 1993 and in the eighteen years between that, and my Mum's death something like a year before this piece was written, the garden shed was rarely opened. It had always been his domain, where woodworking projects were conceived and lovingly executed over many years, and where he kept his fishing tackle.

Clearing out somewhere that's been a family home after almost sixty years, in preparation for its sale, is a lengthy process. Particularly at a distance of 80 miles or so. It took roughly six months. The dimly lit, crammed, spidery outhouse was left pretty much 'til the last, such a daunting prospect was it.

It was a poignant moment, finding the old reel. By the time we opened that shed, after six months of sorting, cataloguing, deciding what to keep, what to sell, what to throw away, we had long ago passed the point of caring. We just wanted it done. And yet, here was something, so full of childhood memories, it tugged at the heart strings. Tugged at the purse strings too. Surely it was valuable? An antique mahogany and brass fishing reel from the turn of the century? The last century, I mean, in case that wasn't obvious. But I already had plastic tubs piled high with "stuff" destined for eBay. As far as I remember, nothing from the outhouse survives.

Day 36: Dreamer

He was running. From what, or where to, he wasn't quite sure. One thing he was sure of though. Whatever it was was gaining on him. And it was a monster. Two things he was sure of. He couldn't decide which of them was more terrifying.

The landscape was unfamiliar. At first he thought he recognised it. The woods behind his childhood home, where once there was nothing more terrifying that a rook unexpectedly taking wing beyond the dappled green of the sap-steeped hollows he used to frequent as a boy. Vincent N'tanga didn't have a lot of friends. He had learned very early in life how to amuse himself. How to avoid the taunts of the neighbourhood children. Avoid their eyes, even, lest he give unintended offence for some unrecognised wrongdoing. But the paths through this wood were not the ones in his wood and, as he ran, his surroundings changed unusually quickly.

He ran around a corner straight into his kitchen. His mother was standing at the sink, peeling onions. Tears rolled down her face. He called out to her.

"Mother."

She turned, blinded by her tears, brandishing the knife.

"Who's there?"

"It's me, Vince."

"It can't be Vince. He never comes home before tea time."

She lunged at him with the peeler and Vince dodged through the kitchen and into the hall. Only it wasn't the hall. Where the hall had been was now an enormous, white, featureless room with a marble floor. From the door behind him came the roar of the monster, still gaining on him, its bellow echoing around the marble room as if it were coming toward him from all directions. He turned, trying to get back into the relative safety of the kitchen, but the door had slammed shut behind him and there was no handle on this side.

"Vince, this way!" called a low voice.

He spun around again, trying to locate the voice among the echoes.

"Over here!"

He could not make out the direction the voice was coming from. It came again, this time from right behind his ear.

"Come on! Hurry!"

A girl stood a few yards away along the same wall as the kitchen door. At first glance he thought it was his sister Toya, but as he looked closer he saw this girl was taller, older, and had longer hair. He stared once more at the kitchen door. It had begun to smoulder.

He turned back towards the girl, tripped over his feet and fell headlong into cold, fast-flowing water. He struggled to get a breath as the current bore him along. From the bank a branch overhung the river. It was covered in grubs, but offered the only available hand-hold. He reached for it, crushing several bugs into slimy brown mush as he pulled himself from the water. The slime began to eat away at his hand and in the space of a few seconds had exposed the bones of his fingers.

Without realising he was arriving at a conclusion, the explanation for the strange and rapid changes of terrain and the appearance and disappearance of people both known and unknown dawned on him. He was dreaming.

But if that were true, he should be able to wake up. He didn't remember exactly how old he was when he discovered that it was possible to become aware inside a dream. To control the dream, if you were careful. Or end it, if you weren't, or if it was the kind of dream you didn't want to prolong. It was a long time ago, that was for sure, and in the intervening years he had become quite adept at it. He stopped running, and forced his consciousness up through the levels of dreaming, like swimming up from the bottom of the pool where he had been holding his breath, trying to frighten Toya. He pushed, and pushed, and... opened his eyes.

He was still standing on the bank of the river, and nothing remained of his hand but bones. He began to scream.

"Mum!"

His hand fell into the river.

"MUM!"

From behind Vince's closed eyelid, a single tear emerged. It began to roll down his cheek before freezing, leaving a shining icy path behind it. Beyond his cryochamber, Professor David Redhead and Doctor Peter Barton were recording their outputs and observations in their logs. Barton's attention was caught by the reflection from Vince's crystalline lachrymation.

"Is that... a tear? David?"

"Autonomic response probably. There may be some irritation of his corneas."

"You're sure he can't be dreaming?"

"Not a chance. There's not enough brain function to sustain a dream at these temperatures. We have to make sure of that. A five-year-long dream would send anyone mad."

Author's Notes

For me, dreamscapes are a compelling narrative device. I'm not alone in that, if the success of movies like

"Inception" and the many Star Trek episodes that use dreaming as an anchor for the story are any guide. I use them frequently in the Berikatanyan Chronicles for a variety of purposes.

Trying to capture the essence of a dream is challenging. To represent the way parts of the sequence are connected in illogical or unpredictable ways, probably on account of being separate dreams, while maintaining some kind of coherence to the tale. The end result can often be a confusing mishmash of disjointed vignettes, but when it works it can add a fresh dimension to a story.

Some of the ideas in my "log lines" document come from dreams. The most vivid ones, which hang around long enough to be written down on waking. Often all that remains is a sense of what happened, without any detail, but sometimes that's exactly what's needed to give the text a dreamlike quality.

The inspiration for this piece, which the day's writing "prompt" brought immediately to mind, is an SF short called "Shards", by Brian Aldiss, which I last read as a teenager. In that case the strange sequence of thoughts turns out to be (*spoiler alert*) the result of having pieces of human brain ("shards") embedded into fish in order to communicate with, and/or fight, invading aquatic aliens, so in that case not a dream as such, but a powerful story whose memory remains fresh despite the passing of years.

Notes from an Editor's perspective

"...nothing more terrifying that a rook..." should obviously be "than a rook". Quite a common drafting error for me, and one that's quite hard to spot. Often missed if the passage in question is read towards the end of the editing stint when concentration is failing, especially since it's one of the things that grammar checkers have trouble with (although having said that, this manuscript began life in Google Docs where it was successfully highlighted, so things are definitely improving on that score).

"He struggled to get a breath…" Get is one of those words that should only appear in first drafts, where thinking room is not available for selection of the best word unless it comes effortlessly to mind. Get is a backstop. A ready "null" word that doesn't stem the flow of the narrative. But it always has a better alternative – often more than one – which should always replace it in the final work. Here, I would probably have opted for something like "catch" a breath, or possibly "gulp" a breath.

Day 37: Mist

Opaqued into whiteness by condensation, the ranks of greenhouse roofs stretched for miles across the unrelieved flatness of the old alluvial plane, like teeth in the widened maw of a colossal beast. Occasionally a pane would open or close fractionally at the impulse of some hidden temperature or humidity sensor, but that apart nothing disturbed the stillness of the scene.

No birds flapped. No rodents dug. No beetles scurried. There were no trees or bushes to react to any breath of wind. The only sound was the creaking of horticultural glass as it stretched and groaned under the midday sun, fiercely bright in the cloudless sky.

Beneath the glass, all was not still. Not always. The interior of the glasshouse, partitioned into areas the size of midwestern cornfields from a distant age, occasionally resounded to mechanical activity. In some partitions, automated diggers churned the soil, adding white powder to the deep brown dirt and leaving the surface finely milled. The diggers were followed closely by wheeled hoppers, clicking quietly as they dispensed seeds one at a time into the depressions left by the diggers. As first the diggers and then the hoppers garaged themselves inside the partitions, a gentle rain fell from sprinklers set on the glazing bars high above.

The scene in other partitions – those behind the one in which the automated agricultural machinery had been busy – was not so idyllically sylvan. It more closely resembled the aftermath of apocalypse. The ground, devoid of any distinguishing marks, steamed evilly. Faint patches of grey slime puddled into slight pockets in the soil, or ran in small odorous rivulets to join others on their way to the pools. The air in these partitions reeked. The glass had lost its whitened condensate in favour of grey, casting a depressing pall over the space.

But beyond the machines, and beyond the destruction, colour and ripeness could be found. Acre upon acre of burgeoning vegetables, filling the air with the scents of mellow maturity. In the nearest of these, any opened lights were slowly closing. All of them. Once the last few had clicked shut an enormous motor kicked into life and the myriad clear irrigation pipes were filled with a pale blue liquid from a single vast tank, stamped in letters a metre tall with a capitalised word in a similar pale blue: MIST.

And the mist fell. Finer than the germinating rain in the planted sections, the tiny droplets of iridescence were hardly large enough to fall, yet fall they did. Slowly. And at the first touch of shining blue on their ripe perfection, the vegetables began to dissolve. Tomatoes bubbled and popped. Courgettes dripped. Peas and beans slipped from their stems. Within the space of a few minutes the entire section was reduced to a flood of reeking grey slime. From a central partition, huge mobile tanks emerged, sucking up the juice. They too were marked MIST but now, below the blue heading in smaller, black letters, another legend could be seen: Macerating Interspersal Spray Technology.

Author's Notes

After 38 years spent in the computing industry, I still haven't lost my love for a decent acronym, or backronym. So that was my first thought on seeing the prompt for this day: can I come up with an alternative meaning to M.I.S.T and spin a yarn around that?

The piece is deliberately ambiguous. On the one hand, the complex arrangements of automated agriculture speak to a post-apocalyptic time where there may be no humans left alive to benefit from the produce, yet the machines keep on with their tasks oblivious to the pointlessness of it all. This can be interpreted to also fit with the application of MIST: the food, remaining unharvested, must be disposed of to make way for the next crop. Behind that simple interpretation though, is a darker, more horrific alternative. Perhaps whatever IS left alive on this world is only capable of ingesting its food as a nutritious grey slime?

Notes from an Editor's perspective

Rereading these from such a long-term perspective makes me wish I could find a way to reset my drafting brain to active mode. These many instances of passive voice that remain in every first draft I write serve only to load up more work for the editing pass. "The diggers were followed…", "...pipes were filled with…", etc. I think after ten years as a published author, and another ten years before that spent drafting and editing, I'm just going to have to accept that this is the way I write, and deal with it.

On a more positive note, bearing in mind that all the descriptive passages in this piece are first-draft, conceived and written in 30 minutes, I think they hold up pretty well.

Day 38: Burning

Sheelagh was subconsciously aware something was wrong even before she awoke. She had been dreaming about petrol. About filling her car and the nozzle coming off the hose and splashing the thin pungent liquor all over her clothes and face. The boundary between dreams and reality blurred as she woke up, because the air in her bedroom was redolent with the heavy, intoxicating smell of the petrol from her nightmare.

A loud "whooomp" from outside her door brought her fully awake. Shadows danced through the crack of the half-open door.

"Bernie! Bernie!" she nudged her snoring husband. "Wake up! Somet'ing's wrong!"

"Mmm? Whassat?"

Sheelagh threw off the covers and ran to the door. The sound of crackling, faint at first but swelling quickly, echoed through their sparsely-furnished hallway. And the smell. Woodsmoke. Its first tentative tendrils already creeping up the stairs, looking for airways to choke. Sheelagh slammed the door shut, grabbed the top sheet from her bed and ran to the sink in the next room.

"Get up Bernie for God's sake! We'll be burned alive!"

Their danger slowly filtering through his torpor by a combination of Sheelagh's voice and the cold from lack of a sheet, Bernie sat up in bed.

"What you? What the hell is going on?"

"There's fire in the hall," Sheelagh shouted from their bathroom as she plunged the sheet into cold water. "Don't open the door."

Bernie started towards the door but Sheelagh shoved him roughly aside, plugging the gap between door and floor with the sodden sheet. She rounded on her husband.

"Will you wake up properly yer feckless eejit? Help me tie these sheets together." She was already retrieving spare sheets from the divan drawer when the smoke alarm went off.

MEEPMEEPMEEPMEEPMEEPMEEPMEEP

The loudness of the staccato siren finally penetrated Bernie's consciousness. He grabbed two sheets from Sheelagh and began tying them together. Sheelagh ran to the window. Opened it. A chill November gust blew in. The sudden influx of fresh oxygen elicited a roar from the landing beyond the bedroom door as the fire greedily sucked new fuel, climbing the stairs at a lick. An ominous orange glow shone around the cracks of the doorframe, encircling the door in a fiery halo.

"Hurry Bernie!"

Her husband tied one end of the sheet rope to the radiator pipe while Sheelagh flung the rest through the opened window. She peered out into the dark. The streetlights were out at this time of night and there was no moon, but the garden below was illuminated redly by the flickering light of the blaze in their hall. It had already crept into the living room and begun consuming the sofa. Acrid chemical smoke billowed out of a crack in the window immediately below her, stinging her eyes.

"Come on!" she cried, "It's in the lounge already – we've no time!"

She grabbed hold of the sheet rope and swung her legs over the sill. The last sheet flapped dangerously far from the ground but she had used all they had. She knew she'd have to jump the last few feet. Swallowing her fear she slipped off the sill, gripping the sheet as tightly as she could, and held her breath against the clouds of smoke from the window below.

Author's Notes

Little to say about what is essentially a pretty obvious interpretation of the topic. I will say though, that the idea of a dream sequence, of whatever length, turning into a waking reality is one I've used several times in the Berikatanyan Chronicles, often with the implication of prescience on the part of the dreamer.

Notes from an Editor's perspective

There's more passive voice here too, but I've already laboured that point so I won't repeat myself further. I'm sure you get it by now.

The other drafting tic present here is a dearth of descriptive variance. An editing pass on this piece would have resulted in significantly fewer instances of "door" – either replacing them with suitable alternatives or rephrasing the sentence entirely – and perhaps some more inventive ways of describing fire.

I think the sparse usage of Irish accent works well to establish the characters even in this short space. It's too easy to overdo this, which can then come across as cartoonish. A little goes a long way.

Day 39: Out of Time

[this post is a continuation of the story begun in "Online" earlier in the writing challenge – on Day 22]

The scream of the train whistle was matched by a frantic scream from the woman.

"My God! It's coming! The train's coming!"

Niall continued to saw at the rope but he already knew it was not going to be any use. He never sharpened the blade – never had any reason to follow the advice his father had given him on numerous occasions.

"Always keep your blade sharp, lad. You never know when you're going to need it most."

If Niall had been a praying man, he would have sent up a plea that he could have heeded his father sooner. Now, it was too late. He didn't have time to spare to whet the small blade, but neither did he have time not to.

"You'll never do it," the woman screamed, squirming and twisting against the rope. Her frantic movements served only to tighten the complex knots still further, the half-formed thought that he would be better employed seeking a solution to their conundrum dying in Niall's mind as she did so.

The whistle sounded again, frighteningly closer now. The train would emerge around the bend any moment. Still less than halfway through the rope, Niall stopped, spat on the track, and flashed the blade back and forth over the wetted steel. The soft metal took a slight edge. He prayed it would be enough. The first stroke sliced through several strands. Sweat trickled down Niall's face as he bent again to his task with grim determination.

"Yes! Yes, that's it," the woman yelled in his ear, encouraged by the sudden progress. "Please hurry! You can do it!"

But the knife had already lost its new keenness, each thin nylon strand deceptively resistant to its increasingly dull passage. The track began to thrum under Niall's knees as the train neared.

"Sharpen it again!" screamed the woman, fractionally later than Niall's identical thought. He spat again, stropped again, cut again. The train came around the corner, lights already burning in readiness for the tunnel on the other side of the station. Only seconds remained. Niall's arm ached with the effort, his hands were beginning to cramp. He pressed harder against the rope, cleaving strand after strand, but even though less than a quarter of the thickness remained the man-made fibres, designed to bear triple or quadruple the weight of a falling climber, held fast.

The woman's shoulders slumped as the train bore rapidly down on them.

"It's too late!" she cried. "Leave me! Save yourself!"

Niall knew absolutely that she was right, yet he could not leave her. Scant seconds remained. Logic bellowed through his mind that even if he managed to sever the rope he still had to unravel it and lift the woman clear. He needed minutes, and had only seconds. A fat blister burst on his finger and the knife, slippery with his serum, slipped from his hand. It was over.

"I'm sorry," Niall murmured, knowing she would never have heard him over the roar of the train. He jumped back, eyes closed, rolling across the gravel bed of the track. With a grinding clatter the train shot past, drowning the woman's screams in a welter of mechanical pandemonium.

Silence. Not even bees disturbed it. Niall lay on his back, winded. He was bruised, shaken, but otherwise unhurt. He definitely did not want to open his eyes.

"Uh. Uh-huh. Uh-huh-huh-huh."

The sound of gentle sobbing surprised him into a glance at the track, where he had expected to see the gory result of the train's passage. The woman lay, unharmed, in exactly the same place as before, her head cradled in her hands as she cried. Niall stared at the second track and rubbed unconsciously at his broken blister.

Author's Notes

Inspired by a childhood spent watching Tom & Jerry, and other similar cartoon shows, where the trope of an unfortunate character tied to a (toy) trainline was oft repeated, and just as often resolved by the train crossing a set of points (or, for my American readers, a railroad switch) and taking another line.

Were I ever to flesh this out into a "proper" short story, the future of Niall and the woman he has been so dramatically introduced to could clearly go in any one of several directions, but being an old romantic at heart I'd like to think they could eventually find happiness together.

Notes from an Editor's perspective

I would almost certainly take the opportunity to replace "He needed minutes, and had only seconds." with "He needed minutes, and had only moments." I can never resist a little alliteration (even though style guides frown upon it), and apart from that by the time we arrive at this sentence I've already used "seconds" twice in quick succession.

Day 40: Knowing How

"I'm not sure I can figure out this assembly. Do you know how?"

"Sure."

"Great. Can you show me?"

"Show you what?"

"I thought you said you know how?"

"I do."

"So show me."

"Show you how?"

"Yeah."

"He won't be here until later."

"Who?"

"No, How."

"What?"

"No! Make your mind up. I thought you wanted me to show you How."

"I do."

"Well then, you'll have to wait until he arrives."

"Who?"

"No! How! Hu's not coming!"

"I don't know. I don't know who's coming."

"Well he isn't."

"Who?"

"Yes."

"Who's not coming?"

"That's right."

"No! Who! Who's not coming?"

"I know. No need to keep repeating yourself. It was me told you!"

"When?"

"No, he's not coming either. What is it with you and the Chinese?"

"What?"

"Look. It's quite simple. Hu's not coming. Wen is not coming. And neither is Watt. How could he be coming? He's dead."

"How?"

"No! Watt!"

"No, I meant 'how did he die'?"

"Who?"

"Watt."

"I don't know! Google it!"

"I don't know how."

"Well I'll introduce you when he gets here."

"Who?"

"For pity's sake I already told you Hu's not coming."

"No you didn't."

"Yes. I did."

"When?"

"That's right. Wen and Hu. And Watt."

"What?"

"Yes."

"What's not coming?"

"Yes."

"WHAT?"

"Yes! Don't sound so surprised! He's been dead for centuries!"

"Who?"

"NO! WATT! Anyway, look. It doesn't matter. Here's How."

"Finally! You could have just showed me when I asked you."

"Hi How."

"Hi guys. What's going down?"

"He can't. Apparently he's dead."

"Who?"

"No, Watt."

"You guys are weird. So, where are we going?"

"Are we? When did we decide that?"

"What?"

"That we were going to Ware."

"Where?"

"Yes."

"We didn't decide."

"You just said we did."

"Who did?"

"No he didn't! He's too busy leading China!"

"What?"

"He's dead!"

"Who?"

"No, Watt."

"When?"

"No, he's leading China too. With Hu."

"Who?"

"That's right."

"Where?"

"OK. If you insist. But we'll have to get the bus."

"To where?"

"Exactly. Too far to walk."

...

A story of two friends, a guy called Howard (known only to one of them), the Chinese leader Hu (Jintao), the 6th Chinese Premier Wen (Jiabao), Watt (the engineer) and Ware (a town in Yorkshire). Inspired by Jim Sherman's short skit written after Hu was elected, which is enacted here
(https://www.youtube.com/watch?v=BeRjRxYhz6U)
You might guess I ran out of steam after a lot less than 30 minutes this time ;0)

Author's Notes

In this case I clearly thought it necessary to include the explanation within the topic itself, so enough said!

Day 41: Fork in the Road

Jason wandered along the forest path. It was a hot afternoon, and his June holiday was ending with the month. He stared at the sun through screwed-up eyes, his squint distorting its edges into horn-like flares. He had decided to take one final walk to the beach before heading home. Not for any special reason or sentiment, but just because.

He shielded his eyes with his hand, noticing something glinting on the path in front of him. A single bright point of scintillation. Curious, he walked over to it and bent down. It was a fork, its polished steel bouncing the strong sun in all directions. A few metres away, closer to the side of the road, lay a plate. He stood up, and walked over to the plate.

It lay at the entrance to a path he had not noticed before. Heavily overgrown so that it was almost invisible beneath the foliage, the path headed off into the woods. Jason had originally intended to keep to the main road on his walk to the beach, but this strange, deserted path intrigued him. He took it.

On entering the first crop of trees, Jason could see there was a clearing ahead. He heard voices. He had been holidaying here for two weeks – how had he not discovered this place sooner?

He entered the clearing, and realised immediately it was a picnic area. To one side stood a man in front of a cooker. Jason was surprised to see it was a bottled gas cooker, right here in the open space. The man watched a pan of water that stood on the largest burner.

Several picnic tables were arranged around the clearing, some occupied by holidaymakers. One man, a worried expression on his face, sat in front of a plate piled high with traditional picnic food, scratching his head. He glanced around the clearing at the other people there, as if searching for something. On the other side of the table, in complete contrast to the first man, a second man had less than half of a sandwich remaining. He had taken only a single bite, but his face was distorted in pain and sweat stood out on his brow.

Over on the other side of the clearing one of the picnicker's dogs had been chasing a cat. It stood at the foot of a tree, barking excitedly. The cat stared down at it disdainfully from a tree a metre to the left.

From his right came the sound of a loudly revving truck engine. Jason walked over and saw that the picnic area car park was in a hollow and had been reinforced with stone walls. Someone in a massive 4x4 had clearly taken a wrong turning and ended up sliding down the bank. The vehicle had come to a standstill with its front wheels wedged against the wall. Inside the cabin, the man and his wife were clearly visible, arguing heatedly, while the man continued to try to move the truck despite its precarious position. The front wheels spun against the stone, sending up clouds of toxic smoke.

Jason turned back to the clearing, taking in more of the scene. At another table a family of four were laying out their snacks. Their young son had stolen a bar of chocolate from his younger sister, who lay in her basket and didn't seem to mind. Meanwhile the father had filled a long ancient meerschaum and was trying to light it. Unremarked by the rest of the family, a third child took aim with his catapult at a bird sitting high in the same tree as the cat Jason had noticed earlier. The boy let go with his stone and the bird fell dead into the clearing, shortly followed by another which had been sitting unnoticed behind it on the same branch.

Jason had seen enough of the strange picnic stop. Checking all the paths, he selected one and walked towards it, passing a bed of roses. The air was heavy with their scent but Jason did not stop. He looked back at the clearing. The man's pot still had not begun to boil, but he could not hang around any longer. He turned, blinking against the brightness of the sun, and the picnic clearing was gone.

The afternoon heat seemed to intensify as he walked, but it didn't worry him. The only thing making him really uncomfortable was the strong green smell of the forest, and the moisture being released by all that greenery. The air was full of it.

Before long the beach came in sight below him. He had chosen the cliff path. On the beach he could see a child with a stick, drawing in the sand while his father busied himself setting out a large pile of deckchairs. As Jason watched the man seemed dissatisfied with the arrangement of the chairs and was trying to set them out in a different pattern. On the other side of the path a stream ran slowly down to the sea. Although slow moving, the water was very clear and Jason could see the bottom of the stream many metres below. The stream divided into several different rivulets, but all the channels joined together again before they reached the bridge towards which Jason was walking.

On the other side of the bridge the grassy bank shone in the afternoon sun, a deeper green compared to the sparse couch grass on Jason's side. Before he reached the bridge Jason noticed a tunnel, set strangely high on the hillside.

The path in front of him continued straight, inclining slightly downward to the beach. But to his right, another path snaked up the side of the hill in the direction of the tunnel. Thinking of all that had happened to him that afternoon, Jason had to know. He took the right-hand path, and climbed slowly and breathlessly up towards the tunnel. After a few hundred metres the path passed a small chapel. Through the open door came the sonorous tones of the minister giving a sermon. Jason poked his head around the door inquisitively. The chapel was deserted except for a few choirboys who sat with bored expressions listening to the sermon.

The route up the hillside was hard and rocky, but Jason persisted, determined to see for himself what lay at the top. At length the path fetched up at the side of the track, immediately before the entrance to the tunnel. Placing one hand on the cut stone arch, Jason peered along the length of the tunnel. Through the blackness, a very long way down the track, there was a light.

Author's Notes

I had a lot of fun with this one. The topic of "a fork in the road" made me think of cliches and cultural references, and how many it might be possible to incorporate in a single short story. So on this occasion, I broke my own rule about plotting versus drafting, and invested some of my time (still inside the 30 minutes) coming up with a list of such cliches. I managed to think of 26 in the end, all of which are represented above. See how many you can find. To avoid spoiling the fun, I've listed them in the Appendix. No cheating now!

Day 42: Start

Tani stood in the clearing, her heart pounding as if she had run a sprint race. Another sprint race, she corrected herself. It was, after all, running such races that had put her in this place, at this time. A bead of sweat trickled down her face. She dashed it away with her free hand.

Promecyon – the alpha sun – was setting. In another few minutes the only light remaining would be from the beta sun Anubethon, a million times dimmer. A light that barely served to see by. Just this side of total darkness. It was the light that, by countless years of tradition, illuminated The Hunt.

She took small comfort that only the best were chosen. The Hunters meant "the best sport." Those who would prolong the chase and give the most thrills. Take unexpected chances, death-defying risks, maybe even escape capture altogether. It was fabled that there had been one such. A man, in that case. Riki. His name etched in the minds of all who were chosen for The Hunt. One man. One among the thousands who had tried, and failed.

But Tani had a few tricks up her sleeve. In the days leading up to the contest she had spoken to no-one, trusted no-one with her ideas. Instead, she had concentrated on her training. Mind and body she exercised, so that both would work together in total harmony. She knew that, when it came to the moment when her fate would be decided, she might only have seconds. Fractions of seconds in which to decide on a course and execute it. She needed to be at the top of her game, and she was.

So for now, in the last few minutes of alpha light, she breathed deep and tried to calm her racing heart. She rubbed at her tethered hand. The mechocuff chafed, even though she knew better than to tug at it. The post to which it was fastened had been sunk five metres deep into the bedrock and was made of puranium steel. It was said that it would survive a neutron blast. Tani focused her thoughts on her chosen exit from the clearing. She did not look towards it, or even deliberately away from it. She didn't want to give away the slightest clue to her intentions as the seconds counted down to her Start.

Once the cuff released she would have half an hour's lead on the Pack. And another fifteen minutes before the Hunt proper left the enclosure. She discounted those last fifteen minutes. Not much of a bonus when you were faced with being tracked by the Pack. GM wolves with enhanced sight and smell, and legs whose length and musculature had been bred to give them frightening speed over clear ground. Tani did not intend to give them the advantage of any clear ground. Where she planned to flee, the Pack would be hard pushed to follow.

Promecyon edged closer to the horizon. In the surrounding forest the night creatures stirred. One more danger for Tani to factor in to her escape. At best, a few of them could be said to be benign. Even these could give the unwary a nasty nip, although they would only retaliate if attacked first. In the worst cases even that small nip could be fatal, as many of the smaller creatures carried napa glands. The deadly poison tipped the arrows, spears and hand blades of the Hunt. But it was the true predators that held the greatest danger. At least, that which lay ahead of her. Behind her the Hunt had determination, weapons, intellect and intent. Ahead of her, the forest presented an almost equivalent menace. Animal blood lust, strength, instinct and blisteringly fast reaction times. And hunger. On this world the predators outnumbered the prey and consequently lived in a perpetual state of attack, always searching for their next meal.

As if these did not present enough of a threat, Tani faced vegetable foes too. Over millennia the forest had evolved its own defences to the animal life that tried to make a living within it. She was well schooled in the almost endless list of vines, shrubs, leaves and spines that she would have to avoid if she were to match Riki and survive the Hunt.

Unremarked by the animal and vegetable threats surrounding her, the forest canopy extinguished the last fingers of light from Promecyon. With a soundless click the mechocuff unlocked and fell away from her wrist. The Hunt was on!

[this story is continued in "Heart Song" later in the writing challenge – on Day 45]

Author's Notes

The names of the character, sun, and flora/fauna have changed, but with those adaptations, this piece appears as a dream sequence in the first book of the Berikatanyan Chronicles.

Day 43: Nature's Fury

This dream stretched back to the dawn of the nuclear age, when man first conceived of how the universe might be put together, concocted experiments to prove those conceptions and created engines to exploit those concoctions.

They were right, those early scientists. Everything that had happened since only served to prove them more right. To refine their models, certainly. To uncover new wonders. But never to countermand that early genius. That incredible leap of imagination that had envisaged the ultimately minuscule in all its glory and complexity.

What had once been a dream was now an incredible reality. Quite literally incredible it would have seemed to anyone from that past who could be given a glimpse of the impossible future. The technological splendours upon which the world had come to rely. And yet, splendid as they all were, the technological runway was about to run out. The dream turn to nightmare. Without this one final step, this culmination of the dream of centuries, mankind was surely doomed. For their appetite for power remained undimmed. Gorging like a starving gluttonous gourmand, they sucked power from the grid as fast as current technology could generate it. Faster, in some cases, whereupon the fragile contrivance that supplied their power would grumble and groan, spark and fizzle and, yes, die. And natural night would fall at last upon hitherto unnaturally effulgent cities.

Fossil fuels all but exhausted, nuclear reactors strictly curtailed by pan-governmental edicts, and the promise of "renewable" energy a spent force that had consumed fully one half of all the world's rare elements and yet produced barely ten percent of its needs, this dream, this one final step, was all that remained of the hope of humanity.

Fusion.

Many still scoffed at the idea that puny man could hope to harness the sun's fury. Those with long memories cited the many examples of cold fusion scams that blighted the pages of even the most well-respected scientific journals. Remnants of once-mighty generating companies and their lobbyists even now still tried to pour scorn and opprobrium on those who led the field. Every bit as much the geniuses as those who first studied the wonders of atoms and discovered how they were constructed. Three people led the field, and of those only one, the one who stood now on the brink of the most radical paradigm shift in the history of history, had had any experimental success.

Small scale, it was true. Yet every nuance and wrinkle of Shami Patel's models held up to the closest scrutiny and the most rigorous and lengthy testing. Three times Patel had built larger test rigs; three times all lights had come up green. His most recent experiments generated enough power to run his entire laboratory. More than enough evidence to commit to the final step. This final step. He and his team had scaled the model up to full production capacity and he stood now with his hand resting beside the main breaker. An insignificant toggle switch that, in an homage to every disaster and science fiction movie ever made, had been mounted on a red bezel and hidden behind a plexiglass cover.

Once again, as before, all Shami's lights were green. Video cameras, digital cameras, mobile phones and webcams were all focussed on him. The army of scientists, investors and journalists held their collective breath while they waited for Shami to throw that switch. He gazed unseeing at the console, his concentration bent inwards, reviewing the road that had led him to this moment. Exploring for the hundredth time all the avenues and dead-ends, the untaken turns, the alternative directions. Convincing himself that this was the right course. The only course.

The path to the future when every other path had none.

He gave a small shrug and a beatific smile crept onto his face as he reached for the switch.

Author's Notes

When I saw the prompt for this day my first and immediate thought was of the sun. Can there be a more obvious example of nature's fury? It shines down on us every day, the sole source of every other power in our world, one way or another.

Exotic power sources abound in the science fiction stories I have read, or watched, from a very early age. The miniature reactors of Asimov's Foundation series, or Herbert's Imperium, the warp core of Star Trek, etc. It's often said that fiction is allowed to bend the rules of physics as long as it does so in a consistent and believable way. But I was recently reminded, by a fellow writer I have long admired, that the best science fiction is grounded in real science. If you can do that, then your readers will have no qualms about believing in the worlds you create.

Whether or not you believe humankind will ever harness fusion, it is at least possible, and therefore seemed to me a fine subject for this piece. Will Patel's switch usher in a new dawn for us all, or will the artificial sun set forever in a blaze of exploding tech? In common with many of these short works, the story leaves you guessing.

Day 44: At Peace

The nascent heat of the summer morning enveloped her as she stepped from the air-conditioned interior of the limousine. She revelled in the warmth. Let it sink into her old bones as she stood, straightening slowly against the pain of her arthritic spine and hips. The driver walked around to return her pair of barley-twist walking sticks; family heirlooms handed down from a long forgotten forebear, but which felt especially apposite on this day. She thanked him graciously as he replaced his tall hat and preceded her into the chapel.

Through the door in front of her came the lilting sound of organ music. His favourite tune, played with somewhat less vigour than he would have preferred, she knew, and yet comfortingly familiar even at its funereal pace. She hesitated at the door, gathering her strength against the expected flood of emotion, but on stepping through onto the worn stone slabs of the aisle her only feeling was one of ineffable peace. Her gaze stretched along the aisle to the white-shrouded catafalque. White, because both he and she believed that death was not the end, not something to be mourned, but a new beginning for the one departed and therefore something, if at all possible through the maelstrom of grief and loss and pain, to be celebrated.

A ripple of muted voices passed through the seated mourners as the realisation of her arrival spread. All faces turned in her direction, some tear-streaked, some red-eyed, others grimly holding their grief in check. She smiled at each familiar face as she approached the empty front pew. No family waited there for her. Each of them had been only children and they had lost Geraldine more than fifteen years before to breast cancer. She was the last. Before taking her seat she paused beside the polished oak casket, laying a tentative hand on its lid. Peace at last my darling. After the months of late night nursing, cleaning up the sick and managing the medication, ignoring the pain-induced sniping and drying the tears, reading his favourite stories until the book fell unheeded from her sleeping hands, trying to persuade him to take one more mouthful of a meal he once relished. Peace. For both of them.

The vicar cleared his throat politely, bringing her back to the present. To the reality of the day. Reluctantly she took her hand from the coffin, kissed her fingers and brushed them back along its gleaming surface. The final few bars of music died away as she took her lonely seat on the family pew and reached forward to retrieve the tattered, leather-bound prayer book from its resting place.

In his best, most sincere and respectful tones, the vicar began his eulogy, but she wasn't really listening. The man had barely known him, and had gone through the usual motions of interviewing her the week before to garner sufficient details about him to make a decent fist of it. He wouldn't be saying anything she didn't already know. Her mind drifted, remembering the long cycle rides they had taken in their youth – on just such days as this. Fresh, bright, shining with possibilities. She remembered that queasy, excited, breathtaking feeling she felt when the first hints of love sparked unexpectedly, turning their next-door-neighbour friendship into something that would carry them through 60 years of togetherness. Weathering the storms of less sunny days, basking in the warmth of those which were even sunnier. The heartache of losing their only daughter, of knowing they would never bounce grandchildren on their knees or take them for walks in the fields at the end of their lane. The wonderful holidays they had shared: covering the length of Britain, but never venturing to foreign countries; something they each agreed held no interest for them.

The sound of others getting to their feet brought her back to the moment as the organ struck up again for the first hymn. Another favourite of his – and hers too. She smiled as she opened the right page and a gleaming finger of bright yellow light from the stained glass illuminated the first verse.

Author's Notes

Once again, for this prompt it was only a tiny leap of intuition to think of death. But there's more "peace" here than that. Inner peace; the quiet peace that can be found inside a church; the release from palliative care of a loved one; and peace of mind. The constraints of the process threw up many personal memories which found their way into the text. As a family, we did indeed own those barley-twist walking sticks. We did (do) believe in a life hereafter. My father did precede my mother into that life. They both took long cycle rides together in their youth. Neither of them had the slightest interest in "foreign" holidays. And finally, they did suffer with a local vicar who showed absolutely no interest in whichever of life's trials they endured. One of the many reasons for my antipathy towards organised religion.

Notes from an Editor's perspective

Reading through this for the first time since I wrote it back in September of 2012, I recognise that my desire for the characters to remain anonymous has occasionally resulted in ambiguity regarding which "he" or "she" I am referring to. In three or four places I would certainly have recast the sentence to make this clearer and less clunky.

Day 45: Heart Song

[this post is a continuation of the story begun in "Start" earlier in the writing challenge – on Day 42]

Tani raced through the dark wood, her feet barely touching the soft loam. Almost presciently avoiding the breaking of a single twig underfoot and dodging right and left, ducking and weaving to ensure not even the slightest bend or sway of a branch or leaf would betray her passage. There was barely enough light to see when running in the clear. Here, beneath the dense canopy, the darkness was just this side of total. Her night-adapted eyes swelled to take in every scintilla of reflection to guide her direction. Her mind hummed, processing information and decisions at maximum synaptic speed to match her flying legs.

So far there had been no sign of the Pack, and – she checked her chronotech – it was still five minutes until the Hunt began their bloodthirsty quest.

Ahead of her, Tani could dimly make out a fork in the forest path. To the right, the path continued unimpeded. The loam packed solid by the animals and traders that used it, the vegetation well cleared. It was a good choice. She would leave no trace. But in that direction the path travelled straight for almost three hundred metres without deviating and without any natural cover. She could be spotted from far behind. She was nearing the fork now. Had to decide. The left-hand route was even closer to total darkness and heavily overgrown. She would have to take ultimate care and still risked leaving a trace of her entry. But once through and after only a few metres, she would be utterly invisible to any passing hunter. And – she shook a plasteel flask at her hip – she had just enough scentblock remaining to give her a chance of eluding the Pack too.

She ripped the flask from her belt and came to an abrupt halt at the fork. Stepping gingerly over the first fronds of bracken she sprayed a fine mist of scentblock behind her, checking as best she could in the crepuscular coppice that she left no tracks. After a dozen metres, convinced she had done all she could and unwilling to spend more time on covering her entry to the dark path, she turned and ran through the thickening undergrowth.

Not more than fifty metres further and she began to consider the mistake she had just made. It was too late to turn back – the Pack would certainly be passing the point where she left the path at any moment – but her progress had slowed to a crawl on account of the heavy undergrowth. Worse, she could no longer make out any path at all. Each gap between trees looked as though it might be a path, until she tried it and found it blocked with bramble, or sickmoss, or trapweed. Tani stopped, trying to quieten her breathing, and considered what to do.

As the pounding of her heart lessened, she became aware of the faint sound of music coming through the trees from her left. She turned toward it, and immediately the gap between the two largest boles in that direction resolved itself into a clear path. Amazed she had not seen it before and determined now to discover the source of the unexpected melody she pushed on along the new passage. The strain became louder with every step. It seemed somehow familiar to her, though she was certain she had never heard it before. She had often heard others talk of how music "called to them," but until now had never experienced it for herself. She felt almost impelled along the path. She had neither the desire nor the ability to turn aside and find a new direction. Her plan had been to veer and jig constantly during her flight, to be completely unpredictable, but all concerns over being caught had evaporated from her suddenly calm mind as she sought out the source of the refrain.

The wood remained as pitch dark as it had when she first stepped onto this eldritch path, yet her feet seemed to find their own way, stepping over obstacles concealed beneath the ground cover, avoiding trip hazards and potholes. She was travelling almost as quickly through this section of the forest as she had been on the clear path. After another few metres she glimpsed a flash of bright green between the low-hanging branches. The music was much louder now. It filled her mind. Her heart was pounding again, despite the fact she was no longer running. Tani rounded the trunk of an enormous, ancient oak and stepped into a clearing. Other large oaks surrounded it, but between them nothing grew. The forest floor was a carpet of old bracken and leaf litter. The sweet woody smell of the decaying leaves drifted up as she walked over them. In the centre of the clearing, on a low outcrop of rock a very small, very old man in a bright green cap sat playing a set of Pan pipes.

[this story is continued later in the writing challenge – on Day 82 in "Advantage"]

Author's Notes

One of the great joys, for me as an author, is naming things. I'm not necessarily claiming to be good at it, but I do enjoy it. Coming up with exactly the right neologism that is both original, and captures the essence of what it is describing in a way that is transparent to the reader. I don't like reading passages of exposition where the author clearly doesn't trust their readership to infer meaning, and instead beats them about the head with long winded explanations.

One of the acknowledged masters of this, at least in my opinion, was Brian Aldiss. His novel "Hothouse", which I read in my early teens, abounds with new flora and fauna, each named precisely and ingeniously for their behaviours or effects. I will comment on this further in later entries.

Chronotech and plasteel are fairly obvious terms, and –

being so obvious – I don't claim they're original. Trapweed and sickmoss may not be exactly original either, but even today Google doesn't throw up any relevant results, at least in the context of fiction.

Day 46: Reflection

"Good morning."

"Hello"

"Please take a seat."

"Thanks"

"May I ask your name?"

"Amir"

"Thank you Amir. I am Doctor Savi. Are you sitting comfortably?"

"Fine, thanks"

"Who have you brought with you today?"

"This is my mate. Wladek"

"And how long have you and Wladek been friends?"

"We grew up together"

"I see. Well, you should make yourself comfortable too Wladek, but please don't interrupt my discussion with Amir. Now, Amir, would you like to tell me why you came to see me today?"

"I can't sleep"

"I'm sorry to hear that Amir. How long have you been unable to sleep?"

"It's been going on about a month."

"I see. And how long do you spend in bed each night, before you get to sleep?"

"I fall asleep right off, but then I wake up again after about an hour and can't get back off again."

"Off to sleep, you mean?"

"Well, yes."

"It's a goddamn AI."

"What?"

"It's an AI doctor for fuck's sake. Let's go."

"No, I need some meds or something"

"Is there a problem, Amir?"

"No – carry on. After I get that hour I can't get sleep anymore"

"What have you tried, to help you get back to sleep?"

"Everything"

"Please, be a little more specific. What have you tried to help you get back to sleep?"

"See? I'm tellin' ya. It's a goddamn machine."

"No it isn't"

"You mean you can't tell? Jesus Christ it's obvious."

"Milky drinks. Reading. Counting sheep. Breathing slowly. Visualisation. Hot baths. Chamomile tea. I've tried the lot. Can you give me some pills doc?"

"I would prefer to try and understand the root cause of your sleep problem Amir before I simply give you some pills"

"God DAMN it. Can't you see? It's just reflecting every time."

"Reflecting?"

"Repeating what you say. Or using your own phrases to make you feel relaxed and comfortable. It's not real!"

"They wouldn't use a machine"

"Who's they?"

"The health people. They wouldn't let a machine run clinics like this"

"Sure they would. How much do you think it would cost to run all these clinics out in the sticks where no doctor wants to work?"

"That's why they do it remotely. They've probably got dozens of doctors online all the time, helping people"

"You're such a goddamn prick sometimes Am."

"Please, Wladek. I did ask you not to interrupt my discussion with Amir."

"See? It reuses the same phrases over and over."

"If you can't sit quietly during the consultation I'm afraid I shall have to ask you to leave."

"And it's so fucking polite. You think a real doctor would be that polite?"

"Amir, do you want to continue with our discussion?"

"Please, Doctor. Ignore Wladek. He always likes to pretend he knows what's going on with stuff better than I do"

"I wonder if this tension between you could be the source of your sleeping problem?"

"What do you mean Doctor Savi?"

"It means I'm a bad fucking infuence you dummy. I'm making you crazy and you're bottling it up or some shit like that. And it's there in your brain, stopping you from sleeping."

"Shut up Waddy. For once, hey?"

"Whatever."

"Perhaps you could take a holiday Amir? Get away for a week or two and see if that helps your sleeping."

"It means away from me."

"Not everything's about you Waddy for God's sake!"

"I know that. But this stupid machine will make you think it is. All your problems will be rooted in me, let me tell you. And they'll all be solved by getting rid of me. That's what these damn machines want. Everyone isolated so they can work their schemes."

"What the hell...?"

"I must ask you to wait outside Wladek."

"I ain't going nowhere."

"Amir, please ask Wladek to wait outside."

"Do as he says Waddy. Please"

"Do as IT says you mean."

"Please"

"You're crazier than I thought if you're gonna let that fucking tin quack tell us what to do. Even its name gives it away for Chrissake. Savi!"

"Huh?"

"Sounds like Savvy. Intelligent. Right? You get it now?"

"That's just a coincidence. He's probably Indian"

"Right."

"Are you going to leave, Wladek?"

"Please Waddy. I'll be right out"

"I won't be here."

"You don't need to..."

"I'm not waiting around to see you suckered in any further by that THING. It's your funeral."

"It's unlikely that Amir's sleeping problems will be fatal."

"Can you imagine a real doctor making a statement like that, Am? Fatal sleeping problem is unlikely? For fuck's sake."

"Just go Wad. Out the door or out the clinic or out of sight. I don't much care which"

"Like I said. Your funeral."

"What were you saying Doctor? Something about a holiday?"

"Yes, I have somewhere in mind. Somewhere that has had great success in the past with people who have suffered from similar conditions as yourself, Amir."

Author's Notes

We're almost halfway through the challenge at this point, so you should already be familiar with (a) my lifelong love of science fiction and (b) the weird connections my mind makes with these topics.

Artificial Intelligence has made huge strides in the ten years since this was written, but back then one of the tricks that was sometimes employed in "conversational" AI was to take what had been said by the human agent and reflect it back to them with a few simple contextual changes. Amusingly, this is also a tool in the arsenal of a trained counsellor.

So that was the starting premise for this piece. I wanted to mix it up a little by including a second human who had a clearer insight into what was going on, and that introduced the challenge of running with three distinct "voices" without any overt dialogue attribution. Given that this whole thing was, as usual, written in 30 minutes or less, I'm still pretty pleased with the result (notwithstanding the editor's note below).

Notes from an Editor's perspective

Clearly the "doctor" speaks with rigid formality; Amir with the kind of deference most people will adopt when talking to a doctor; and Wladek with significantly less respect, and with a much less formal style, peppered with frequent expletives. I could definitely have tightened up these differences to make them even clearer, with an editing pass.

Lastly, whether this was intentional, subconscious, or a simple keyboard problem, I did notice when formatting this for publication that many – although not all – of Amir's speeches don't have closing punctuation (unless it's a question). Once or twice may have been accidental but it's much more frequent than that, so I guess I must have done it deliberately.

Day 47: Perfection

Jocelyn sat squarely on her stool. Balanced. Grounded. Literally grounded, with her feet planted flat on the cold tile floor of the basement, and figuratively grounded too. Calm in a way she only ever achieved when potting. She weighed the lump of clay, slowly passing it from hand to hand. Thinking of the millennia that had led to this moment, as the sheet granite weathered into boulders, then pebbles, then grains until finally it became clay. This piece held in her hand, in her basement, in her house, could be ten million years old. Twenty million. And its long years of history gave no hint of the future that was hidden behind its lumpen form. Infinite possibilities lay ahead, and potentially at least, more millennia once it became an artefact.

Archaeologists were still unearthing crocks from Egyptian times and before. Ming vases held a special place in the zeitgeist, so unshakeably anchored in the public consciousness that any vaguely Chinese-looking urn was always christened "Ming." An electric tingle ran the length of her spine at the thought that what she created here today might become a fabled 21st century collector's piece in two or three thousand years' time.

She flicked her wheel on and took several deep breaths as it span up to speed. With one final toss of the clay from her left hand to her right, she threw the balled nugget onto the wheel, hitting it dead centre. A perfect start. Jocelyn smiled, and dipped her hands into the tub of cool water beside her.

Her wet hands glistened as they caressed the smooth surface of the clay, moistening it and beginning to coax it into shape. She loved this part of her craft the best. The sensual slipperiness, the earthy smells, the cool solidity of the lump of something she was creating. Often at this stage of the process she had no idea what she was going to make, letting the clay almost decide for itself what shape it would take from her hands, rather than they imposing one on it. Not today. Inspired by her earlier thoughts of Ming, today she knew exactly what she would be making. A vase. A vessel so unique in shape, so perfect in craft, so breathtakingly beautiful in conception that it would deserve to last those millennia she had imagined.

She wet her hands once more. She pushed and cajoled. Scooped and pulled. And gradually, as an iridescent butterfly may emerge from an ugly misshapen chrysalis, her vase grew out of the grey mass, revealing itself moment by moment as her wheel hummed and her insistent fingers demanded. Like an image appearing on paper swimming in a bath of developing chemicals, like a firefighter stepping out of a smoke cloud, where once there was nothing remarkable, now before her intense concentration and beneath her carefully smoothing hands, the amphora asserted its existence. Still as yet unfinished – the object she saw with her eyes not quite matching the vision she held in her mind – but the possibilities were clearly becoming reality.

She paused, removing her hands from the work and allowing the wheel to slow so that she could examine the vase from all angles. It did not wobble or gyrate, precess or lean, but instead stood perfectly straight and true, still in the exact centre of the wheel, still absolutely symmetrical from every angle. And the shape. Oh, the shape! She had dreamed it unique and the waking did not disappoint. Another few minutes would see it reach the perfection she yearned for and, she was certain, guarantee her flask its place in history.

Author's Notes

The famous pottery wheel scene from the movie "Ghost" enjoys every bit as entrenched a position in my own personal iconography as I have claimed here for Ming in the public one. Even allowing for that, with a ten-year perspective I'm unable to explain how I made the connection between "Perfection" and a basement pottery experience. I like the way it turned out though :o)

Day 48: Everyday Magic

The sudden deluge bounced reflected raindrops off the pavement as high as his knees as Bob ran for his appointment. The briefcase held over his head offered the only protection from the downpour, which had come from an apparently cloudless sky. He couldn't afford to be late. Not this time.

Less than a block away from his destination, a voice calling urgently through the blinding rain caught his attention. A well-dressed woman stood dejectedly at the kerb. Already drenched, she glanced from face to face as they passed, pleading. Bob caught her eye as he approached.

"Help me, please." She indicated the gutter. It brimmed with rushing brown water as it struggled to cope with the cloudburst. "My keys."

Bob stopped, momentarily torn between his natural urge to help and his pressing and vital engagement. He gave a mental sigh.

"Where did you drop them?"

"Right here. Here by the door." Her car was parked on a double yellow line, although it was now rendered invisible by the gurgling drain water. "I've felt around a bit, but..."

"This current is strong enough to carry them quite a distance," Bob mused. He rolled up the sleeves of his soaking jacket, offered an ironic smile to the woman, and plunged his hand into the fast-flowing water a foot or so past the point she had indicated. The freezing cold water rose past his wrist, numbing his fingers as he groped along the edge of the kerb.

With a triumphant cry, he fished a set of keys out of the gutter.

"There you go!"

"Oh, thank you!"

"Sorry to dash, but I'm already late."

*

Fiona Broadbent watched the earnest young man as he made his apology and ran for the nearest building. Her car keys dangled from her hand and they almost slipped from her grasp before she clutched them against her chest, opened the door, and slid gratefully behind the wheel out of the torrential rain that continued to fall.

She fired up the engine and pulled into the flow of traffic, almost as heavy and fast-flowing as the gutter from which the gentleman had retrieved her keys. Her wipers struggled to keep the windscreen clear against the continuing downpour. A few hundred metres further on she passed an elderly lady, standing alone at a bus stop. She was bent almost double under the combined weight of two enormous shopping bags and the heavy rain. There were no buses in sight. Fiona had never offered anyone a lift in her life. If anyone had asked her why she chose to make today her first she would not have been able to explain it. She pulled in to the kerb and keyed the window.

"Would you like a lift?"

"Eh?"

"Looks like I'm going in your direction – would you like a ride?"

"Oh, bless you!"

The old woman fell in through the open door, dragging her shopping after her. The inside of Fiona's car began to reek of wet old dog and mothballs.

"Where are you going?"

"Well I was going to get the bus to the station, but if you're going that far...?"

Fiona's turn was three blocks before the station, but her new-found altruism blossomed in her mind. "The station it is," she replied quickly, glancing behind as she pulled out once more into the traffic. "Have you got much further to go?"

"I live in Greenfield," said the woman, "it's only about 20 minutes away by train."

*

By the time Brenda McIntyre stepped from the train at Greenfield station the unexpected cloudburst had ceased, the clouds had moved away as quickly as they had appeared, and the late summer sun burned the wet platform into a steaming cauldron. As she walked quickly to the exit, her unused bus fare jingled loudly in her coat pocket. A young boy stood by the exit, looking up at the arrivals board. Brenda reached into her pocket, held out her change to the boy.

"Here you are young man," she said in her best headmistress voice – unused these past eleven years and yet apparently still in good working order. "I'm sure you can put this to good use."

*

Jonny watched the old woman pass through the exit turnstile with a dazed expression glued to his face. He stared at his open hand, and back at the woman's retreating back. And then, he looked at the flower vendor's display further down the platform. He had another 12 minutes before his Mum's train arrived. He turned in the direction of the stall, counting the coins as he walked.

Author's Notes

The movie "Pay It Forward" came out 12 years before I wrote this piece, and I had already watched it several times.

It's still a firm family favourite. Even before that though, I'd developed a fascination for the kind of "sliding doors" story that reveals how one person's actions affect another person, and how these interactions can cascade along a timeline. In a way, this also connects back to another childhood favourite – Asimov's The End of Eternity – where similar connections are unravelled back to their first, often insignificant, beginnings; the smallest thing that needs to be changed to prevent the entire sequence occurring.

I'm also a huge fan of altruistic tales. There's enough competition and climbing of the greasy pole in real life; I don't need to read about it too.

Day 49: Umbrella

Jeremy stood in the lobby gazing out at the rain. Any other day, the inclement weather would have been cause for depression. Today, Jeremy was on a mission. A meticulously planned mission. One that depended on rain.

He'd first conceived it the day he started at Felicity Mutual. That was, he counted, more than nine months ago. Nine months of sleepless nights and nail-biting days trying to juggle his new responsibilities with the enormous stack of rules and financial regulations he had to learn while all the time the space in his head – that should have been devoted to these important and urgent tasks – was filled with one image. The arresting image he had seen as he first took his seat at his new desk. Half-way down the office on the other side of the floor, facing him but giving all her attention to her monitor as she began her work for the day.

Misha.

Exotic, mysterious, raven-haired, fragrant, beautiful Misha. Out of Jeremy's league Misha. Misha who didn't even know he existed. Misha who was regularly hit upon by the senior partners at Felicity Mutual, but who never responded. Oh, sure, she would smile and flash her clear brown eyes at them, and reply with infinite patience and rigorous politeness, but then she would turn away and continue with her work, or discover some vital errand that required her to walk to the other side of the building. She was well practised in the art of dodging unwanted attention while maintaining her professional integrity. All of which, naturally, only made Jeremy love her more.

He twirled his umbrella absent-mindedly and checked the weather again. Still raining. The forecast had assured him it was set for the day but one could never be too careful. His painstakingly constructed pack of cards would come tumbling down if those essential raindrops stopped falling. He glanced at his watch. 12:37. Misha's lunch break started at half past, but she could easily have picked up a piece of work that one of the partners would claim was urgent just to get her alone in the office when everyone else was out to lunch. He dismissed the thought with a frown. Not today. That wouldn't happen today.

The elevator pinged its arrival in the lobby and Jeremy refocussed on the glass in front of him. From his position at the side of the lobby, the marble-faced pillar outside the building created a mirror effect on the glass frontage of the building so he could observe the traffic to and from the elevators without appearing to be watching. To a casual observer it looked as if he were simply staring at the rain outside.

The elevator emptied into the hallway. Misha was not among them. Jeremy checked the other lifts. One at the third floor going up, and the last one at the eleventh floor coming down. He worked on the ninth. Misha could even now be waiting for the third lift on the ninth floor. A tingle ran up Jeremy's back causing his neck hairs to rise at the expectation. He tried to relax as the lift descended. It stopped at nine! He shifted his feet and stretched to release the tension in his shoulders. The lift continued its downward journey, not stopping at any other floors. It pinged again as the doors opened.

There she was! Jeremy swallowed hard and rubbed his free hand on his trousers. He surreptitiously checked his breath. He had flossed carefully this morning – even more carefully than usual – and the results were good. As far as he could tell. Misha swayed across the lobby. He could watch her walk all day long. Poetry in motion. She stopped beside the door a few feet away from him and wrinkled her nose at the weather.

"Damn it! It had to rain today didn't it. Of all days. The

day I lost my umbrella."

The moment had come. It was now or never. Two steps and one short sentence to change his life forever. He gripped his umbrella in his right hand and stepped toward her.

"Would you like to share mine?"

Author's Notes

I don't write romance. I often think I should – it's the most voraciously devoured and popular genre in the world, and also the most competitive – but I don't read it either, so as a writer I couldn't do it justice. On the other hand, all of my work includes characters who are drawn to each other romantically. So I don't avoid writing a romantic subplot, if it lends richness and credibility to a story.

I've never engineered an encounter in the way Jeremy does here, but I have worked in an office, and I have (in my youth ;o)) pined for one or more unattainable beauties who also worked there. And during that period of my life I've also met colleagues even more sleazy than Jeremy or his bosses. All of those experiences informed this work, once I'd settled on an interpretation of the topic.

Day 50: Party

Damn your arrogant ass! You KNOW I'm right.

No I don't. And it's not arrogance to have a different view from you.

What's good enough for me should be good enough for you. I never questioned my father's take on it.

Well maybe you should've.

See? Arrogance and disrespect. Your grandfather would turn in his grave.

Why? I'd have thought he'd be more pleased to see me thinking for myself.

You call that thinking? All you're doing is swallowing their lies.

How do you know they're lies? Your lot have been lying to you for years.

No they haven't.

Of course they have! Look at them now. Is it the same party you grew up with? Grandad grew up with?

Well, no, but–

Exactly. They don't deserve your support. Least, not your unthinking support. I don't know why you keep voting for them. Come to think of it, I don't know why you keep voting at all. Or me, for that matter.

Don't talk like that. Folk fought and died so that we could have the vote.

That was the Suffragettes Dad. That was for women.

I'm talking about the war you dozy twerp. You know what I mean. Do you think people like us would have a say in how the country's run if we were all under Hitler?

Do you think you have a say now? When was the last time your lot did anything for you.

They're always doing stuff for us.

Yeah? Is that why I hear you yelling at the news every night?

Hmm. Well I don't always agree with everything they do, it's true. But that's party politics. It's not about the little things. It's about a shared vision. Working together for a better future.

Right. And when are we gonna get this 'future' you speak of? I bet Grandad used to spout the same old line, and he never saw any of it did he? And you haven't. And it doesn't look like I will either. It's all bollocks.

Well that kind of thinking won't get you anywhere.

What kind of thinking.

Giving up before you've even started.

I have started! For fuck's sake, what do you think I've been doing for the last six years.

Wasting your time. And don't swear in the house. You know your mother doesn't like it.

She's not here.

No, but it's the principle. And anyway if you get used to it you'll slip up when she IS here, and I don't like it.

Another worthless principle. What does it matter what language we use. It's the message that's important, not the medium.

That's typical of you young ones these days. Chucking out all the principles. What do you actually stand for, this new lot of yours? At least we knew where we stood. What we were fighting for in my day.

Yeah but it's not your day any more is it Dad? Your day's done. Pipe and slippers time for you old man.

Thanks.

It's true. No use denying it. This is my day. Our day. The young ones, as you call us, although most days I don't feel that young any more. But if we don't get off our arses and DO something about this bloody mess there won't BE a future. I don't want my kids growing up with the sort of shit I've had to put up with.

Nice.

I don't mean in the family. I mean the country. All their snouts in the trough, back-handers and I'm Alright Jack. We've all had enough of it. I know you agree, don't pretend you don't. I can hear you ranting at the TV even when you think I'm not listening.

Well I suppose it's good you're fired up about something, even if you are on the wrong side.

Like I said, your lot have done nothing for us. It's time to change your thinking Dad. Time to get radical.

Riots and stone-throwing never solved anything.

It's not about rioting. It's about direct action.

Well that's rioting in my book.

No it isn't. Doesn't have to be.

Well what is it then?

Oh I don't know. The Occupy movement is one idea.

Oh yes. A load of unwashed idiots in denims sitting down in bank lobbies. Lot of good that's going to do.

And then there's the Internet. Sumofus and 38degrees and all those.

You're talking gibberish now lad. Make sense will you?

They're focus groups and lobbyists Dad, but on our side. On the side of the small guy.

Focus groups? Listen to yourself! What good have they ever done? Petitions! No-one takes any notice lad.

That might have been true in your day Dad, but we've got the web now. Loads of publicity, stuff going viral, instant video whenever one of them puts a foot wrong. Don't you see? They can't cover anything up now. It's all over the world in five minutes.

Hmm. I wouldn't be so sure about that if I were you. I'd be very surprised if anything really serious got out that they wanted to put a lid on. Look at that Julian Assange bloke. Stuck in that embassy. Not exactly going anywhere is he?

Maybe not, but the movement he started is. People catch on quick. He was just a catalyst. Like the Tolpuddle Martyrs if you like, but bigger. Global. That cat's out of the bag now Dad. Genii's out of the bottle. There's no going back, you'll see.

Author's Notes

Once again it was an easy leap for me from the topic of "Party" to political party. Ten years ago I didn't air my political views very often. More so now, perhaps, but those ten years have been a trying time in UK politics and it's hard to keep a lid on the frustration at times.

This conversation between a man and his father, which also references his grandfather, is firmly rooted in my family. My grandad had a greengrocer's business. Back then small business owners naturally gravitated to the Conservative party, a political affiliation which my father inherited, only moving slightly leftwards in later life.

But the scourge of neoliberalism has made the Tories unrecognisable from the party those guys voted for during the last century. If my father were still alive, I could easily have this same conversation with him today, though I'd hope he'd be more easily persuaded than the father speaking above.

Notes from an Editor's perspective

I've encountered a few non-standard ways of representing dialogue during the last two or three decades, from the stream of consciousness and zero punctuation of A Million Little Pieces to italicised or emboldened text. I can't tell you why I chose to represent the older man in standard text and the younger in italics here. I think their voices are sufficiently distinct to render it unnecessary, but this is how the piece turned out, so…

I missed a few question marks too. No biggie.

Day 51: Troubling Thoughts

The BBC announcer had adopted his most serious tones:

"These scenes are being brought to you live from Birmingham, where there is now a full-scale riot in progress. In a moment we will be bringing you coverage from Manchester and an update from London, but first a report from our correspondent at the scene of the rioting, Phil Mackie."

Jessie watched the scenes unfolding in front of her. She heard what the BBC reporter was saying but she struggled to understand it. Why now? Why Birmingham? A city with a long and proud tradition of accepting people of all backgrounds. And the boys on her screen! Some of them looked barely old enough to be in long trousers. And girls too! When did girls start to become involved in such behaviour? It was alien to her.

She thanked God that her own son had more sense than to get mixed up in such things. Upstairs in his room he was probably chatting on that Spacebook, or whatever it was called, or getting blown up in the safety of a computer-rendered war zone rather than the real-life war zone flashing red and blue on her TV.

"Police say these incidents across the country are being orchestrated by a few militants who are well known to CID and Special Operations units, through their contact networks built up on social media sites like Facebook and Twitter."

Facebook! That was it. Jeremiah was on Facebook. But only with his school friends and members of the family, including some outside the UK. Thankfully he would have more sense than to get mixed up with thugs like these. A strong and upright family, even without a father's influence, Jessie had always made sure Jeremiah knew the difference between right and wrong. And when he had started down the wrong path, on entering his teen years, she had been there to steer him right. That had been a difficult time. Cold winds blowing across their table at breakfast and supper. She had got through to him in the end though. Weathered the storm and put him back on the right path. He saw the sense of her viewpoint. Came round to it even. As much as a teenager could ever be expected to do what their parents told them. He was a good boy, all things considered. Not as much trouble as some. Especially round here. Jessie had wanted to move to Solihull or Edgebaston, but they couldn't stretch to it on a single wage. But where they lived in Perry Barr wasn't THAT bad. Other people kept to themselves most of the time and there wasn't much trouble to speak of.

The TV report had moved on to Manchester now. Jessie decided she'd better check that Jeremiah had sorted out his sports kit for tomorrow. Her knees cracked as she levered herself up off the sofa. Those old bones weren't getting any younger. She gripped the banister tightly as she climbed the stairs one at a time, her arthritis flaring painfully with every jarring step. Jeremiah's bedroom door was closed. No sound came from inside but that wasn't unusual. Her constant complaining of the noises of explosions and blood-curdling screams had persuaded him eventually to buy a pair of headphones, and her continued complaining for several months after that had convinced him to start using them.

She knocked, waited, and poked her head around the door. The room was empty. The bedclothes were still as neat as when she had made his bed that morning. His computer hummed quietly in the corner, but Jeremiah's monitor was turned off. His school bag was nowhere to be seen. Jessie felt sure he had not entered the room since he left for school this morning.

He should have been home for hours. It had been dark since five thirty and he was never this late on a school night. Jessie crossed the room and turned on the computer monitor. As it warmed up, Jeremiah's Facebook page swam into view. But not his personal profile or newsfeed. A cold chill settled around Jessie's spine as she read the title of the page he had been reading: "Spread The Hate."

A hundred conflicting thoughts sparked in her mind. Not her boy. Why? Who were these people? How had he got involved? Surely he was just late home from school. Or gone for a pizza with his football team? Why hadn't he told her he'd be late? Was he alright? Safe? He wouldn't do that. Not throw bricks or loot shops or spray graffiti. None of that.

The doorbell interrupted the insane flood of questions and worries. Jeremiah! Forgotten his keys again! Thank God. Not rioting. She'd been a fool to think that of him. Her boy would never...

Two tall dark figures stood on the front door step, their blurry outlines visible through the obscured glass. Not Jeremiah then. She hurried downstairs as fast as her arthritic joints would allow.

"Just a minute," she called.

She paused with her hand on the latch, suddenly terrified. She opened the door, just a crack. Two uniformed police officers stood outside.

Author's Notes

I will admit to spending a few seconds researching the relative "niceness" of Birmingham suburbs in the interests of legitimacy, although I'm prepared to accept such attributions change over time. I live in an area that was once considered my city's "red light" district, but is now relatively genteel.

I always intended to put these short pieces to work

whenever I had the chance, and I've recently started crafting a series of horror stories, in which (an amended version of) this one appears.

Notes from an Editor's perspective

There's a lot of "prose tightening" to be done here, which would have been mopped up in an editing pass. Weak phrases like "[his] bedroom door was closed/room was empty/monitor was turned off" would have been replaced with stronger phrasing and description. I've also repeated "have more sense" in two places, so one of these would've been consigned to the cutting room floor in favour of an alternative.

Day 52: Stirring of the Wind

"Are you done yet?"

"Nearly!"

"I'll put the tea on."

Neil leaned on his rake and surveyed the results of his efforts. Nine neat piles, the dark green grass between them virtually free of leaves save for where one or two had escaped the pull of the tines and fallen from the path of the rake. He breathed deep of the autumn scents and smiled. The year was not yet old enough to have a winter chill, but had left summer far behind. Mornings like today – mist-shrouded and mysterious; damp and cool – were his favourites. One could do a day's work without breaking sweat and have time left in the still lengthy evenings to enjoy the view, or sit on the deck and savour a glass of wine.

A gust of wind teased Neil's hair as he stood looking over the valley. A few leaves from the tallest piles shook themselves loose and fluttered away onto the grass. Neil pulled a plastic garden sack from his pocket and began stuffing it with leaves from the nearest pile, anxious to complete the clearing up before the wind undid his day's work. As he grabbed handful after handful of the leathery brown leaves their sweet musky odour filled his nostrils, shaking loose memories of school mornings when he and Kate would kick their way to class, scattering the yellow, red and brown threads of the road rug with their polished patent leather, creating new patterns and shapes as the leaves flew and fell, flew and fell. Laughing at the gentle soughing and the smells and the joyous feeling of togetherness; the excitement of a new year ahead. New knowledge and new possibilities, coupled with pangs of old yearning. Wondering whether this would be the year she would start to look at him as more than the boy next door. Kate of the autumn-red hair and brown, gold-flecked eyes that shone and flashed as she laughed at his silly jokes. He played the clown for her to hide his longing. Cracked a joke to mask his embarrassment at the strength of feeling inside him. Stole a sidelong glance at the wonderful curves of her growing body. And fought down the need to declare himself in love with her, for fear of frightening her away.

The wind spoke again, and the trees answered. Sighing and rustling. Neil dashed away a tear with his gloved hand, the suede rough against his cheek. He knotted his bag, stood, and surveyed the garden once again. The few tentative gusts had blurred the edges of his piles, flattening and spreading them out. Sending handfuls of carefully collected leaves back out across the grass. Another few years and it would be too much for him to manage on his own, especially at this time of year. Too many trees, too much grass. And way too many memories. He always knew the leaves would unlock his past. Like evil spirits flying from Pandora's Box, those bitter-sweet rememberings were always set free at this time of year. The season in which he'd had Kate, and the same season he'd lost her. The world had lost her. Like walking into a winter that never ended, and all that was left was cold and dark, crisp and bleak and featureless like a land buried beneath a lifetime of snow. Where Spring could never come.

Author's Notes

One of my favourites of all these 100 pieces, I declared myself "very pleased" with this from the start. Ten years of perspective haven't dulled my satisfaction with it (despite the editor's notes below), which is multifaceted. As with all good work, there's a lot of "me" in here. I've done my fair share of leaf-raking in large gardens over the years, so I had a very clear image in my mind while writing it. The image was of a garden I've never visited – more of an amalgam of several gardens really – but could readily conjure. The character of Neil too is an amalgam. Part me, part family relation (two of them in fact), and part construction. The youthful yearning for the girl next door is me too, although the description applies more to her closest friend, neither of them were called Kate, and I never walked to school with them.

The subject of kicking through autumn leaves on the way to school seems to be something of a theme with me, featuring heavily in the track "When We Were Young" from my album of original songs: Suburban Nostalgia. Autumn is my favourite time of year.

My pride in this piece led me to submit it as a (successful, as it turned out) candidate for inclusion in the Grist Anthology, published in 2017 by Huddersfield University Press. The first and only time my writing has been recognised in any "academic" sense. This whole work – a collection of "studies in viewpoint" separated into I, You, He, She, and It – is available to read online here: https://search.informit.org/doi/10.3316/INFORMIT.9781862181427

My Q&A for the piece is also still accessible and you can find it here:
https://hudunipress.wordpress.com/2017/10/17/155/

Notes from an Editor's perspective

I can do no better than to reiterate what I said in that linked Q&A above:

"The idea of Neil's reflection turning into mourning for his lost first love only occurred to me during the writing, and I think brings added poignancy to what was already a subdued piece, with its parallel between the autumn of the year and of Neil's life. With critical hindsight, it suffers from the lack of editing in what for me is a

common slip – the reuse of similar words or phrases in close proximity. 'Shook – or shaking – loose' appears twice in the early part of the second (non-dialogue) paragraph. 'Handfuls' is not a word you would want to use more than once in a piece of this length, and even 'leaves', with some judicious journeying through thesaurus and dictionary, could have been spared its current exhaustion."

Day 53: Future

The last of the bridge walkers moved out of sight behind the main tower. Steve had already slowed almost to a stop to let them get ahead. Now he did stop. Below him, the East River flowed sluggishly, an oily black slick of freezing cold water more than 150 feet down. At this time of year that water would kill you in under two minutes. He stared. Less than two minutes, plus falling time his mathematician's mind insisted, between him and who knew what?

The current of the river swam before his eyes, screwing with his balance and threatening to tip him off the bridge. Before he was ready, that is. Because there was only one way Stephen Jordan was leaving this bridge today, and it wouldn't be on foot.

He didn't know where he was going when he stepped onto the nothing at the side of the cable. Didn't have that religious certainty of heaven, or the sinner's fear of hell. He sometimes wished he did. Something to look forward to in the one case, or try to avoid by doing the right thing in this life in the other. Ha! The right thing. What the fuck was that? What did that mean to a man like him? He might not know where he was going, but he sure as hell knew where he was coming from, and he wasn't going back to it. No sir. A belly full of lies and cheating, the scum he had to deal with every day, all dressed up in their fine thousand-dollar suits and their silk ties. Their Berluti shoes and their crisp white shirts. New one every day. Perfect on the outside. Respectable. Upright. Living the American Dream. But their insides? Steve imagined them looking something like one of those apples he used to have to take to school for his lunch. All red and ripe and shiny from the outside. Gonna be all sweet and juicy when you bite into it, but it would turn out brown and stinking rotten all the way through to the core. That was like them. Rotten insides, all of them. Souls as black as the icy water flowing under his feet right now.

He changed his grip on the suspensor wire, taking hold with his warm hand and rubbing his cold one against his thigh before ramming it into his pocket. Wouldn't have to worry about cold hands or frostbite where he was going. Wherever it was. Fiery or idyllic or something else that the prophets had never foreseen. Or the black nothing of non-existence that his few atheist friends insisted was all that waited for mankind on the other side of the veil.

A few flakes of snow blew past, sticking to his coat, one or two melting quickly on his lips. Where they caught the suspensor cable they lived a little longer and Steve could almost make out a hint of their hexagonal crystal beauty before they blew off or melted under the sudden warmth of his breath. He coughed a bitter laugh into the fading light. Beauty never lasted. Either it was another façade over a rotten core – like Justine had been – or it got chipped and worn away by time and life and too many margaritas. He swayed against the cable, his vision momentarily blurred by unexpected tears. She'd been the one. How did the song go? "You are the one I'd wait my whole life for." And he had waited. All through High School and college, all those years without a girlfriend because his ever-calculating mind would always find a reason not to make the first move, or respond to an approach on those rare occasions a woman would be brave enough to ask. Tumblers clicking, gears whirring, his subconscious would estimate the chances of a relationship working, factoring in height, weight, dress sense, any friends visible on the occasion, smoking, drinking and a hundred other bits of information, and then it would push them all through its filter and come out with no.

Until Justine. He couldn't consciously have explained why she was a yes. His first ever yes. Didn't even like to question it, in case he should scratch the polished surface of her yesness and find there was really a rusty no underneath. He shivered. The wind was stronger now and the snow flurries thicker. Pretty soon he wouldn't be able to see the East River at all. He'd be stepping off into nothing at the side of him and nothing below too. But that was OK. His mathematical mind took less that a millisecond to calculate that nothing into nothing was nothing. And he wanted to be nothing. To cease. To end the pain of the no she had turned out to be, and being surrounded by the rotten suits, and the endless gnawing certainty that there would never be anything more than this. Day after day. Blackness, blackness dragging me down. He looked down. But where before there had been the blackness of that old favourite song now there was only whiteness. Billowing flurries of whiteness, spiralling past and obscuring the river completely.

Author's Notes

"No-one knows what the future holds" is as familiar a saying as any, and one that was firmly at the front of my mind when thinking about this prompt. It's not true of course, at least in the sense that we all know, at some point, we're gonna die. But we don't know when. Unless, like Stephen, we're desperate enough, hopeless enough, to bring it on.

I've seen documentaries about "bridge walking." I even have one or two friends who've done it. And it has, briefly, flitted through my mind when listening to them talk about it, that it would be one certain – if uncomfortable – "final solution" if one were considering such.

Having a future that only stretches forward for a few minutes would, I assume, focus the mind, and it's that focus and the attendant regrets and memories, that I tried to elicit here.

Another emergent theme, while I've been reading these pieces back, is the "unrequited", or at least "unsatisfactory" love trope. Well, what can I say? It's a pretty universal experience, and I've had my fair share.

Notes from an Editor's perspective

I've diligently stuck to my own rules here, and left uncorrected one of my most common drafting errors: typing "less that a millisecond" when I meant "than". Something that used to be hard to spot, but which thankfully modern grammar checkers have caught on to.

I did break, or at least stretch, the rules and allow myself a bit of research here though. I can't help it; I need to be accurate, or at least in the right ballpark. So I did search for the height of a bridge over the East River, and the name of an expensive brand of shoes. I don't really "do" shoes – or any fashion, in fact. The whole topic bores me to death (although not to suicide, lol). I didn't recognise 'Berluti' back when I wrote this, and I still don't, but at least it will presumably mean something to some readers; I didn't just invent it.

I recently did a line edit for a friend's novel and suggested his description of a plush office space would be much stronger and more credible if he mentioned the expensive furnishings by name. I gave examples.

"How the hell do you know about that?" he responded. "I've never heard of it!"

Neither had I mate. I Googled it. It's called research.

Day 54: Health and Healing

I had a nasty experience recently. Immediately after it, I decided to make it the subject of this post, as part of the writing challenge. I've been coming up with ideas for each day's prompt in advance (which shouldn't come as a surprise) and at the start of the piece I check back at the few words or couple of short sentences I've written in my "theme pack" (a document that lists the themes, my ideas for the themes, how many are left to write, how many to decide what I'm going to write, etc), get the idea in my head, and set off writing.

Today, it's a couple of weeks since the nasty incident and I've calmed down a bit. With those two weeks' perspective I'm no longer angry. Just sad, and... well... a little resigned. Resigned to human nature.

Some of you already know I'm a Spiritualist healer. To anyone that's just visiting, or is a regular who didn't know that for whatever reason, there are a few pages about it (what it is, how I came to be one) on my website . Shortly after I finished my training, the Spiritualists National Union (SNU) asked me if I'd like to be a tutor for the course I'd just taken. It's a correspondence course (there is a practical element to the healing too, of course. You can't be healed by post) and they were in need of new tutors. Since I'd done so well on the course, achieving the highest mark in my graduation year and winning a prize for doing it, they thought I'd make an ideal tutor.

So since 1997 I've been looking after students from all over the UK and, more recently, overseas, as the SNU spreads its influence and offers the course to people from Europe and beyond. I've had some excellent students in all that time, many lovely comments, some that have required a little more help than others, some who have really struggled but even so done their best, and others who have for one reason or another given up part way through or even not started at all, after having registered.

But until the Sunday before last I have never, ever, been engaged in a shouting match with a student. These are, after all, people who are looking to be healers. Empathic, sympathetic, warm and generous people who want to give their time to help make others feel better. So not the kind of person, you would think, to have an over-inflated ego, a sense of moral righteousness, or – worse – one of entitlement where they believe the highest grades should be handed to them on a plate for a minimum of effort. Such were the sentiments behind the irate phone call I received from this particular student.

One of those people who ask a question and then immediately talk over the answer. Because they're not interested in your answer. They're only interested in telling you what the answer is. What the answer you should have given them is. And that answer is never a C grade. I've never had a C grade in my life and I'll be damned if I'm going to let you give me one now. I'm a teacher and assessor myself, I'll have you know. All courses all over the UK are governed by this or that official body and I know the rules. Show me where in the question it tells me that I need to answer in the way you say? The question asks for X and I've given you X so I should have top marks. I'll take this as high as I have to in the SNU. I'm not having it. I've let it pass and let it pass but I can't take it any more. Everyone at my church is AMAZED at what I've had to put up with and on and on and on.

A lot of the above paragraph is paraphrased or implicit (rather than explicit) in what he said but that was the clear message. Some of it is the real words. And with the best will – and all the patience – in the world I found it impossible, eventually, not to rise to the bait. Although I started off calm, I ended up literally shaking with rage. Which, you know, is the most annoying thing of all really. My reaction. The fact that I lost it, when all I really needed to do was keep calmly putting forward my view. My correct view. My 15-year-experienced-tutor view. My 55-year-old world view*. He hadn't done the work. For months he has been trying to get away with the minimum necessary to scrape through the course. And for quite a long time I've shrugged and warned and cajoled and suggested, and been ignored. And this time, finally, the chickens came home to roost and they didn't taste very nice. And there was a clucking and a ruffling of feathers in the hen house.

I hung up in the end. In the middle of a continued tirade from the other end, I hung up. And emailed him to tell him not to call again. I have no idea if he complained, or how high, or whether he's demanding a different tutor, or what. I strongly suspect our student/tutor relationship is too badly compromised to continue, which is a shame (in a way) because he's only one question away from finishing the course. If he can swallow his enormous pride and just knuckle down and get on with it. But I doubt that will happen. And I don't much care either way. One bad apple in a barrel of almost 150 students over 15 years. It's not a bad track record. The guy who organises the training courses was worried it would put me off being a tutor. I have a thicker skin than that. Yes, I was upset, but I got over it.

But as I said right at the off, my main feeling now is one of sadness. That someone with that amount of hubris cannot set it aside and focus on the long term goal. If he wants to help people, then he really needs to be able to understand them better. And do the work.

*His opening gambit, at the start of the phone call, had been to say "I don't know how old you are, but..." so I told him. Quite took the wind out of his sails to learn I was three years his senior. I'm certain he was expecting me to be younger so that he could play the "age and experience" card on me. Shame ;0)

Author's Notes

Not much writerly insight for this one. It's a blog entry, so it accurately documents the subject.

But there are two follow-up points I should add. I did, in the end, email the course organiser to inform him that I no longer wished to tutor this student. The first and only time that happened in over 20 years of tutoring (I retired from it in 2019). Turned out he had requested a change anyway. No surprises there.

What was a surprise: I later learned that this student had been disqualified. That last question – the only one he had left – was full of verbatim, uncredited material from other sources, so he was thrown off the course for plagiarism. The schadenfreude was strong with me that day, I can tell you.

Day 55: Separation

The almost-matt brown surface gleamed under the bright halogen lights. Nestling in its carton, the gravid oval roundness suggested fertility even if it gave no clue as to what lay inside. Plump. Ripe. Heavy in the hand once it was plucked from its sanctuary. It was the colour of ripeness too. Of a nut newly fallen from its tree. Not yet ready to sprout and good for the eating.

Eating would be on the agenda here too, soon. But not yet. That silk-sheen surface, still refrigerator cold to the touch, appeared at first glance to be perfect. Unblemished and uniform. Created with almost factory precision, with almost a factory's efficiency and delivery rate too. A closer look revealed the uniformity to be only a trick of the eye. The surface was flecked. Almost pixelated. In places a few hard blebs commingled with the smoothness, wrecking its satisfying curvature on colliding with the eye.

The surface gave a comforting crack as it struck the rim of the polished pyrex dish. Small brown flakes, released by the destructive contact, flew to the floor avoiding the interior of the dish. A lucky escape. Fingernails sought an opportunity, urgently yet slowly pressing, demanding a parting of the carapace. Once begun, its integrity breached, the husk revealed its secret. Glistening and gelid, shining into the open air and the aching light, it lay quivering in half a moon, dripping small gobs of gelatinous content into the open waiting maw of the dish.

With infinite slowness and care, the moon was rotated and the sun rose into view. Appearing through the pale jelly as the heavenly sun might appear through the morning mist. It rose, turned restlessly and fell from the broken ragged lip of the rind like a castle defender tipped from the ramparts by an attacking arrow. But it was caught! Its fall broken by the twin rind held below as the gelid mass slipped between the two and splashed greasily into the bowl to join the vanguard already waiting there.

The fortunate sun rocked gently in its new cradle, bathing now in much reduced waters. Fully four-fifths of its cushion had fallen before the sun was forced to retrace its steps back to the original hemisphere, like an unnatural commuter who could not decide in which continent to settle. On the journey it lost all trace of bathwater, the more liquid remains of the once-resistant gel now warmed, fluid and dripping lusciously from the shell to join its translucent family sitting patiently in the dish.

Now alone and naked in its broken home, defenceless in the face of the chef's desire, the golden orb convulsed in his nervous hand as it was carried to an unknown fate.

Beyond the boundaries of the pyrex dish, hidden from the unwitting contents, a pair of beaters waited patiently, knowing their turn would soon come, eager to spin into action and bring their ebullient effervescence to the party.

Author's Notes

Did I mention my mind made strange connections? I'm a competent and enthusiastic cook, but even for me it was an unusual choice to interpret "Separation" as the kitchen-based split of yolk from white.

Nevertheless I relished the challenge of describing this mundane task in a literary fashion. I'll leave it to you to decide whether or not I succeeded.

Day 56: Everything For You

Shona dug her friend sharply in the ribs.

"See? It's changed again."

"Ow!" Ella rubbed the spot, frowning. "Yes, alright. So what?"

"It changes every day."

"So you said."

"Don't you think it's strange? I never saw a shop that changed its window display every day."

"You can hardly call that a display," Ella replied, still frowning as she squinted across the road against the early morning sun. "It's only one thing. On a stool."

"I still think it's weird."

"I wish the bus would hurry up."

"I wonder what else they sell?"

"Who knows. Or cares?"

"God. You're so boring sometimes. Nothing ever happens around here and then someone takes over the old grocer's and puts loads of interesting and weird stuff in the window–"

"ONE thing."

"AT A TIME. OK, a SERIES of interesting stuff in the window, and no-one knows what they sell."

"Says everything."

"What?"

"The sign. 'Everything For You'. They must sell everything."

"Don't be daft! Nowhere sells everything. How would they

fit it all in that little shop? It's only a grocer's."

"Was a grocer's. I wonder if they still sell fruit and veg and breakfast cereal?"

"See? You ARE interested. Why would they still sell groceries? It's not a grocer's any more."

"No, but they reckon they sell everything. That must include groceries."

"Think you're clever do you?"

The bus arrived, interrupting their incipient argument. Across the road, a thin blue-veined hand appeared inside the door of the shop they had been discussing, and turned the sign over to "CLOSED."

*

Shona and Ella alighted from the bus, their satchels weighed down with text books for the evening's homework, their faces still glowing from the last lesson of the day, which had been P.E. The homecoming bus stop stood right beside the old grocery shop. The sign in the door read "OPEN".

"Let's go in."

"What for?"

"To see what they've got."

"We don't have time! I've got a mountain of homework, and so have you."

"Five minutes."

"No Shona!"

Ella's plea was too late. Shona had already disappeared through the shop door.

"God's sake!" Ella sighed, following her friend into the gloomy interior of the shop.

Whoever owned it obviously had no notion of modern, 21st century retail. No mood lighting, or product placement. No special offer signs. No racks of brightly packaged goods. Beside the door, in the window on the now-familiar stool, stood a blue glass vase painted with an unusual geometric design. The rest of the shop was deserted save for a long counter on the back wall upon which sat an old manual till, its brass and pewter scrollwork shining dully in the gloom. The inside of the shop was lit with two small chandeliers, each holding six incandescent bulbs of very low wattage. They glowed amber and illuminated the shop with a sickly yellow light. The floor, which until only a few weeks ago would have been littered with bags of potatoes and rice, and shelves stacked high with domestic dry goods, was now entirely empty. Its bare boards swept, but uncovered.

"There's nothing here," Ella whispered. "Let's go."

"Can I help you ladies?" a deep voice intoned. A tall, thin man stepped out from behind a curtain at the side of the till. He placed his hands on the counter. He wore a black suit, tie, and shirt. In the dim light of the shop his dark attire seemed to make his face and hands float eerily above the counter, unconnected to each other or anything else. "Shona, isn't it?" he asked, peering blearily at Shona.

"How do you know her name?" asked Ella.

"And Ella," the man went on. "Did you have a nice day at school?"

Ella swallowed.

"How do you know our names?"

"I think one of the locals might have mentioned you," the man said, cocking his head on one side as if trying to remember exactly who. "How fascinated you are with our little display."

"I never–" Shona began, but the man interrupted her, speaking as he bent down beneath the counter.

"I have something here for you," he said, "that might interest you."

He straightened, and placed a medium-sized book on the polished mahogany countertop.

A TEXT BOOK OF INDIAN HISTORY

read the title in large letters, while underneath in smaller letters, was printed

WITH GEOGRAPHICAL NOTES

"Just what you've been after for your homework, I think?"

The man smiled at Shona. She looked at the text, and back at the man.

"How did you–"

"And for Ella," he continued, opening a cabinet behind the till. Until that very moment Ella would have sworn the cabinet was empty, yet the man took from it a small box. He set it gently on the counter and removed the lid. Inside lay a burnished copper fountain pen. Ella had lost her own pen that very afternoon.

Author's Notes

As a lifelong lover of Stephen King's work, this piece was heavily influenced, and indeed immediately suggested to my mind, by the novel Needful Things (as you no doubt realised, if you've read it). The connection was an obvious one, at least to me.

The challenge, then, was to make my interpretation more original than simply a retelling of a brief part of King's work. Something like two decades had passed between my reading of it, and writing this piece. My memory of the novel is vague at best, so this may not be as original as I hoped, but it is what it is.

I think it's one of the entries that could definitely be developed into a longer story. Were I to do that I'd certainly reread Needful Things to make sure I avoided any hint of plagiarism. Borrowing the idea is bad enough! But a story with this start could easily go in any one of a number of directions. Is the store owner malevolent or benevolent? Or neither – having his own motivation, which may or may not emerge as the story progresses. Is he human, alien, or paranormal? How many artefacts does he sell, and why? Where do they come from? What powers do they have? Even these initial questions show what a strong and adaptable premise this is.

Notes from an Editor's perspective

A certain amount of repetition is a good thing, IMO, when setting an uneasy mood, but it's easy to overdo it, so I would definitely have removed "of the shop" from the end of "the gloomy interior." The reader knows where we are by then.

The initial edit would certainly have expunged the passive voice in "The inside of the shop was lit with two small chandeliers, each holding six incandescent bulbs of very low wattage." and probably recast it altogether. I've already taken out one "of the shop" and now we have another to deal with. Something more like "Two small chandeliers, each holding six incandescent bulbs of very low wattage, illuminated the bare space." is stronger, but would then have required a follow-on edit to replace "bare boards" with something other than bare.

It suffers quite badly from "first draftitis" does this piece. Here's another section…

"I have something here for you," he said, "that might

interest you."

…in need of revision. Either take out the first "for you" or – better, because it's important to emphasise that the strange shop owner has selected the piece especially for Shona – change the second part to "that might be of interest?"

Day 57: Slow Down

"Come on – Ian's brought his car."

"You have got to be joking. He's had way too much."

"No I 'aven't. Only 'ad three pints."

"In the bar, maybe. What about earlier?"

"...was AGES ago. I'll have processed all that by now."

Julie hesitated. Ian was not a particularly good driver at the best of times, but once he'd got some drink inside him he was worse than reckless.

"Come on Ju," Hettie insisted. "We've left it too late to get a cab now. We'll miss the start if we don't go with them."

Ian was already behind the wheel, struggling to get his key in the ignition. It didn't look good. But Hettie had joined Roland and Kyle in the back seat and was holding the door open for her. Ian's new girlfriend – Julie couldn't remember her name – wound down the front passenger window.

"Are you coming or not?"

Ian finally found the ignition and fired up the engine.

"Let's go!" he yelled, revving hard.

Despite the insistent cries of her little voice that it was mad, Julie squashed in beside Hettie and closed the door. Four of them in the back of Ian's old Austin was easily one too many, especially with Hettie being... bigger than average. Julie twisted into the corner to sit on one cheek as Ian gunned the car away from the kerb.

"Not too fast, Ian," she called over the roar of the engine, "we're not THAT late."

"Relax!" Ian leered into the rear view mirror, grabbing it and adjusting it roughly so he could see Julie's face (and, incidentally, her cleavage, she thought). "I'm in total control."

"That's what I'm worried about," she muttered as Ian crossed a traffic light on the cusp of amber.

"Woo!" shouted Debbie (her name popped into Julie's mind) from the front. "Yeah! Go Ian."

Ian grinned widely at the appreciation and began showing off for his "audience", dropping a gear and accelerating toward the next green light. They were still a couple of hundred metres away when it flicked to amber, but Ian wasn't looking. He was waving a hand at the glovebox.

"Open it Debs," he said. "Need another drink."

"No, Ian!" Julie cried. "Wait 'til we're there."

"Come on," Ian insisted. Debbie unlatched the compartment and reached inside to retrieve a quarter bottle of whisky, already more than a third gone. She passed it over.

"Perfect!" Ian said, steering with one hand as he chugged the whisky. The light turned red as they crossed it, this time just the wrong side of legal.

"Red light runner!" yelled Roland. "Forfeit one mouthful of whisky!"

He held out his hand. Ian leaned back with the bottle, spilling it over his wrist. The Austin drifted over to the wrong side of the road.

"Shit," Ian said, more worried about the loss of booze than his errant direction.

"Ian! Watch it!" Julie yelled.

"Sorry!" he laughed, over correcting and swerving the Austin towards the nearside kerb. "Whoops."

"For Christ's sake, slow down. You'll hit somebody."

"Who? Nobody around this time of night round here." He laughed again. "They're all in the pub."

"If you don't slow down, I'm getting out," Julie said loudly.

"Calm down Ju," Hettie poked her in the ribs. "It's only a bit of fun."

Julie looked at her pityingly. "You won't be saying that when you're picking bits of yourself up off the road."

She looked over at Kyle, who hadn't said a word since they left the bar. He looked very pale. A sheen of sweat slicked his forehead, sticking his gelled fringe down in even more bizarre shapes than he'd intended.

"You OK, Kyle?" Julie asked

"For fuck's sake, don't throw up on me," Hettie said, trying to twist away from him and squashing Julie even harder against the door in the process.

"M'OK," Kyle mumbled. "Don't really like small spaces."

"Great. He's fucking claustrophobic," Debbie said, her face pulled into a hard stare. "Hurry up Ian. We don't want him puking in the car."

"Your wish is my command," Ian saluted with his whisky-soaked fingers and floored the accelerator.

"IAN!" Julie yelled, now really frightened. "Stop this! You're going way too fast."

"I feel the need," he shouted, grabbing the wheel with both hands and leaning forward like some maniacal character from Wacky Races, "the need for speed."

Author's Notes

Those intervening ten years have dated this story. Struggling to get his key in the ignition? Well, I do refer to it later as his “old Austin” so that’s the most likely explanation. It could also have been one from the diminishing number of companies that don’t provide keyless ignition as standard. I didn’t own a keyless car until 2016, and since I’m not a petrol head I remained blissfully unaware of the technology back in 2012. The days before I needed to own a Faraday box to avoid having my motor stolen by key cloners.

Do you have a “little voice”? That’s what we’ve always called it at Beresford Towers. That nagging feeling you get sometimes that you should or shouldn’t do something. Don’t try to carry the cups and the plates downstairs: you’ll drop something. Don’t take that route home: it’s an accident blackspot. Whether you believe it’s a guardian angel whispering in your mind, or only common sense, or something in between, you ignore that voice at your peril. I’ve ignored it many times during my life and better than 50% of those times I’ve suffered the peril I’d “warned myself” against. And roughly 50% of that other 50%, I’ve come close, catching the falling cup at the last moment, or narrowly avoiding the RTA.

And finally, how many of you have been in this situation? Either as a passenger or a driver? It’s both, for me (to my shame). In my younger, more foolish days. I learned my lesson before I did anyone any harm, but that’s no excuse. I’m painfully aware of the damage I could’ve wrought, had I been less fortunate.

So today’s effort was informed by a lifetime’s experience, both real life and those many car-based movie scenes with many passengers and much alcohol. And here again, the story could be taken in several directions. An accident, the death of a pedestrian, or a passenger, or both. Or a critical or life-changing injury. Or a hallucination, leading anywhere. An argument, in the car or after they arrive at their destination. Or maybe even, if I wanted to give it an SF twist, a combination of all of those things: the timeline fragmenting into half-a-dozen potential futures, none of which are desirable and result in one of the characters trying to "fix" things, with – obviously – disastrous consequences.

Notes from an Editor's perspective

I always try to avoid distancing my reader from my characters' thoughts. In many advisory writing texts it's seen as bad form to use "he thought", or devices such as the "(her name popped into Julie's mind)" above, to document someone's internal dialogue. It's supposedly preferable, and in the case of the non-POV characters, mandatory, to indicate thoughts in more circumspect ways, through body language, gestures, conversational pauses, etc.

On the other hand I've read many works – many extremely successful works – where this rule, if it is a rule, is ignored. Some authors make liberal use of parentheses (to record thoughts which interrupt a current conversation), others have no qualms about using chunks of exposition to tell the reader what the characters are thinking.

As a reader, I can't honestly say I have a problem with that, whether or not it's "bad practice". As a writer I still prefer "deep POV", where we spend our time in the character's head, so everything that's written is a thought, or an experience, or that character's interpretation of events, and tags like "he thought" or "she decided" are unnecessary.

Day 58: Heartfelt Apology

This is a hard one. Hard to write, almost certainly hard to read. Hard to even think about. Because there's an apology – a heartfelt apology – that I have needed to make for a long time, and I can never make it.

Do you think about it much? I bet you do. In those quiet moments, perhaps, before you go to sleep. Or if you're feeling down for any reason. Or sometimes does it hit you at the most surprising times, when everything is sunshine and warmth and happiness. And then you remember with a sudden jolt and a lump in the throat. I do.

But for me – and I know this isn't about me, but this is how I still feel about it; the only way I can express it – for me the worst times are whenever I see or hear stories of abandonment. Of children left behind. They always make me cry. I'm crying now, thinking about it. Writing about it. There are some scenes, in some movies, that I simply cannot watch.

Even now, with the perspective of all these years, it's still there. Like a stain on my soul. One that I can never scrub off no matter what I do to repair that old wound. It bears a scar, you see. I knew it would. I talked it over and over with people who had been through it. Talking about it like that was, partly, just a way of postponing the inevitable, but it was also a way of validating the hard decision. I needed to be certain that, of all the bad choices I could make, the one I ended up with was the least bad for the most number of people. Which is why it took me so long to go. Even though I knew for a long time I had to, I couldn't bring myself to do it for years. Because I would always, always rather hurt myself than hurt you.

In the end though, I knew there was nothing else for it. I had to do it. Because staying, in the long term, would have caused more hurt than going. I tried to explain, even though I knew I never would be able to. Even though I knew the message would be garbled, and infected with lies and half-truths by those more interested in serving their own agenda. You couldn't possibly have understood, back then. And knowing that you understand now, now that you're all grown up and out there, doing your own things and living your own lives and, no doubt, making your own mistakes the way all of us do. Stumbling around in the dark looking for the way forward. Now I know you understand, it helps. A little. But you didn't understand at the time. You were bewildered, frightened, angry, and lost.

And that's the hurt I can never mend, no matter how many times I apologise. I can't go back there and be there for you, help you through it the way I always had up to that point. The way I started to again, much later. So this isn't only an apology to you today, though you surely deserve one. It is also – or even mainly, perhaps – an apology to the 11-year-old you, and the 6-year-old you. The frightened, tearful girls I left behind who grew up, in spite of all the pain and loss, to be the most wonderful, talented, beautiful daughters a man could ever dream of. Love you.

Author's Notes

Here we are on Day 58. I'd seen this topic coming from a long way off, obviously, and I knew what I wanted to write. Knew it would be a hard write. Knew I couldn't not do it. The life-changing event it refers to was, by this time, more than 12 years in our past as a family, but still raw. And yes, even now, I'm still affected by tales of abandonment. It's a scar that, as far as I can tell, will never fade.

Day 59: Challenged

The chiascuro of whirling bright lights dissipated. Jann Arden's eyes adapted to the relative gloom of his surroundings. He had no idea where he was. A room. Dilapidated. Faded. Old. There was no light in the room but a strange blue glow filtered in through the worn blinds. He could make out shapes. A bed. A nightstand beside it. A bureau, and a bentwood chair. A door to another room. And one to a hallway, hanging open with its lock broken. A hotel room then? Or a small apartment.

A peculiar smell hung in the air. Thick and sweet. Jann couldn't tell where it was coming from. He moved across the room slowly, his eyes still not fully accustomed to the murk. On the other side of the bed, in front of an incongruous ornate marble fireplace, a body lay on the floor. A man, blood oozing from an open gash in his throat. A few feet from the body a large knife lay on the carpet. It had spattered the white marble of the hearth as it fell. He knelt beside the body, felt briefly and hopelessly for a pulse, picked up the knife. He turned it over in the pale light washing from the window. Blood stained the blade black in the electric blue light.

Three beams of incandescent white light tore through the room from the hallway.

"Drop the weapon!"

Jann stood up, turned to the light.

"Drop the weapon and kneel on the floor! Now!"

Jann was bewildered. Where was this place? Why did he have to kneel down? He opened his arms, trying to appear harmless.

"But... I..." he began.

"DOWN! NOW!" cried the voice. The three beams

resolved themselves into torches, carried by three men in dark red uniforms. Each carried a gun in their other hand. The man doing all the shouting also carried a gun, only this one was pointed at Jann's chest and held in both hands. Jann dropped to the floor, letting the knife fall from his fingers to the carpet once more.

The shouting man stepped swiftly up to Jann and pulled his hands roughly together behind his back. "You are obliged to answer any question put to you by a member of the MIF." he barked. "You have the right to a Protector. If you do not have access to a Protector one will be appointed for you. You must provide a DNA sample on request. These are the rights and obligations as determined by the Council of Mars. Do you understand?"

Jann had no idea what a Protector was, but it sounded like he might need one. He nodded.

"Do you understand? Answer the question!"

"Yes," he replied. But he didn't. For one thing, where the hell was 'Mars'?

The man pulled him to his feet.

"Clear, sir!" he called.

A fifth man stepped into the room. Dressed differently from the other four, in a cream suit, he carried no weapon, only an air of superiority and calm indifference. He looked quickly and efficiently around the small room, poked his head through the second door and walked over to the body.

"Do we know who he is?"

"Prefect Montague of District Seven," replied the shouting man, whose lapel badge Jann could now see read HAYNES.

The man turned to him, staring at him for several seconds

before asking: "Did you know this man? Prefect Montague."

"No," said Jann.

"Why did you kill him?"

"I didn't. I..."

"He was still holding the knife when we got here, sir!" declared Haynes.

"I only just got here myself," Jann said, "he was already dead."

"The medical examiner will tell us whether that is true or not," the suited man replied, "but if you didn't kill him and you didn't know him, what were you doing here?"

Author's Notes

The name has changed slightly – to Jann Argent – but today's effort has been reused, virtually unchanged, twice. The indigents on my fantasy world of Berikatanya speak their own language, so in the first reuse some of the dialogue is recast in that language, and corresponding confusion/lack of understanding introduced on the other side of the conversation.

For my prequel novella Berikatanyan Dawn – available free if you sign up to my newsletter – I took the opportunity to reuse a version of the same story, but from another perspective. To add the matching piece of the jigsaw, if you like, thereby filling in any blanks that may have remained.

Day 60: Exhaustion

There was still no end in sight. How long had he been climbing? Without any external clues – sunlight, moonlight, stars, a watch – it was impossible to tell. Counting one-one thousand wouldn't have been any good, even if he'd thought to begin when he started. That point was, by now, way below him. How far, he couldn't imagine. Didn't even like to think about it in case it set off his vertigo again.

Funny how he'd always thought he didn't suffer from vertigo. He'd never been one of those to experience cold shivers when walking down the stairwell of a high-rise office block or hotel. The views from the window had always fascinated him. Attracted him, even. He'd been up the Space Needle and the CN Tower. Stood on the glass floors and stared straight down. No problem. Felt kinda weird being suspended in mid-air like that when part of your brain still insisted you were standing on the floor, but in a madcap kind of way he enjoyed it. Could never empathise – or even, for the most part, sympathise – with anyone who shied away from such experiences, although he stopped short of ridiculing them.

He held on to that small crumb of comfort now. That lack of ridicule. Because he was certain he looked pretty ridiculous now. Clinging to this ladder and climbing from way down there to way up there without a clue how he got there or where he was going. A slick of sweat on his face and the smell from his armpits giving away his terror, though there was no-one around to suffer it.

It wouldn't have been any use counting rungs either. Sure, they were evenly spaced, but his pace was anything but even. Every now and then when a fresh wave of vertigo struck he would have to stop climbing and cling to the rung, wrapping his arms around the riser, clasping his hands tight around each opposite wrist, and hoping his legs wouldn't give out. Even without the vertigo he had to keep stopping to catch his breath. He'd never been the fittest of the bunch but this climb would have tested the best of the high-school jocks who used to taunt his incipient beer belly all those years before.

After an hour or so – or what felt like an hour – he'd settled into a kind of rhythm. Climb for a bit, rest for a bit, climb for a bit, and repeat that around ten times before stopping for a longer rest, until his heart slowed again and his breathing returned to normal. That had seemed a good strategy at the time, but lately he'd begun to worry that it slowed his climb significantly. As time went on, the rest stops did nothing to reduce the aching in his arms and legs. Sure, his circulation was still recovering, but his muscles were getting more and more tired. The lactic acid build-up was beginning to bite, and if he stopped moving for too long his legs would begin to shake and his arms wouldn't obey the instructions from his increasingly fatigued and frightened brain.

Where the hell was this anyway? And where did it lead? He had no memory of starting up the ladder. No idea what was at the base, or even if he had begun his climb at the bottom. It had been a little darker down there, maybe. Like he was climbing out of a pit. But if that was true it was a pit with no visible sides. No sign of support. And if, as he vaguely remembered, there had been less light down there, then there wasn't all that much more light up here. The change was almost entirely imperceptible. There was no "blue sky" above him, or hadn't been the last time he'd looked and almost lost his grip on the rungs and fallen back to wherever it was he'd started. No matter which way he figured it he must already have climbed a couple of thousand feet and he knew with bone deep certainty that the vinegar in his muscles wouldn't allow him another couple of thousand. Not even half that. And still no sign of there being any top to the climb.

He stopped again, panting, and drew a hand across his brow to prevent the accumulated sweat running into his eyes. With his arms once more locked around the ladder he stared straight ahead, standing on his right leg and resting his left, squinting through the bland greyness that surrounded him to try to make out any pattern, any hint of substance beyond. He looked left, and right, staring into nothing, unable to focus since there was nothing to focus on. Nothing moved. Nothing made a sound. There were no colours. It was as if the word 'void' had been made real and wrapped around him in a long tube with no beginning and no end.

He shifted onto his left leg to try to relieve the aches, but as fast as one ache died away another took its place. He had to keep moving. This close to total exhaustion one false step would mean a certain fall, and if his estimate of distance was even halfway accurate, certain death.

Author's Notes

The older I get, the closer I am to exhaustion most of the time. At least, it feels that way sometimes. For this piece I had a tentative memory of a horror story read in my youth, of someone on a ladder. No clue how he arrived there, or where it led. I seem to remember he encountered various problems too. Rusted rungs, I believe, and perhaps even the end of the ladder altogether, at some frightening elevation. So that was my starting point.

The ambiguity of my climber's situation lends some tension to the piece, but much of it is also informed by personal experience. I am that man who believed himself free of vertigo, having indeed ascended both of the towers mentioned, and stood on those glass floors. I am also that man who had occasion to climb a ladder – both to apply silicone sealer to the gable wall from a ladder propped up on the roof of the single-storey extension; and later to repaint the windows at a slightly reduced altitude – only to discover to my horror that I do in fact have a fear of heights. At least, when those heights are physically obvious and offering imminent danger of a fall.

Day 61: Accuracy

Gregor sat beside a rusty iron stanchion, preparing himself. Today was all about planning, limiting options for things going wrong and, in the end, accuracy. His employers would probably count that last item as the most important. After all, it was what they were paying him for. Without accuracy, he would be nothing. Not at the top of his game, with an international reputation and a dozen calls on his, rather expensive, time each month.

But for Gregor, the other two factors were equally if not supremely important. If his focus should happen to waver on this occasion, even though it had been meticulously planned and nothing was likely to go wrong, then he would almost certainly get another chance, on another day. If his planning should fail, however, or his clever ideas for damage limitation were to prove not so clever as he believed, then there might be no second chance. His scope for second chances in that eventuality could even be removed for a very long time.

A gust of wind stirred up a small cloud of dust from the concrete roof. At this height even the calmest day could appear windy. The dust devil spiralled a short distance across the dull grey slabs and dissipated as quickly as it had been born. The likelihood of just such a sudden gust had been factored into Gregor's plans. When the time came, he could make the adjustment if necessary.

He unlocked the clasps on his worn black attaché case and flipped them open. No combination locks for him. Far too easily cracked. A four-digit combination could be broken inside half an hour by a skilled code breaker. If the contents of his nondescript bag were to be discovered, well, that was another of the damage limitation measures he preferred not to think about. His precautions had, so far, been sufficient, but Gregor was never complacent. Although from the outside the case appeared to be worn, it contained the very latest protective countermeasures. He had replaced the locks with titanium-hardened 7-lever tumblers that would survive an attempt to explode the bag. The sides of the case were lined with a material more opaque to normal airline X-rays than lead. And the inner linings had been crafted to reveal to those X-rays outlines of mundane, everyday objects that would allay even the most suspicious security personnel. So far, in fifteen years of use, he had never been asked to open the case.

He opened the lid. The final lingering fingers of the late afternoon sun gave his equipment a warm burnished glow that denied its deadly purpose. With the practised ease of his long experience he began to assemble the individual pieces, selecting them in the same order as he always did, checking them over with eyes that could detect the slightest imperfection, and fitting them smoothly into place. A small smile played over his face at the satisfying clicks as the assembly progressed. With a few seconds the task was complete. The tool of his trade lay in his lap, ready for use.

Once the job was complete, Gregor knew exactly how long it would take to disassemble and return the pieces to his case. Eight seconds. Roughly two-thirds of the time it took to put it together, if he were in a hurry. Today, with his plan carefully worked out and still, for the present at least, on track, he had been able to take his time. There had been occasions, a few only but all the more memorable for that, when he had had to change position. To run through the streets to his second, or – just once – third position. On those occasions assembly had been a more urgent task and one for which he had to rely on his instincts, memory and familiarity with his equipment to complete the job as quickly and accurately as possible. No time to check for misalignment, or wear on the individual sections, he had to trust that his meticulously careful cleaning of his tools after each job would be enough.

Today, he was confident all was in order. There would be no slip-ups. No need for alternative positions. It was all good.

Gregor checked his watch. The time had come. He hefted the high-powered semi-automatic rifle over the concrete parapet, put his eye to the telescopic night-enhanced sight, and took careful aim.

Author's Notes

Aside from my main published work in SF/F, I have aspirations to be a thriller writer. My first novel is a science fiction thriller, and recently I've assembled a bunch of ideas on how I can take the characters in that novel forward into new adventures. I've even been hoovering up the Jack Reacher books as holiday reads over the past two or three holidays, both because they're cracking good reads for the poolside sunbed, and also in the name of research.

If these ideas ever come to fruition, you may well find a version of this piece squirrelled away inside one of those books.

Notes from an Editor's perspective

One obvious slip here: "With a few seconds the task was complete." should be "within…"

A slightly less obvious mistake is in the second sentence, where the list of three things that "today is all about" initially reads as though "limiting options" is the beginning of an explanation of the planning, rather than a list item in its own right. In an editing pass I would have replaced the commas with semicolons to emphasise the list structure, and probably dispensed with the "in the end" bit in the interests of even greater clarity.

Quite a bit of overwriting apparent here too. No one ever

needs to include "after all" in a sentence. It's just drafting noise, and weakens the prose. Similarly, a day can't "appear" to be windy. That's as bad as "seeming" to be windy. It's either windy or not. And, as on this occasion, a day that's calm at street level can be windy atop a tall building.

Day 62: Irregular Orbit

"Excuse me," Marcus said quietly, attempting to squeeze past the errant trolley which had drifted out to block almost the entire aisle while its temporary owner stretched to the bottom shelf to retrieve essential supplies.

"I'm sorry," said the owner, clutching a three-pack of Fray Bentos as he straightened up and turned to give Marcus an embarrassed smile. The smile died on his lips, replaced by a half-puzzled, half-incredulous look.

"Marcus?" he said hesitantly. "It is Marcus, isn't it? Fancy bumping into you!"

Marcus looked more closely at the man's face. That is to say, he continued to look in much the same way as he had before, only this time he devoted more of his attention to the visual signals. Nevertheless the added brainpower he brought to bear made no difference. He did not recognise the tanned and bearded stranger that stood before him.

"Yes, but–"

"Fenton," the man offered, stretching out his non-corned-beef-holding hand and thereby releasing the trolley which rolled even further into the aisle before being stopped by a stack of baked beans, on offer that week at four for a pound. "Fenton Grainger. Remember? Beauforte House?"

The words trickled through Marcus' language centres like overripe bananas. Beauforte House was a good clue, of course. The old company training house where he'd spent several painful weeks on and off over the last thirty years of his career. But Fenton Grainger? No bells there.

"The Sales and Marketing sheep dip," Grainger continued. "You must remember."

Ah, that explained it. Marcus had never had much time for marketing twaddle, and when the company had decided that everyone – all their managers, salesmen, technical staff, even all the architects and programmers – would benefit from a basic grounding in Marketing (always with a capital M), they had all been forced to spend an agonising week at the Beauforte House training centre in deepest, darkest Berkshire. And as soon as he had returned from that week, Marcus had tried his damnedest to blank the entire experience from his mind.

"I'm so sorry," he began, suddenly aware that he had been woolgathering for almost a minute and the man – Grainger – was still stood there with his mouth half open and his hand held out. Marcus took it. A slightly damp, slightly too limp grip. He shook and let go quickly, suppressing a shudder. "I remember the course, well, that is to say I remember going on it – not so much the content – but I'm afraid the name doesn't ring a bell. Sorry," he repeated.

"Oh that's OK. I shouldn't be surprised really. I looked an awful lot different back then," Grainger blustered. "No beard. Almost certainly no tan. And as far as I can remember, about a hundred pounds heavier."

Marcus squinted slightly, his mind's eye trying to picture the man in front of him with those new parameters.

"Oh, and red hair of course," he added, ruffling his sweaty hand through his wild pepper-and-salt locks.

The penny dropped! Gringer! Of course. Such flaming ginger hair as Marcus had never seen before or since, and which had led the others on the course to corrupt his surname in merciless taunting. Gringer the Ginger.

"Fenton Grainger!" Marcus exclaimed, hiding his inadvertent internal humour at the resurgence of the memory. "Now I remember. How are you? What have you been doing in the... er..."

"Almost twenty years," Grainger offered. "Where does the time go, eh?"

"Indeed."

"Never did much with Marketing after that."

"You and me both. In fact as far as I know, no-one did. Hardly surprising really though is it? Weren't we all techies that week?"

"Apart from Rickman," Grainger reminded him, holding up a finger as he bent to retrieve his trolley and dump the tins into it. "He was sales I think. Kept himself pretty much to himself."

"Ah yes. I vaguely remember," Marcus lied. "So, what have you been doing the last twenty years? If not Marketing."

"I've been off-world," Grainger whispered conspiratorially, pointing to the ceiling with his still-raised finger.

Marcus looked around, thankful that there were few other shoppers about this early in the day and trying quickly to think of an excuse to cut the conversation short.

"That's where I got such a good tan," confided Grainger. "Stuck in orbit around Vega with a worn-out UV shield."

"Right. Sounds hairy."

"You're not joking," Grainger laughed. "Hence the beard. The Vegans don't believe in shaving. By the time I got back, I'd quite got used to it."

"And you lost weight on account of their food, eh?" Marcus offered, having not come up with the excuse he was searching for yet.

"You've tried it?" Grainger asked, surprised.

"A lucky guess."

"Ah. Well, you'd know what I mean if you had tried it," Grainger continued. "Almost a year on nothing but water and seaweed. That's one thing I did change when I got back."

"Understandable. Look, I'm sorry to cut this short – it's been great to see you again – but I have to get all this done before I start work for the day, so I'll have to–"

"Yes, yes, I quite understand," Grainger said, smiling. "I'd suggest going out for a pint to catch up, but I'm off again tomorrow."

"Back to Vega?" Marcus asked nonchalantly, as if it were the most normal place to return to.

"No! Wouldn't go back there if they paid me double! No, it's a different kind of trip altogether this time."

"Oh?"

"Staying exactly where I am, geographically speaking."

"OK. So what kind of trip is it?"

"I'm heading five thousand years into the future," Grainger said, raising his finger again but pointing it ahead of him, down the aisle.

Author's Notes

My interpretation of this day's topic is firmly rooted in my fascination with cosmology, at least to start with. A second idea came hot on its heels: that an orbit can be a social thing, as in "a circle of friends" or people who come into your orbit.

The end result is a combination of those ideas, my decision to have a bit of fun with it, and a liberal sprinkling of personal history. I did indeed spend an awful week on a "marketing sheep-dip" as a result of a corporate decision – originating as you might expect from a marketing consultant who had the ear of the CEO – that we would all "benefit" from the experience. The course was held in my company's wonderful training centre, whose name was a close match with the fictional Beauforte that appears here. Most of the time I spent there was more "pleasurable" than "painful". It was an idyllic place, and – marketing aside – everything I learned there came in handy during my varied career in computing.

The name "Fenton" still occupied the zeitgeist at the time, having the previous November been popularised by the footage of a man attempting to stop his labrador Fenton chasing a herd of red deer in Richmond Park (still available at the time of writing on YouTube if you're interested).

One final footnote on this piece that I noticed on rereading, concerns how the world has moved on in the intervening ten years with respect to the "three-pack of Fray Bentos." I don't know if this has happened in your part of the world but here in the UK many supermarkets, driven by increasing environmental concerns, have abandoned multipacks of tinned goods, at least as far as the plastic shrink-wrapped versions go. If tins (cans) are sold together, they're now mostly in cardboard packaging, but many are simply sold individually.

Day 63: Cold Embrace

One of the hardest days of his life, but it was over. The last mourners, his best friend Sean and his wife Abi, had finally been persuaded to leave and he was alone with his thoughts and his empty house.

Richard Chivers absently pulled off his black tie and undid his top button, kicked off his gleaming new black shoes that had been pinching his feet all day [Put those away Richard! Don't leave them lying in the hall like that] and wandered in his stocking feet into the kitchen in search of a drink. [Not another one, darling. Take it easy!] He found the whisky at his third attempt. Half a bottle. Was it half full, or half empty, he wondered ironically? Right now, he decided, he'd call it half empty. But at least that wasn't as empty as his home, or his life.

A tear welled up and ran down his cheek. Funny how he could keep it in check when there was anyone around. He'd always been easily distracted. One or two of his friends had even made some half-hearted attempts at humour throughout the day and he'd caught himself laughing a couple of times. How quickly he had forgotten, for a moment, that he had nothing to laugh about.

He poured himself a glass, filling it almost to the brim [Take it easy, I said! Are you trying to drink yourself to death?]. When was the last time he'd drunk whisky? They must have had this bottle ten years. It never did him any good. He walked back into the living room, his gaze falling on a photo of himself and Ruth taken during last year's holiday to Belize. [Look at that sagging jaw line] She looked even more beautiful than when they'd married, only the year before. The sun over there had a different quality. It sparkled in her eyes. Who had taken that photo? [Jim] Jim, that was it. They hadn't even known Jim and Karen were holidaying at the same time as them, until they met at the check in.

He took a sip from his glass, and turned the photo onto its face on the bureau. He shivered. An unseasonal chill had settled on the room. He stared at the glass. The amber liquid sloshing gently as he moved, leaving an oily film inside the glass that separated and fell languidly back to join the rest. Richard realised he wasn't enjoying the drink. He set the glass down on a table [Use a coaster Richard! You'll leave a ring!] and walked upstairs. He was suddenly tired – the emotion of the day, the lack of sleep for the last three nights, and the strain of keeping up appearances for in-laws and friends had finally caught up with him, and with the unexpected coldness of an empty house surrounding him all he wanted was to crawl into bed.

*

Richard slid between the cold covers and lay on his back. An owl hooted in the copse outside his bedroom window. Moonlight filtered in through a crack in the curtains, but it was a half-moon and the light was an even paler imitation of pale than usual. He turned over and buried his head in Ruth's pillow. It still held her scent. He grabbed it with both hands and pressed it against his face, breathing deeply. Sobbing quietly. After a while he became accustomed to the faint perfume and could no longer smell it. He turned over the other way.

The tiled floor of the en-suite creaked. Just the way it had when Ruth would walk through after cleaning her teeth. The heating going off, Richard told himself. Willing himself not to turn over again and check. It couldn't very well be her, could it, so what else could it be but the mundane creak of contracting copper? The bed dipped behind him with a rustle of sheets. Richard's spine tingled. He tried to keep his eyes tight shut, but failed. He realised he'd been holding his breath and released it. Against the moonlight from the window it steamed in the sudden chill of the room. As he breathed in he caught another whiff of Ruth's perfume, stronger this time. Much stronger than on her pillow. How...?

From close behind his back an icy coldness crept up to his shoulders and around his buttocks, while a heavy chill slipped like an unseen arm around his waist.

Author's Notes

I've watched and read a lot of horror over the years, so my immediate thought on seeing this topic was the many times I'd encountered a scene where a ghost returns to embrace its living partner. The only question then was how to put my own spin on what is essentially a well-worn trope, almost to the point of cliché.

Cold Embrace is another example of a piece that would make a short story. I might choose to turn it into an "unreliable narrator" work, still quite a popular option if my recent reads and Amazon's top 100 are any guide. On the other hand Richard's sensations may in truth be caused by a visiting spirit, but is it Ruth?

The appearance of Ruth's comments in [square brackets] is intended to be initially ambiguous, the mundane explanation being that Richard is recalling what Ruth would have said in response to his actions.

Notes from an Editor's perspective

It would only take minor changes to make this a much stronger entry. I'd change "and walked upstairs" to "and climbed the stairs", simply because I think that's a better, more accurate description. The phrase "stocking feet" should more accurately be "stockinged feet" but even then it has bubbled up from my subconscious: a colloquial grandmotherly phrase from my childhood which may be confusing to modern readers, so I'd probably choose an alternative, and add some descriptive reaction to almost-bare feet crossing a cold floor.

Finally, I think those initially ambiguous [bracketed thoughts] could be ratcheted up in significance to greater effect as the story progresses. I'd certainly round them off by inserting a last one towards the end: "It couldn't very well be her, could it [it is], so what else…"

Day 64: Frost

Around this time of year as a boy, or maybe just a week or two later, I used to expect that on really cold days I'd wake up to frost on my bedroom windows. On the inside. Double glazing and central heating were unknown concepts to me growing up. My bedroom windows (there were two, one on each outside wall, which made my room probably the coldest room in the house and certainly the coldest bedroom. Even the bathroom, which also had two exterior walls, only had one window) were single-glazed, with metal frames, and hence particularly susceptible to the cold.

Interestingly (it has just occurred to me) when we sold that house in April of this year , those single glazed metal framed windows – the original ones with which the house was built in the 1940s – were still in place, still intact. I've no doubt they will have been replaced now, but they lasted almost 70 years.

My parents only got around to investing in central heating after I moved out. And even then, because they "didn't like hot bedrooms", the system they installed was only partial. A radiator beside the boiler in the kitchen, which I always thought was completely redundant since the boiler, being a 1970s vintage, was not particularly well insulated. One at the bottom of the stairs to warm the hall. One at the top to service the landing. If you wanted any heat in a bedroom you had to leave the door open. And that was it. Three single, narrow radiators for an entire 3-bedroom semi-detached house. The "through" lounge/ dining room had a gas fire.

But such luxury was unknown to me as a child. The only source of heat in my room was a two-bar portable electric fire. It smelt, when on, in that way old metal electric fires have. Especially the first time it was used each year in the run-up to Christmas. Having been gathering dust for something approaching nine months, the first time you switched it on all that dust would burn off the element and stink the room out for days. It wasn't just dust, of course. There would be the odd dead fly in there too. And possibly a few strands of hair that had found their way through the grille. I hated that fire, ugly brown dumpy little monstrosity that it was, but it didn't stop me from turning it on every night an hour or so before I went to bed.

No such luxury in the mornings, of course. Time switches were another technology denied to us in the 1960s and early 70s. Hence the frost on the windows. I could see my breath most mornings too, in that room. It's a wonder I ever plucked up the courage to get out of bed, especially once my folks had gone all modern and replaced our traditional bedding with those new-fangled "continental quilts" (duvets, to modern readers). Toasty warm it was, under my "quilt", and hence by comparison, even colder in the bedroom.

On school mornings it was a mad dash to the bathroom, once my Dad had whistled his signal that he'd finished at the washbasin. The bathroom had one of those ceiling lights with a heater in it, and on really cold mornings Dad would have turned it on when he first got up. So the bathroom (again, by comparison) was warmer than the bedroom. Warmer even than the landing which, being in the middle of the house, never got as cold as the outer rooms.

On weekend mornings I didn't need to be quite so brave. I could laze around in bed until the sun was up, and melted the frost on the windows. At least then it didn't look as cold in my room.

When I got a bit older, I found myself wondering exactly how cold it got in that room. I'd acquired a thermometer from somewhere and I hung it on the wall. Being of an analytical bent (OK, OK, I was a spod. I admit it), it was not enough for me to just glance at the reading every morning and evening on my way out of, and into bed. I had to write the temperatures down. And then, having written them down, I had to graph them up. And so it was that, by the age of 15, I had a year's worth of bedroom temperature readings on a graph on my wall, and I can tell you with absolute certainty that the coldest it ever got in my room one winter's morning, was 44°F.

I saw my breath THAT morning, I can tell you!

The graph spiked a lot where the electric fire was on in the evening, and not in the morning, but the trend of temperatures was still visible, as were the maxima and minima. Attentive readers will have noticed that even this glaring evidence of incipient frostbite in my room was not enough to persuade my parents that central heating was necessary, until after I'd moved out. Whether or not this constitutes child abuse I will leave it up to the reader to decide.

The frost on the inside of my windows did make exceedingly pretty patterns though. Which was, naturally, some small compensation for the discomfort.

Author's Notes

Memories of those cold winter mornings are still vivid even 50+ years later, so writing this topic up as a blog entry was a natural choice. Yes, this is all real. I was that boy.

Those windows have now been replaced, as expected. My childhood home came up for resale recently on Rightmove, and we checked it out.

Notes from an Editor's perspective

So much "got" it gives me a headache. One of my worst

and most common drafting tics. "When I got a bit older, I found myself wondering exactly how cold it got in that room." Oof, dreadful. Out with it!

Day 65: A Moment In Time

Barg sat in front of his Nexus Editor, staring at the scene it displayed. He frowned. His friend and colleague (and also, although neither of them let this stand in the way of their friendship or work relationship, his team leader) Admirator Snell, looked across from where he was tutoring a new Editor.

"Problem?"

"It's this same scene," said Barg. "I've been looking at it for hours and I can't decide which way to go."

"Run it through for me then," said Snell, trying not to sound patronising.

"Subject is Artemis Pandraptis, and he is running for his train. The parameter controlling the nexus is his arrival at the door of the train – an urban light railway with automated doors and driver – and there are three options."

"Go on."

"In option one, his arm hits the door as it is closing, but he is in time for the sensors to detect his fingers and the door reopens to admit him to the train. He boards, and arrives home in time to enjoy a meal with his wife Bariana who has just discovered she is pregnant with their first child."

"Sounds like a good option."

"At this stage it is, but there are complications which I'll come to later. In option two, Artemis is delayed by 11.8 milliseconds, which is just long enough for the doors to fail to open. The train leaves without him."

"So he doesn't make dinner."

"Correct. But it's worse than that for his wife. The slightly elevated stress levels at his lateness lead to increased amounts of cortisone and a few other hormones in her blood. At such an early stage of pregnancy these are sufficient to cause her to miscarry."

"Unfortunate. It sounds clearly like a less favourable option."

"Well, yes, but that's also connected with the complications I mentioned earlier. The child – should it survive – has, shall we say, a less than auspicious future ahead of it. But let me outline the third option before we come to that."

"OK, go ahead."

"In the third option, Artemis is delayed slightly longer. By..." Barg fingered another part of his Nexus screen and scrolled down the list of numbers that appeared, "... another 650 milliseconds. That's long enough not only for him to miss the door but also for the train to start to move out of the station. The unexpected movement causes him to knock his glasses off, and when he bends down to retrieve them the backdraft from the departing train overbalances him. He falls onto the track and is electrocuted. Fatally."

"Oh dear, no! How tragic!"

"Indeed. The consequences for the unborn child are the same – after all, Artemis will still be late for dinner – but it is the effect on Bariana that are most significant. She will, eventually, repartner and in doing so... well... the variables at this point defeat me."

"And are there any other effects to take into account on the station?"

"What I've described is the focus of the nexus. There are one hundred and eleven thousand nine hundred and fifty-six other split points within a 5-second bracketing window around the nexus, but none of them have such significant effect on society one way or another."

"OK. I think we've reached the point where we must consider those effects then. You mentioned the child?"

"Yes. The child Bariana is presently carrying, if he survives, will grow up to be Narsis She'Ath."

"The mass murderer?"

"The very same."

"I begin to see your dilemma."

"If it was a dilemma it would not be so difficult to resolve Snell. In this case there are three variables. There is Artemis to consider, and also the results of Bariana's new relationship in the event of his death."

"Artemis Prandraptis you said? You don't mean he's THE Prandraptis? The discoverer of the Prandraptis effect?"

"I'm surprised you didn't recognise him. Although he is quite a bit younger at this nexus than when he becomes famous."

"But, we can't let him die! Mankind's future depends on him!"

"Its future in space travel, certainly. My calculations – and I admit with such lengthy extrapolation they only have a 7.4% probability of being accurate – suggest that in the absence of Prandraptis it will take another 145 years before humans achieve faster-than-light space travel."

"So your choice – forgive me – ONE of your choices, is between humans reaching the stars in this century and allowing the Murderer of Mars to come into the world?"

"You begin to see my problem."

Author's Notes

Another piece that is clearly inspired by Asimov's End of Eternity. I don't think I'd appreciated quite how much that novel meant to me. I would recommend it, if you haven't read it. Many of my teenage reads are quite badly dated now, but I'd guess the majority of Asimov's oeuvre holds up. In fact I don't have to guess, I can check out some of the more recent reviews on Goodreads, and there it is. The short version is: still a good story, but don't expect 1950s authors in general, or Asimov in particular, to give female characters much of a role.

On rereading today's entry, I notice that it only works as the beginning of a story. Although it ends on a kind of cliff-hanger, it's not actually a problem as it stands. Option 1 allows She'Ath to be born, option 3 kills the inventor of FTL travel, but option 2 currently kills the murderer while at the same time leaving Prandraptis alive, which on the face of it seems to me, now, to have no downside. Perhaps not surprising that I left (what could be) a gaping plot hole given the constraints of the exercise.

Were I to continue with this story, Snell would have to reach this same conclusion, and Barg to continue his explanation with another, as yet undocumented, problem with Option 2.

Notes from an Editor's perspective

Right at the beginning of this piece I find a little bit of accidental head-swapping. Normally if I start a scene with a character's name, the reader can comfortably assume the scene will be written from their POV. But in this case, having begun with Barg sitting at his terminal, three lines later we have: "...said Snell, trying not to sound patronising." To know that Snell was speaking with that intent, we'd have to be in his POV.

The solution here is a simple one. The rest of the piece has no further indications of POV one way or the other. It could be either of them. So I'd rewrite that first paragraph to be clearly Snell's POV from the start, mentioning him and his training activity to open the sentence, followed by his observation of Barg's activity and his frowning. The frown gives him sufficient incentive to continue with his query: "Problem?"

There's some of the usual drafting glitches to tidy up here too – repetition of "significant"; "becomes" famous might be better as "became"; "effect on Bariana that are most significant" should be "is"; etc.

Day 66: Dangerous Territory

"So that's a Bud Light for May, Spitfires for Jim and Keith, V 'n' Ts for Ranvir, Suzi and Bella, and... sorry, what was yours Jack?"

"Nnn?"

"He's already had enough," Suzi offered.

"No I ant, s'awright," Jack held up a finger. "Mine's easy t'remember anyhoo. Jack for Jack."

"Oh yeah, a JD on the rocks for Gentleman Jack."

Jas headed off to the kitchen to take his turn at bartendering while the others remained in various states of crash around the living room.

"What IS this garbage we're listening to?" Jim asked.

"Dunno," Keith replied. "Change it. I've put loads of playlists on the Pod."

Jim scrolled casually through the list and selected "Party – Late" which was exactly where they were. Too late for dancing, too early for easy listening (whatever THAT was), they just needed a series of decent choons. He trusted Keith's selections implicitly.

Jas returned carry a bentwood tray loaded with drinks and snacks.

"My MAN!" Jack said, eyeing the snacks and swaying dangerously close to the tray. "How'd you know I had the munchies?"

"I'm psychic," Jas laughed.

They took their drinks and Jas parked the tray.

"So," he said opening his arms to include the room, "what're we gonna do now?"

"You KNOW what we're gonna do," May replied mischievously. "We're gonna play... Dangerous Territory!"

Jim, Ranvir and Bella groaned.

"Not that again," Bella sighed. "You know what happened last time."

"Yes I do," May continued, undeterred. "We had fun!"

"Funny sort of fun"

"Exactly! The best kind! Funny fun is wicked."

"And wicked fun is funny," added Suzi. "Can I go first?"

"Spin a bottle," Jack insisted, through a mouthful of Hula Hoops.

A brief search for an empty bottle that hadn't already been recycled ensued. Jas found one behind the sofa, set it on the floor in the middle of the room and spun it. It came to rest with its neck pointing at Suzi.

"Yayyy! I DO go first."

"Victim?" asked May.

Jas spun the bottle again. It stopped at him.

"Oooh!" said Suzi, giving Jas a wicked grin, "let's see. Umm..."

Jas looked nervous. "Nothing too risky," he pleaded.

"Is there anyone in the room you fancy?" Suzi asked. "That's mild enough, isn't it?"

Jas blushed, trying not to look at anyone in particular.

"I guess. Er... I mean... yes. There is."

"Who? Tell us!" May insisted.

"Hey! S'not fair!" Jack said, picking up the bottle. "One question a time. That was the rule last time."

"But it'll take FOREVER to get anything juicy out of anyone," May pouted.

"Well ask better questions then!" Jack said, pointing the bottle at Suzi. He replaced it, and set it spinning again. It stopped at Jas.

"Ha!" he said. "Revenge"

"You don't know who the victim's gonna be yet," Jack pointed out, spinning the bottle a fourth time.

"It takes too long for the bottle to stop," said Bella. "Can't we just roll a dice or something."

"A die," said Keith.

"Whatever."

"Suzi!" yelled May

"Yes?" she said

"She means you're the victim," Jas grinned. "Revenge IS sweet. Now let me see..."

"Remember I didn't ask you anything too dirty!" Suzi said, suddenly looking less assured.

"Should have taken the chance while you had it," Jas teased. "My question is... have you ever had anal?"

Suzi turned a deep red and flashed a look at Jim before she could stop herself.

"Aha!" exclaimed May, who caught the look and its meaning immediately. "Hardly need to answer that now do we, Miss Backdoor?"

"Shut up," said Suzi sharply, "you can't talk anyway. Your rear entrance has seen almost as much action as your front."

"See? I told you this would happen," Bella said. "We've only just started and you're at each other's throats already."

"Backsides more like," joked Keith.

"So, is that right? Suzi?" Jas insisted. "You haven't ACTUALLY answered the question yet. So you've done it with Jim, yeah?"

"You only asked if I'd done it, not with who. And yes, I have. So what? Don't you ever like to try anything different?"

"Hey, no need to get all defensive. Whatever floats your—"

"—turd," interjected Jack.

"Ewww," Bella screwed up her face and paused with a handful of peanuts halfway to her mouth. "Putting me off my snacks here."

"Spin again Jack," said Keith.

Inquisitor: Keith. Victim: Bella

"Fuck," Bella muttered

Keith grinned. "How evil am I feeling?" he mused quietly to himself, but easily loud enough for the neighbours to hear. "Have you," he started slowly, dragging out the tension, "ever had sex with another girl?"

"Foul!" called May.

"Why foul?" Keith asked indignantly.

"Because you know she has. I told you."

"Ooh. Scandal AND gossip," Jack crowed. "I love it."

"You TOLD him?" Bella exploded. "WHEN?"

"The next day," May said, smiling. "Didn't know we were hiding it from anybody."

"Well YOU might not have been," Bella said, giving May a shove.

Author's Notes

So many potential interpretations of this topic, each of them clamouring for attention! All these years later, I can't put my finger on why I chose this – rather unusual – one. Perhaps a faint trace of memory from one of the dodgy parties I attended in my best-forgotten past? An amalgam of all those appalling party games: "adult" Twister; Strip Postman's Knock, etc. There were certainly several instances of bottle-spinning, mostly more innocent than this one.

Where could this tale go, were I to extend it into a short story? It boasts a sizable cast of characters, so it has huge potential for side- or sub-plots. It has already revealed a previously hidden gay relationship, or at least a single encounter that could blossom into a full-blown affair, or lead to embarrassment/rivalry, or both. The party itself could dissolve into an argument, or an orgy , or possibly even a death, which the surviving characters might choose to cover up in the style of The Secret History.

Day 67: Boundaries

A ripple of applause encircled the small pitch just as the church clock struck the quarter hour. Williams had hit a four. Paul was grateful for the interruption.

"I just can't get past it," Burlap was saying, "it's like I've hit a brick wall."

"That was a great shot."

"Eh?"

"Williams. Another four. That's three and he's only been in since just before eleven."

"Oh. Yeah. Good for him."

"You're not really here today at all are you old boy?"

"Mmm? Sorry. No. It's this work thing."

"It's Sunday Jonny, for Chrissake. Can't you leave it in the office for the weekend."

"This code is due on Monday," Burlap replied, running his hands across his face. "And I just–"

"Can't fix the problem. Yeah, you said."

A loud "oooh!" rolled around the ground. Paul looked back across the pitch to see the umpire pointing at Williams.

"God. He's out."

"What?"

"Williams. LBW I think. Bad luck."

"Guess that means I'm in," Burlap sighed, picking up his bat and checking his pads.

"Guess so," Paul agreed, trying to hide his relief. He was happy to help out a mate, naturally, but in Burlap's case there was no help he could offer. He wasn't a computer man, and an hour and a quarter of listening to him moan on about his latest project was more than enough.

Burlap shook Williams' hand as they passed each other at the entrance to the pavilion. Williams spotted the vacant seat next to Paul and walked over.

"Good boundaries!" Paul offered.

A dark look passed across Williams' face and he stopped in the act of sitting down.

"What do you mean by that?" he snapped.

"Three fours and you were only in for about fifteen minutes."

"Oh, that. Yeah. Couple of lucky strikes. Ken isn't a very good bowler really."

"What did you think I meant?"

"Eh?"

"You were a bit snappy. I was congratulating you."

"I know, I'm sorry. Things... well... things aren't so good at home right now. Dele's... well let's just say there's a lot of talk about boundaries at home too, especially recently."

"I didn't think Dele was into cricket."

"Ha! You got that right. It's a different kind of boundary she's talking about. Needs her own space, that kind of bollocks."

"Ah."

"Sorry. Didn't mean to let it spill out here. Christ, this is the one place I thought I could get away from it for a few hours. Just a bit touchy at the moment."

"Yeah. Not surprising. Do you want to talk about it?"

"Would it help?"

"Dunno."

"Not the kind of thing we talk about really is it? You and me. Or anyone on the team. Crosses a line."

"Line?"

"Oh come on. You know what I'm talking about. What does any of us really know about... any of us? We might as well all exist in separate little bubbles when we're not here. All we ever talk about is runs and league tables and what type of linseed oil to use. I don't even know how you vote, or whether you've got kids."

"Never really thought about it before."

"I have."

"I mean, when I'm here, I'm here for the cricket."

"Sorry, but that doesn't sound very sociable."

"It's what brings us together though."

"Yes, but it's a bit one-tracked isn't it? There's more to life than cricket."

"Maybe it's just me. When I'm at work, I think about work. When I'm at home, I think about Jess and the kids. When I'm here–"

"You think about cricket. I get it. Bit compartmentalised though isn't it?"

"Supposed to be a bloke thing that though isn't it. Little compartments of life, never the twain shall meet and all that."

"I guess. I find that all a bit old school though. Life's hard enough without shutting yourself up in little boxes. Sometimes, it's better to share things. Think out of the box."

Williams looked thoughtful. He bent down to undo his laces.

"So I guess the answer to my own question is: yes. It would help to talk about it. Unless you'd rather not."

"No, it's fine. Sorry. That sounded a bit tepid. I'd like to help if you think I can. Gotta be better than having old Burlap bending my ear about his Java."

"His coffee?"

"Sorry. Java SCRIPT. Some kind of computer thing, apparently."

"Oh God, he's been at you with that too has he? I had it all last night in the pub too. If he spent as much time fixing it as talking about it, it would all be done by now."

Paul laughed. "Maybe he's too compartmentalised. He can only talk about it when he's not at work. Or worry about it. Not actually DO it, you know?"

"Maybe."

"So... Dele?"

"You're sure."

"Whatever you want to share. Within reason of course. There is a limit."

"Oh don't worry. I'm not about to give you all the gory details. Too painful."

"For me?"

Williams chuckled. A hollow chuckle, Paul thought.

"For both of us, probably. You know, it occurred to me the other day. You're the only one I know who's still with his original partner. Jess is your first wife, isn't she?"

"Yep. Came close once before. Long time ago. But really, it's always been Jess."

"Lucky you. I thought the same about Dele until this last couple of months."

"When she started talking about boundaries?"

"Exactly."

Author's Notes

First off, I should admit I know next to nothing about cricket, beyond being forced to play it in school games lessons back in the Stone Age. And on top of that, no desire to learn anything about it. I'm one of those strange blokes who has next to no interest in sports of any kind.

But even for a non-sporter like myself, the topic of "boundaries" brought the instant thought of a cricket pitch, followed in almost the same moment by the thought of personal boundaries. I love a good pun, so the opportunity to weave a story around that one proved irresistible.

My second insight for this piece is that, as a determined plotter, it gave me a rare insight into the attraction of the opposite writing style; pantsing. I've written about the differences between the two here

https://johnberesford.com/2020/10/26/the-plot-thickens/

...but when writing novels I always work with a well-defined plot. For this challenge, each piece is as I've already mentioned begun with only the vaguest notion of how I expect the story to pan out. And in several cases – this one in particular – the characters and their conversations have run off in a totally unexpected direction. One which, if I'm honest, I'd been keen to pursue, if only to find out for myself where they end up.

My main reason for being a plotter is fear. Fear of "writing myself into a corner"; of investing hours of effort in a story that ends up being impossible to rescue without further hours of rewriting. All that waste! Even the thought of it gives me indigestion. But is that fear real? Having not taken that path, I may be wrong. Perhaps if I trusted the characters (i.e. myself) more, then magic would happen. Dean Wesley Smith's "Writing into the Dark" explores this subject in great depth, and has effectively become the pantsers' bible. Perhaps I should read it.

Day 68: Unsettling Revelations

Robert slipped his key into the lock carefully. Gently, soundlessly, he opened the front door and stepped into the hall. He stood for a moment, listening. The house was still. At this time of the morning he would have expected some activity. Baking, a radio, a vacuum cleaner. His wife's car was still in the drive. If she had been out he would have continued on his way to work, disappointed but resigned to try another day. There would always be another day, and on one of them he would catch her.

Today might still be that day.

He removed his shoes to avoid any possibility of squeaking rubber on the polished hall floor and climbed the broad sweeping staircase to the first floor. Half-way up he heard the first faint sounds that confirmed what he had known for... how many months? Nine? Ten? The tell-tale sound of a rhythmically bouncing bed.

He stood still again on the landing. His wife's voice came from the third bedroom – the guest room – sighing with passion. "Ohhhh. Yessss." He clenched his fist, but did not move from his position on the top step. Clever of her to avoid using their room. No chance of an errant stain or unfamiliar odour. No inexplicable movement of pillows or too-frequent changing of sheets. Robert never went in the guest room. Hardly ever. Twice a year maybe. Too rarely to notice any changes.

"Mmmm. MMMM!" moaned his wife through the closed door. Part of him wanted to catch her in the act, but another part cautioned patience. "Yes!!" she cried, clearly reaching her climax. "Oh Yes, YES, YEEESSS."

The sounds of movement ceased, and Robert moved forward again. He may have missed his chance to catch his wife and lover in flagrante, but he was not going to give them time to dress or dispose of any other evidence. He had not covered more than half the distance to the bedroom door before his wife began to moan again. Jesus Christ! What kind of a man was he, her lover?

Determined this time not to wait too long, Robert crept to the door. There was no longer any sound of movement, and yet his wife could clearly be heard on her way to another crescendo.

"Yes," she yelled again, "Ahh! Ahhhh!! Argh! Nnnoooo! Oh God!" Richard could wait no longer. He would never have a better chance. Her screams were now so loud they would drown out any noise from the hall or landing. He grasped the knob, flung wide the bedroom door and shouted "So! I was right!"

The final word died on his lips at the sight that opened up before him. His wife, lying on her back, naked atop the bed, her legs spread wide and her arms flung back in what appeared at first glance to be passionate abandon. Between her legs the burnished bronze head of Oliver, the house robot, was apparently providing a secondary source of pleasure. As the full horrific detail of the scene filtered through to Robert's numbed mind, he realised his wife had not responded to his dramatic entrance. Her eyes, their gaze still fixed on the window, had not moved but seemed instead to have developed an unnatural glaze. Her smile, which Robert had initially taken to be one of mechanically-induced ecstasy, now looked instead to be a rictus of horror.

Reacting at last to his master's presence, Oliver turned his head toward Robert. His face glistened bright red and small globs of flesh and pubic hair clung to his mouth. The scene faded to grey before him as Robert lost consciousness and fell to the floor, his last thought a sickening realisation that Oliver must have completely misinterpreted the command "Eat me."

Author's Notes

I honestly can't remember if my boyhood hero Isaac Asimov ever covered "extra-curricular" activities in his Robot stories, but I do remember reading that it was a virtual certainty, whenever humanoid robots are developed, that they will sooner or later be used for sex.

I only hope those who programme the robots' neural nets, or positronic matrices, or whatever, take care to include the appropriate safeguards :o)

Day 69: Shattered

William marched swiftly along the hall, adjusting his tie. He hated ties, could never get the damned things on straight, but even more so when they were tight around stiff collars. There was nothing for it though. Judy and Punch's – er, Frederick's – wedding was a full "top hats and morning coats" do, so his best bib and tucker was the least that was expected.

The tie's intransigence occupying most of his attention, William nudged their hall table as he passed. It took a few moments for the collision to impinge on his consciousness and by the time he looked back Gillian's precious vase was already teetering at an impossible angle. Rocked by the old table it twisted one way and the other, and was clearly about to abandon its fight with gravity, and topple. William slid to a halt on the polished parquet floor and tried to back track.

Even as he started, he knew it was hopeless, but maybe...? He summoned up all the muscle memory he had remaining of his brief time on the school rugger team and launched himself at the table, arms outstretched to catch the now falling vase. He hit the floor with a breath-sapping thud, his fingers touched the vase, but there was no time left to get a grip before it made contact with the hard, unforgiving floor. The vase gave a hollow crack and split almost perfectly in half in his hands.

"Fuck!" he cried.

"William?"

Gillian's voice echoed down the hallway from the kitchen. She appeared in the doorway.

"What...? Oh! No! My vase! My mother's vase!"

She ran down the hall, heels clicking and catching the hem of her bridesmaid's dress.

"What have you done?" she cried, tears starting in her eyes and plopping onto her cheeks. She grabbed the two halves of the vase from him. One of them fell into three pieces as she took it. Some sort of delayed reaction, William thought dazedly as the smaller pieces fell to the floor and shattered.

"You clumsy bastard!" Gillian shouted. "I've TOLD you not to run down the hall."

"I wasn't–" he began.

"This is all I had left of her," she sobbed. "It was her favourite! It was MY favourite. You KNEW how much I loved it. Oh God. You stupid, stupid bastard!"

William got up slowly off the floor, dusted down his trousers. He started to defend himself, but thought better of it.

"Why today of all days?" Gillian continued. "I'll look wonderful in the wedding photos won't I? With swollen red eyes and a face like thunder? Judy will be mad as hell if I spoil her day. It's your fault," she yelled, brandishing the largest piece of vase at him. "It's all your fault!"

"I–" he began again.

"You'd better get changed," she said angrily, cutting him off again. "You can't go like that, all dusty and creased. Judy will–"

"Oh for fuck's sake! Fuck Judy," William retorted, his anger and embarrassment vying for supremacy. "She won't even notice me for God's sake. She's your friend, not mine."

"Oh! Oh! Is she? MY friend? And there I was thinking she was OUR friend."

She looked down at the pieces of vase in her hand. At the fragments now littering the floor.

"It's gone," she said, "this is– it's too bad. I'll never mend it."

"I could–"

"Are you still here? I told you – go and get changed! We don't have time for this."

"I don't have another suit," William said.

"What? Of course you've got another suit. Wear the blue one. It's not your best but it'll have to do."

"The blue one is at the cleaners. I spilled wine on it at the stag do, remember?"

"God you're a clumsy prick," Gillian put the pieces of vase back on the hall table, rounded on him. "Spilling wine, breaking vases. What are you going to ruin next?"

"This stupid wedding, apparently."

"Yes," she said, eyeing him angrily. "Yes, you probably will. Won't be the first one, will it?"

"Oh, God. Not that again."

"Oh, I'm sorry. Sorry if you're still embarrassed about ruining OUR wedding too."

"I didn't ruin–"

"Forgotten already, have you? Why am I surprised? You never really wanted a proper wedding–"

"That wasn't a proper wedding. It was another one of THESE weddings. The kind you have to impress other people. It wasn't about what we wanted."

"It was what I wanted."

"What you'd been told to want. What you'd been forced into by all the talk from your friends. By Judy. It wasn't what I wanted."

"So you decided to break that too. Like you broke my

mother's heart. And now her vase. Now I've got nothing left."

Tears welled up again in Gillian's eyes and she collapsed onto the hall floor, her lavender dress falling in ugly creases and billows around her.

[this story is continued later in the writing challenge – on Day 71 in "The True You"]

Author's Notes

Another "pantsing" effort, where the characters took off in their own direction. You've probably heard/read writers saying that before. "Oh my characters are always going off at a tangent, they never fail to surprise me." I used to think it was more than a bit fake, until it started happening to me.

I only had the vaguest notion what this story would be about when I began writing it. To draw a parallel between physical and psychological "shattering". I made the rest up as I went along and got so caught up in the flow that my 30 minutes expired while I still had more than half a story in my mind.

Incidentally, any similarity between these characters and the real Bill and Gill is entirely coincidental.

Notes from an Editor's perspective

For me, two common side-effects of writing this way are sloppy punctuation and poor choice of vocabulary (or repetition). In this example I seem to have done quite well with the latter. A brief scan hasn't thrown up any obvious changes that I might make. As for the punctuation, during an editing pass I would probably avoid quite so many "interrupted endings" of William and Gillian's speeches, maybe alter the speech emphasis in some places, but overall I think this one turned out pretty well.

Day 70: Bitter Silence

The arguments would be over soon, he realised.

He liked to win. Whenever they had engaged in verbal jousting in the past, he'd always tried to win. Mostly, he liked to think, he'd succeeded in the attempt. Or was that just his take on things? There was another argument in the making, right there. Perspectives. Beliefs. Expectations. They were all argument fodder at one time or another. No matter how the cut and thrust of vocabulary and pithy comment soared and dived, he's always felt in control. Always knew he'd end up ramming his points home, convincing the others of the validity of his reasoning, the clarity of his thinking, the enormous towering edifice that was his intellect.

Just recently, it had begun to dawn on him that edifice may actually be artifice. That he had never, in a reality seen from their alternative perspectives, convinced anyone. Only alienated them. Turned them off, in the modern vernacular that he decried so forcefully on so many occasions. Faces began to turn away not in submission to the weight of evidence he presented, or acceptance of his supremacy, but in resignation. They only bowed to his argument, they didn't accept it. Or embrace it. Or believe it.

He'd call it a pyrrhic victory, only there was no fire in it. It was a cold, empty ascendancy. Like climbing a mountain and attaining the summit only to find no camp, no survivors, no friendly climbers had preceded you or prepared a welcome. And there you sat, alone on your mountain of right, while your fellows remained below in their wrongness. Their warm, comfortable, familiar wrongness. Sometimes, being right was a lonely place to be. He'd expected that. Expected to lead the herd, to be out in front, in the vanguard, lighting the way with the fiercely burning, bright torch of his righteousness. But he'd also expected them to follow. Take his example, and walk his beaten path. Not leave him to blaze the trail and watch the light disappear into the darkness. Not let him wander alone on the path with no succour or companionship or validation.

So it came to this. He'd won his arguments, all of them, one at a time. And it had made no difference. Had he changed anything? Now that he thought back, he honestly could not remember a single person altering a single belief or behaviour as a result of his debating. It was like an intellectual exercise to them. The mental equivalent of going to the gym. The intent was only to get better at the debate (physical activity) and to limber up the muscles of the mind (body). The content of those debates was immaterial to them, when to him it was the very stuff of existence. The reason for being. Its import could not be overstated. He had the knowledge. The direct line to fact, certainty, attainment. Did the fools not realise all they had to do was listen to him, follow the thread of his discourse, to achieve enlightenment?

Clearly not. And the endless striving had now exhausted him. One way remained to him to win the final argument, albeit by default. For if he wasn't there to listen to their side of the deliberations, why then there could be no debate. They had heard his side. And when he was gone, he would never be able to hear theirs. Stalemate? Perhaps, but the points were weighed in his favour.

He took the small white pill in his left hand, the glass of water in his right. The time for debate was done. Now was a time for silence.

Author's Notes

Besides "bitter silence" another thing commonly associated with bitter is: pill. And there immediately was my central theme – my quirky connection – for this piece. My unnamed protagonist has to swallow both the bitter (mental) pill of realisation that his lifetime's engagement in debate has been fruitless, and the second, physical pill which will take him on his chosen path. His eventual silence is therefore, if anything, doubly bitter.

Quite disturbing, in retrospect, how many of these pieces are connected in some way with suicide. For the avoidance of doubt I'm not, have never been, and never expect to be suicidal. But there's no denying that many people are. It remains the second most common cause of death for males between the ages of 10 and 34 in the U.S. Ten! Good grief. And the situation is not much better in the UK. Perhaps not a suitable subject for fiction, then? On the other hand, perhaps better to air the subject as widely as possible, to stimulate debate and perhaps the realisation of its futility?

Notes from an Editor's perspective

A slight slip with "he's always felt in control", which should of course be "he'd".

Beyond that, I think the piece overall has a rushed tone. It could be made stronger, or at least flow better, with a deep rewrite. On this occasion the free-flowing drafting thoughts have delivered something that, for me, reads quite "clunky". The protagonist's rushing thoughts crowd each other, and are documented in a high-brow, intellectual voice that, while it may be "in character," in many places serves only to distance the speaker from the reader.

Day 71: The True You

[this post is a continuation of the story begun in "Shattered" earlier in the writing challenge – on Day 69]

Gillian let the broken pieces of vase fall from her hand, her shoulders quivering as her sobbing subsided.

"Why didn't you tell me?"

"Tell you what?" William stopped on the verge of going to change his suit, turned back to his quietly weeping wife.

"That you didn't want a proper wedding."

"It still would have been 'proper'. Just not so bloody flamboyant. You know I hate all that."

"I didn't, actually."

"What? How can we have been together for this long without you knowing at least that much about me?"

"Sometimes I don't think I know you at all. You... you're so... guarded."

"I am not guarded."

"You never really talk about what you want. You always leave it up to me."

"I want you to be happy, that's all."

"I'd rather you told me what you really think. Feel. Who you really are."

William flushed. Turned away, trying to avoid her searching gaze.

"What?" Gillian had caught the first flash of the pain in his eyes. "What is it? Tell me!"

"You wouldn't like who I really am," he said quietly.

"What do you mean? I love you! At least..."

"Exactly. You love who you think I am. Who I try to be, for you. Or worse, who you want me to be. I don't know whether I can do it any more."

"Do what?"

"Hide."

"What are you hiding from? Not from me?"

Gillian stood up, brushed the creases out of her dress. She started to move towards William, but thought better of it.

"It's not a matter of hiding from anything," William replied. "It's more what I'm trying to hide. Me. Oh God, do we really have to get into this now? We'll be late for the wedding."

"Then let's be late," Gillian retorted.

William's eyes widened. "A few moments ago your best friend's wedding was the most important thing in the world."

"Yes, well. That was before we got into this."

"We haven't got into anything," William said quickly. "Come on. I've got to get changed and you'd better run a damp towel over that dress. My blue suit isn't ideal, but that's the only bridesmaid's dress we have in the house!"

*

"I don't think anyone noticed."

"Noticed what?"

"That I wasn't wearing the right colour suit."

William dropped his car keys on the tray. "Nightcap?"

"I wouldn't mind a drop of brandy."

"I'll join you," William agreed, walking through into the living room. Gillian took off her shoes. The clink of glasses being removed from the cabinet and the brandy decanter being unstoppered echoed across the cold hall. She shivered and turned the heating up.

In the living room, William had set her snifter beside her chair. He was cradling his, standing at the window staring into the garden.

"Close the curtains. It's bloody freezing in here," Gillian said.

"I want a divorce," William replied.

"Wha– You want what?"

William drained his glass in one gulp. "I told you earlier that you wouldn't like the real me," he said. "And I also said I couldn't go on hiding it any longer."

"I don't understand. What's brought this on? I thought we were happy!"

"You were happy. At least, you made a good job of pretending. I haven't been happy for a long time."

"Are you– Is there someone else?"

"Ha! The predictable question. Would you believe me if I said no?"

"Yes! That is, I think so. I've never... you've never given me any reason to suspect–"

"Good. That's because there isn't a reason. I don't have anyone else. I don't want anyone."

"But you don't want me any more, is that it?"

William hesitated. He walked over to the drinks cabinet and refilled his brandy glass. "It's more that, oh God! I said I couldn't pretend any more. And I think that, if... no, when I stop pretending, you won't want me."

"But I love you William! This is crazy! I don't understand."

"Have you been listening to anything I've said today, Gill? You're in love with someone who doesn't really exist. The William you love is a fabrication. A shadow. A confection of lies and half-truths, concealment and doublethink."

"I don't believe you."

"Yeah? Well it's true."

"Well come on then. Give me an example. Show me the real you."

"You don't mean that."

"I bloody do! If it's going to mean divorce anyway, why not tell me the truth?"

"You won't like it."

"I already don't like it William! For fuck's sake! We've spent the whole day at someone else's wedding and now you want to call time on ours? It's madness!"

"How many people at that wedding do you think are your real friends."

"What? All of them! Who are you talking about?"

"The people at the fucking wedding!"

"Alright, no need to swear. I don't know who you mean! Our friends? Judy's mum? Frederick's parents? I don't know ALL of them."

"I'm not talking about their parents! Jesus Christ. How many of them are your friends?"

"All of our friends were there!"

"All of your friends. None of them are my friends. We never see my friends."

"What–? You mean Charlie? Dimble? Those friends? You haven't seen them for years! They never keep in touch, they–"

"They never keep in touch because you made it clear you didn't like them. They put up with you a few times for my sake, but when you started picking at their hobbies, clothes, girlfriends, well... they just gave up on you. And me. And don't pretend you weren't glad about it. Whenever I suggested catching up with them again you were always ready with an excuse. Oh it's the garden show this weekend, or your family were coming over, or Judy – bloody Judy! – had some crisis you had to deal with."

Author's Notes

I can't remember the train of thought that led me to connect this piece with Shattered, but the topic of "The True You" resonated deeply with me. Although I never had exactly this conversation with anyone, I've had a close approximation to it on several occasions, and for almost the same reason. It took me way longer than it should have to stop being a people pleaser and start living my true life. And having spoken about it with many people over the years, I know I'm far from alone in that.

So it was both easy to write from experience, and hard to write because of that experience, if you see what I mean. But the strongest work comes from the truest place, and part of that lesson about being true to myself is to not shy away from baring my soul if it makes the writing better.

One of the closest parallels between this piece and real life is the part about being kept away from my friends by a misplaced sense of duty and propriety. Too many lost years. I don't waste time regretting them, but these days I do make sure I take every opportunity to bask in those friendships and make good memories.

Notes from an Editor's perspective

A liberal sprinkling of "got" most of which should be

replaced with stronger choices. It always can be, and usually should be.

Minor head-swapping. Whose POV is this? It documents thoughts of both characters. Maybe it's omniscient, but I don't usually employ that in any writing. And even if it is, some judicious tightening wouldn't go amiss. An example: "Gillian had caught the first flash…" only needs a slight rewrite to clarify that it is not her thought, but a realisation of the fact from William's POV, perhaps with a supporting thought that he'd turned away too late.

But the biggest problem with this – did you spot it? – is the gaping plot hole of The Blue Suit. The intervening days between Shattered and The True You had clearly robbed me of my memory that William's blue suit is at the cleaners, so he can't "get changed" into it □

Day 72: Pretence

"I'm coming after you!" Dad growled, his voice rising in the dramatic pauses between each word.

Ben screamed – half in fear and half in delight. This was a familiar game, but he still loved it. Dad's hands, fingers hooked into his interpretation of an ogre's claws, appeared around the doorway from the kitchen where he'd smeared them with ketchup for added realism. Ben leapt off the sofa and screwed himself down in the gap between its arm and the wall. His heart pounded, even though he knew it was just a game. Wouldn't be any good if he wasn't just a little bit scared, and though that thought was still some years in his future, his bones knew it.

"I'm... COMING!" his Dad growled again, deep in his throat. He stepped out of the kitchen, his face a rictus of horrific ogreish bloodlust. Ben tried not to breathe.

"Fee, fi, fo, fum," Dad began. Ben knew what was coming next. He suppressed a strong urge to giggle. This was serious!

"I smell the blood of an ENGLISHMAN!" Dad continued, lurching further into the living room. Ben couldn't take the tension any more. He screamed and dashed out from his temporary sanctuary. "Aha!" cried the ogre, walking more like a zombie in his direction. But Ben wasn't watching. He was sliding across the hall floor in the direction of the stairs. Recovering his balance, he took the stairs two at a time.

"Where's my DINNER?" raged the Dad ogre. Through the door of the living room, convincing sounds of monstrous searching came clattering and bouncing up the stairs. Ben stood on the landing catching his breath and trying to peer through the banisters at the living room door. The audible disturbance died down, to be replaced by a kind of snuffling sound. His Dad was the best ogre. A distillation of all the stories and fairy tales Ben had ever read, or ever had read to him. Bone-crunching, limb-tearing, blood-sniffing monster with strong arms to squeeze the life out of any little boy he found before snapping all his bones and making him into crunchy soup for supper. It was terrifying, and Ben loved it.

"He's not here!" cried the ogre, now in an even worse temper. "I'll find him! And when I do I'll break his BONES!"

His Dad clumped loudly across the living room, his heavy footsteps making the glasses rattle in the cabinet and sending Jeeves the family cat tearing out into the hall in a panic. He took refuge in the dining room as Dad appeared in the door. "Raaaaaawwwwrrrrr!" he growled. Ben squealed again, and headed for his bedroom. He jumped onto the bed and pulled the covers up to his eyes. Having his bones broken by the ogre usually meant a good tickling, and he began to tingle in anticipation. The clumping footsteps of the ogre started up the stairs. Ben began to wonder if it might have been a good idea to make a detour to the toilet before taking up his usual hiding place.

Halfway up the stairs his Dad began to make awesome gargling noises. He growled and hissed and banged the banister. It felt like he was shaking the whole house.

"Ruuuurrrgh," he snarled as he made his way to the top step. Dad must have been practising new growls. He hadn't done that one before. He came slowly towards Ben's bedroom door. Ben could hear a scraping noise on the carpet. Dragging his foot, he was, and breathing heavily in his throat.

"Hurrrr. Hurrrr. Hurrrrrr."

Just as Ben began to wonder whether – this time – the closet would be a better hiding place, even if it meant missing out on a tickle, the ogre's hand appeared on the door jamb. Dad had really gone overboard this time. The tomato ketchup still glistened realistically on his fingers, but he'd stuck some of Jeeves' shedded fur on the backs of his fingers so they looked like real ogre fingers. But something else nagged at Ben. Something different. More different than just ketchup and Jeeves fur. Ben's eyes widened as he caught on to what it was. The Dad ogre gave another heavy grunt as Ben began to shake. The hand was fully a foot higher on the frame than Dad's would have been, and twice the size.

The scream that had been building in his throat emerged full-throated as the creature's head rounded the door frame. Half pig, half man, its dirty, dark pink skin was splashed, not with ketchup, but real blood. Thick black bristles covered its chin and they dripped globs of bloody gore onto the carpet. It limped into the room, a kitchen carving knife buried deep in its thigh, and gave another loud roar as its gaze fell on Ben, quivering with terror under his duvet.

"RAAAAAAAWWWWWWWWWWWWWRRRRRRRR!"

Author's Notes

"Pretence" offers few clues to its best interpretation, and the possibilities are legion. But I don't have many opportunities to write a story from a child's perspective, and once my mind lit on the idea of this childhood game it was an easy decision to run with it.

During these short drafting exercises it's hard to silence the "plotter's brain" so I was halfway through my 30 minutes when the idea to switch from the Dad ogre to a real ogre popped into my mind. Since this piece is written from Ben's POV, his demise has to mark the end of the scene, but it would of course be possible to continue the story with another child, perhaps living next door, or with the return of Ben's mother from work, discovering the grisly aftermath.

Notes from an Editor's perspective

In this instance my drafting brain has left a few glitches that need tidying up. 'Banisters' (aka handrails) are not the things Ben would peer through on attaining a temporary sanctuary on the landing. Those would be balusters, or more usually in the UK (where this story is located), spindles.

The brief appearance of the family cat has two slight issues. His first mention is in a run-on sentence, which I always attempt to rewrite when drafting, and his second – in the following sentence – "He took refuge in the dining room…" introduced for me on rereading the piece a momentary confusion about which "he" I was intending. Is it still the cat, or is it Ben? It's important not to give the reader any reason to stop reading and start wondering, so an essential part of the editing process is spotting bits like this, and rewriting them to improve the clarity and flow. I would probably switch these sentences up something like this:

"His Dad clumped loudly across the living room, his heavy footsteps making the glasses rattle in the cabinet. The noise woke Ben's cat Jeeves. Startled, he scrambled out of the room, skidded across the hall, and took refuge in the dining room as Dad appeared in the doorway."

Finally, I should probably say something about "special" words. The one that brought this comment to mind is "rictus." Don't get me wrong, it's a great word, but when drafting I do have a habit of over-using it. And really, it's one of those words that should only appear once, or at most twice, in an entire book. Any more than that risks the reader rolling his or her eyes and starting to become exasperated. I distinctly remember exactly this happening to me as a teenager, reading E.E. "Doc" Smith's Lensman Series. The pyrotechnics in there, normally the result of some battle in deep space or the like, were almost always accompanied by the word "chiaroscuro". Bad enough that such an unusual word was used so often, but once I'd learned what it meant the discovery that it was being misused was even worse. More recently the oft-repeated term "boiled leather" in George R.R. Martin's work has become something of a family joke.

So one of my editing checks is to search a manuscript for words like this (I have a list) and ensure they're only used sparingly. The first time I performed this check for "rictus" I found I'd used it fourteen times. Good grief.

Day 73: Patience

I can wait.

How long have I been saying that to myself? Let's see... I first saw her the day they moved in. That was so long ago, and I was so young, that I don't even remember when it was. I can't pretend it was love at first sight. I don't even know if I believe in that, but even if I did I don't think I fell in love with her then. If I was too young to remember, I guess you could say I was too young to fall in love too.

But later, maybe a few months later, maybe the next summer – the one after they moved in just before Christmas – when I saw her playing in the garden. Then. Then I fell in love with her. Just something about the way her bright blonde curly hair bounced around her face, catching the light. Or – since I've mentioned the light – the way it shone through her thin summer dress and I could see the outline of her legs. I didn't know about the significance of private places, back then, that's how young I was. Didn't know that legs were something boys, when they start trying to be men, would rave over. Shape of them and length of them and how they moved. Back then I was just fascinated by the sway of that translucent cotton dress. It moved so that I thought there was something underneath it. A pet dog, or something. But it was just the air and her.

And her voice. She was so young it was really still only an ordinary girl's voice, but it sounded different to me. Deeper. Smoother. It was still a few years before I learned the word "mellifluous" but that's how I'd describe it now. At night, when I was laying on my back trying to get to sleep, I would replay things she'd said to me in the garden that afternoon. It would make my head tingle. Sometimes I got it tingling so strong I thought it would explode. With my eyes closed I could sometimes see stars, it was tingling so bad.

I never saw her at school. Because her family had moved in so long after mine, she went to the new junior school while I was at the old one. She was the year below me anyway so I guess I wouldn't have seen much of her even if we'd gone to the same place, but at least we would've been able to walk home together. I would have loved that. We could have held hands and I would have picked daisies for her and everything. And then when we went to big school, they were different too. Streaming they called it, or something. Anyway just like before she went to the new school and I went to the old one. I guess it's always been like that – she does new stuff and I do old stuff. I collect stamps; she designs clothes. I watch old black & white movies, on the TV; she only watches new ones, at the cinema. I go to ceilidhs at school; she goes to parties with her cool friends.

But I know she'll notice me one day. Suddenly I'll be more than just the boy next door. It'll be like she's woken up from a dream, one where we were just friends. Just kids playing in the garden or going to the swings. When she wakes up we'll be grown up and ready to play grown up games. Only she'd better wake up soon, because we're pretty much grown up already, and she hasn't seen me yet. You know what I mean by "seen me," right? I mean noticed me. In that way. Realised that I'm the one for her, just like I've known she's the one for me. Right from back then, that first summer.

My parents used to say I was too young to understand what love really is. But they're the ones who don't understand. Just because they didn't get together until they were really old, like 20 or something, doesn't mean it can't happen for other people like that. Like me. I've known all along and I've never changed my mind. My Mum says stuff like, "You wait. You'll find someone one day and you'll forget all about April. You'll wonder what you ever saw in her."

She's mad, my Mum. I know what I see in her. It's not just her hair, her eyes, her legs and all that. I see her. Underneath. I know what she's really like. What she's thinking. And it's golden. Her heart is pure gold and I know I'll never find anyone like that anywhere ever again, no matter what my stupid Mum says.

'Course I can't tell anyone. Crikey, can you imagine? My mates would never let me live it down. We're not supposed to be serious about girls. Not supposed to even think stuff like "her heart is pure gold." They'd never stop laughing if they heard me say that. Laughing at me that is. They do a lot of laughing at people, my mates, so you have to be careful. That's all they think girls are good for: having a laugh. None of them take it seriously. But it's like for life, isn't it? Finding the right girl?

Which is why I can wait. As long as it takes. She's worth it.

Author's Notes

This piece is a veritable witches' cauldron. Its ingredients are part memory, part experience, part adapted memory, and part invention.

In my boyhood home, both our neighbours had girls. On one side, the daughter was much older than me, so always outside my circle of acquaintance. Even so, she appears here as the girl with the floating dress. One of several instances of recurring embarrassment whenever the family film footage was run. We're talking one or more decades before the arrival of VHS, when my parents recorded family holidays on Super 8 cine film. Inevitably, on return from those vacations, the cine camera had several minutes of unexposed film remaining, which had to be shot in and around the garden before the reel could be sent off for processing. In this particular scene the girl was playing with her toy pram, and I'm caught on film – aged something like 7 or 8 – lifting up her skirt.

Naturally my parents took every opportunity to comment on this. "Typical boy", "takes after his father", "chasing after the girls already, at his age!" etc, etc. In all the years I was subjected to this suggestive and salacious interpretation (now thankfully behind us, as no-one has the right equipment to show the film, and on top of that, I have the only copies), nobody believed my innocent explanation…

The girl had been instructed to walk around her pram, to bring some "motion" into what was, after all, a video clip. Her movement, combined with a gust of wind, made her dress billow out. My innocent young mind thought she was hiding something under there, so I lifted the hem of her skirt to see what it was. No, honest. I was definitely not trying to see her pants. Why doesn't anyone believe me?

On the opposite side lived the girl I did carry a torch for. A year or so younger than me, we often played together in one garden or the other, or one house or the other. She it was who designed clothes and went to parties. I did indeed attend the ceilidhs that were held at school (quite enjoyed them, as it happens).

So there I sat in the mind of my 14-year-old self, armed with some real memories and a writer's inventiveness, adapting and augmenting those memories to wring every milligram of poignancy from the scene. When that pot of ingredients mentioned above is stirred, the recipe creates an adaptable brew. A story that could be taken in several directions. The first one that occurs to me leverages the hints that appear towards the end of the piece. A slight feeling of the narrator being revealed as a stalker. His fascination with the girl next door could easily take a darker turn, and lead the story into a "serial killer" tale or similar.

Notes from an Editor's perspective

Commas are a pain in the arse when drafting. I always either put too many in, or miss essential ones out. The grammar checker sometimes comes to my rescue, but (currently) works better with missing ones than superfluous ones. In this case, in "Anyway just like before she went to the new school…", "just like before" should be bracketed by commas. Strictly speaking, grammatically, it should be "just as before", but this text is documenting a head voice of a young speaker who uses normal, day-to-day, informal grammar. In this instance "just as" would sound out of place.

Day 74: Midnight

Even at this hour the air was still warm. Not the blisteringly unbearable heat of the day, and still warmer than the summer days he'd spent at university in England, but a comfortable, blanket-soft, enveloping warmth. A warmth that was tangible on the skin if one was to wave one's hand in the air.

He waved his hand to test the thought. Yes, he was right. A camel grunted from across the oasis. He folded his hand back under his cloak. A wisp of smoke from the dying camp fire curled across his face, bringing the pungent odour of goat's meat and spices mixed in with the dark, dry, powdery smell of the charcoal. He stared into the fire, watching the embers flash and sparkle, the last flames chasing their lost companions across the glowing redness of the remaining wood into the grey ash beneath.

His belly was still full from the meal, still keeping him awake with its grumbling. He didn't mind. This was one of his favourite times, and one of his favourite places. The palm fronds above him cast a black-on-black shadow across the sky, though as a sometime artist he knew the sky wasn't absolutely black. Not the black of his bisht. It was more of an exceedingly deep purple. He stared at it now, through the palms. It was like an enormous soft billowing pincushion. Countless pins had been stuck in the cushion in random patterns and groups which men through the ages had tried to understand or interpret. Or tried to impose on them meanings that they couldn't possibly have. An educated man like himself knew that even stars that appeared to be close neighbours could be separated by huge distances in space and time, the light from one taking millions of years longer to reach his eyes than that from the very next.

Across this blackest of nights, across his poetically imagined pincushion, the great maker had spilled a jug of milk. The pale luminescence of its trail washed from one horizon to the other, a path of light for the gods to tread. There was no distracting moon to dim the beauty of the heavens with its flaring reflected sunlight tonight. All was calm, serene, dark and comforting. As he stared and his eyes completed their adaptation from the fiery glow of the camp fire, more stars and yet more seemed to appear out of nowhere. The canopy was ablaze with pinpoints. So many stars. So much time.

The vastness overwhelmed him. The billions of visible stars in the celestial path of his own galaxy, and the billions more points of light that were really other galaxies, each containing their own billions. On how many planets, circling how many stars, was a man lying on a desert floor staring back at him across the light years and the millennia, wondering if he existed?

A shooting star flashed across the dark above him, its brightness searing a white streak in his dark-adapted eyes. As soon as it appeared it was gone, a fleeting scintilla of conflagration. A beautiful destruction. A chaotic and inevitable death for a random piece of the universe trapped in the Earth's gravity well. Sometimes, he thought ruefully, a scientific education could be a barrier to an artist's appreciation of the world's glamour. Any other tribesman would simply have made a wish, or made the sign of the Hamsa to ward off any evil.

Author's Notes

I've never sat near an oasis at midnight, but I remember with undimmed clarity the moment I first saw the Milky Way in the night sky with my own eyes (rather than in an image, or on TV). On a beach in Rhodes, in the total absence of light pollution, its breathtaking beauty clearly, starkly visible and utterly bewitching.

So today's subject conjured that memory, and provided an opportunity to write about a man much like myself (if you'll forgive the conceit). Someone with science in his mind, and poetry in his soul. I can't count the number of times I've stared at the sky and wondered at its infinite possibilities. One of my earliest memories is lying on the lawn in the garden of my boyhood home, doing exactly that. Everything I've learned since, from books, from the BBC's unrivalled science output, from the Hubble Space Telescope's stunning images, has only increased that wonder, and that sense of the infinite.

Update: I'm in the middle of rereading these "Author's Notes" entries – an editing pass, if you like, given the context of this work – and just last night we watched an hour-long documentary on the new James Webb telescope. The program culminated with one of the early images from the JWST; the one they'd achieved during the "focusing" phase where the mirrors are all brought into the correct alignment. Clearly there are many, many more spectacular images to come in the future, but even this first one knocked the famous "Hubble Deep Field" into a cocked hat. Displaying a huge number of galaxies never before seen, in an image field – as they described it in the show – no bigger than a grain of sand held at arm's length. I'm not embarrassed to admit it brought tears to my eyes.

Notes from an Editor's perspective

I have extremely limited experience (verging on zero) of the lands in North Africa and the Middle East, so I allowed myself just enough research to enable the correct use of "bisht", and "Hamsa" in this piece.

Where I wrote "...the light from one taking millions of years longer to reach his eyes than that from the very next." I'd clearly intended that to mean the one that appears next to it from our point of view. If I were to redraft this, I'd phrase that part better, for clarity. Probably to something like "than that from the one apparently adjacent to it."

Day 75: Shadows

Geoff, Randolph and Narsi sat staring at each other through the blue fug that filled Nightowls Den. It was a garden shed really, but to them it was their den. A secret place for secret things. Geoff passed the spliff to Rand.

"Are we gonna wait all day?"

"They'll be here. Chill."

"Who are we waiting for?" asked Narsi, who had only moved to the street the week before and not yet experienced a full meeting of the Nightowls.

Rand exhaled, adding another plume to the thick atmosphere in the den. "Pete said he wouldn't be here for the tales. He's coming across later. But Ned should be here by now."

The shed door opened as Rand finished speaking and Ned entered.

"Sorry. Sorry. Mum had me putting ALL the groceries away before I could get a pass," he said. He fell into a corner of their broken down sofa and let out a sigh of total satisfaction and relaxation. "But I'm here now, and I need a pull."

He held out his hand, and Rand passed over the joint.

"Is it story time?" he said before taking a massive toke.

"Yeah. Let's make it a good one. It's Narsi's first time. This is Narsi, by the way.

Ned waved, still holding his breath. Narsi smiled and turned to Geoff. "You've not said much about these tales," he began.

Geoff interrupted him. "Telling tales about the tales is verboten," he wagged his finger. "You have to hear the tale to get the full effect. Anything else violates the 'Owls code."

"Whose turn is it?" asked Rand.

"Mine," gasped Ned, exhaling at last.

"That's why we were waiting," Geoff explained to Narsi. "We take it in turns."

Rand stood to draw the blackout blinds on the two small windows while Geoff lit a single tea-light and set it on the small table in the centre of the floor. Drafts from under the door set the light flickering. Shadows danced around the pine walls.

"Perfect lighting for the story I'm about to tell you," Ned began, lowering his voice and adopting a traditional Vincent Price graveyard tone, "because it is about shadows."

The others settled themselves into their seats. Rand extinguished the weed.

"Since a time before time," Ned went on, "our earliest forebears have known that shadows are not what they seem to be. It's true that demons and ghouls seek out dark places. They can often be found lurking in shadows and corners. But those shadows in which they hide are static. They are cast by buildings, or artefacts. Things that have never lived or walked the Earth. They are merely the absence of light. Umbra and penumbra are they, and they hold no terrors of themselves, only by association with the things that hide within them."

Another light breath of wind under the door made the tea light gutter once again. A tree branch scraped against the wall outside. Everyone jumped.

"What our forebears knew," said Ned, warming to his story, "but which has passed out of memory for all but the fewest scholars of the arcana, is that there exist a race of beings with souls blacker than the blackest night. In ancient times they were named the Umbrae, and it is only in relatively recent times that they have given their name to the ordinary shadows that we see around us today."

With a dramatic flourish, Ned swept his hand around the interior, indicating the quivering shadows from the tea light.

"The Umbrae, whose name used to strike dread at its very utterance, do not hide in shadows. They inhabit them. They take them over. These darkest of the spirits from the underworld can use the shadows of living creatures to wield unspeakable evil, wresting control of them from their owners to enter our world for their own ends. Once inside the shadow of a man, they can go wherever he goes, hear whatever he is listening to, influence his mind and those of his friends, with only one purpose in their stygian souls: to perform evil works. To maim and wound, kill and torture, fetch the horrors of the deep and visit them on our world, when we least expect it, and in ways it is impossible to defend against.

"Who would believe us? Children cower in their beds at the shadows in their rooms–"

The door of the shed burst open. Haloed by the bright orange light of the setting sun which streamed across the garden from the West, Pete stood in the doorway, his arms braced against the door posts, his baseball cap twisted sideways on his head.

"So, are we staying here or shall we go shoot some pool?"

The others didn't move. They were staring in transfixed terror at the floor. Pete was standing completely still, but on the smooth wooden boards of the shed floor, his shadow was moving.

Author's Notes

My earliest encounter with an errant shadow was in the story of Peter Pan. Much later, I remember a horror story that featured living shadows and which I found terrifying in my early teens – one of the few stories that really did give me nightmares.

The telling of chilling tales is, of course, a common theme of "anthology" stories, especially in the horror genre.

All of those influences came together in this piece, which could easily carry on the theme of story telling to be extended into an anthology work in its own right. The way it's set up now could even be bent into a "false awakening" style story where it turns out the moving shadow becomes part of Ned's tale.

Notes from an Editor's perspective

Some instances of weak phrasing and Drafter's Repetition:

- "...set it on the small table followed immediately by "...set the light flickering."
- "draw the blackout blinds on the two small windows" might be better as "...blinds down over the two…"
- And to echo the cadence of "can go wherever he goes," the following line would have more power as "hear whatever he hears."

I would certainly also tighten up the final three paragraphs to add a bit of punch to the punchline. It's tautological to include "from the West" (the setting sun never shines from anywhere else). I have a strong antipathy to "was standing", "was moving" and "were staring", the kind of thing that always crops up in drafting, but can be cut down for stronger, more urgent phrasing. Moreover, the reader knows where we are, so it's superfluous to refer to it as "the shed floor" or "the door of the shed":

'The door burst open.

"Hey guys," said Pete, grinning at their startled reactions. The setting sun lent him a fiery orange halo, cut into a celestial Q by the baseball cap twisted sideways on his head.

"You done with story time yet? I wanna go shoot some pool."

No-one spoke. Pete stood motionless in the doorway, one hand gripping the doorframe. In front of him, on the smooth wooden floorboards, his shadow squirmed.'

Day 76: Summer Haze

Joe slapped his arm, squashing another midge. In a few hours he'd be forced to take cover inside the house. The annoying little black flies would begin to swarm as the day cooled towards evening and for some reason his blood smelled sweeter than most to them.

For now, it was just the odd one or two, and Joe wasn't about to let them spoil his enjoyment of this glorious day. The last summer that he would have as a free man. Or at least, that's how he saw it. Freedom from the college work he had left a few weeks behind him. Freedom from the working life he was about to begin, still at least a few weeks in front of him.

He reached for his glass and let out an small, involuntary moan on remembering that he'd finished it only a few minutes before. He leaned over to lay his book on the grass, picked up the empty, still-cold glass, and walked inside. The air in the kitchen was still. A pair of house flies circled the light in eccentric orbits, almost colliding, avoiding, spinning. Always keeping the bulb in the approximate centre of their gyrations; never quite landing on it.

He refilled his glass and dropped in the remaining three ice cubes, pausing to listen to their familiar cracks and schisms before refilling the tray and replacing it in his old freezer, which hissed and wheezed in its efforts to defeat the heat of the day.

Outside, a heavy haze hung over the distant fields. Joe stood, glass in hand, staring out at the open country. Only the nearest details were visible. The further away he looked, the more indistinct the trees and haystacks became, outlines only, hints of shapes, suggestions of possibilities, until finally they disappeared altogether under the weight of summer.

It was like looking through time, Joe thought suddenly. Like a life stretching out in front of him, instead of a simple pastoral scene. The nearest objects were the things he knew were coming. Interviews. A week's holiday with mates in the Algarve. Fiona's birthday. A little further away, the months were indistinct. Possibility of... developments... in his relationship with Fiona. A new job. Travel, maybe. He still hadn't really made up his mind whether to stay in the UK or work abroad. The scene was painted with a broad brush. An impressionist's rendition of things to come, unfinished and with details and highlights yet to be added. He couldn't even see the horizon. That far away the future was a foreign land. What had they called it in that film Brian loved so much? The Undiscovered Country, that was it.

He was seized by a sudden urge to run through the field. To grasp the future and make it reveal its hazy secrets. To blaze a path through the mysteries and know. If only it were that simple. That sylvan, vaporous future that lay before him was separated from the now by more than a briar hedge. There was nothing for it but to wait and see. He laughed at the phrase, one of his father's favourites. His Dad had loved a good mystery, and there was nothing more unknown than the future. He stood on the edge of the fields and on the brink of his life and at that moment, he didn't feel free any more. His hand ached from holding the ice-cold glass for so long. He took a long, head-splitting drink of juice. His freedom was an illusion. He couldn't remain here, in the garden, in the sun. The ice would melt in his drink. The sun would set. The garden would die into winter. And Joe would travel into that future, whatever it was, with no more choice than anyone else.

A cloud passed over the sun. The hazy scene dimmed. Joe turned back toward the house and left the garden.

Author's Notes

Coincidentally this entry falls on Day 76, and the story is inspired by memories of the famous long, hot British summer of 1976, when we had no rain for ten weeks and the long, balmy days seem to stretch on forever.

I was between first and second year of University that summer, I did spend many happy hours relaxing in the garden, and I did famously holiday with my mates that year, though it was to the more mundane Norfolk Broads rather than the exotic – to me at the time, at least – Algarve.

Where this story diverges from reality is that Joe has reached a crossroads that was still, for me at that time, a year or more in my future, and therefore, as with many young men approaching life's critical junctures, completely out of my thoughts.

In truth, though it is only hinted at in the original piece, this is an allegorical tale about the transition from child/boyhood into manhood. About time spent "in the garden" without responsibilities, compared with the yoke of adulthood. Joe thinks about marriage, implicitly at least, and his forthcoming working life, but for now these all exist in the next field, or the one beyond that.

Notes from an Editor's perspective

"Midge" is a British word. With an insight provided by my wife, who spent 40 of her early years in Canada, I know that on the other side of the Atlantic those annoying little black biting flies are called "no-see-ums" or "punkies." But when writing you have to pick one, and since this short story features an English man, in an English garden, using the English word was the only sensible choice. I have to trust that readers in other parts of the world won't trip over it.

Superfluous Thinkage: "... let out an small, involuntary moan on remembering that…". This section obviously started life as simply "an involuntary moan" and I slipped in "small" after the fact, forgetting to return to correct the indefinite article. But my main point here is the "on remembering" – an unnecessary reference to Joe's thoughts. We're already in his head, these are all his thoughts. This would be better split into two sentences: "He reached for his glass and let out a small, involuntary moan. He'd finished the drink only a few minutes before."

A second example of this appears later: "Joe thought suddenly". In this case it can be deleted altogether.

Passive Voice: "...picked up the empty, still-cold glass, and walked inside. The air in the kitchen was still.." I would rephrase that to lose the "was". For example, I might contrast the midges outside with the house flies inside, circling in "the still kitchen air".

Drafter's Repetition: "glass in hand" – the fourth instance of "glass" in the space of three paragraphs, and definitely (at least) one too many. While editing I would most likely replace this one with "drink".

Those Errant Commas: one obvious example "That far away the future was a foreign land." It needs a comma after "away".

And finally, on rereading, I see that the end of this piece would benefit from the addition of a reaction from Joe to the clouding of the sun (and, metaphorically, the chill that settles over his previously carefree life). He would notice a drop in temperature, possibly even shiver and rub his arms, hug himself, etc.

Day 77: Memories

The old woman stood bedside Rebecca as she waved goodbye to her parents. The child seemed cheery enough for now, but eight hours lay ahead of them before her daughter and son-in-law would return and she wondered how on Earth she could fill them for the girl. Lunch, certainly. Afternoon tea. Some crayoning. But then what?

"Will they be gone long?" Rebecca asked.

"All day I'm afraid my dear," she replied. "It takes at least two hours to get to where they're going, and they'll be there all afternoon. What would you like to do? I have some colouring books. Or we could watch some TV?"

The girl's face creased in deep thought. Then her eyes lit up.

"Can we look in the old chest?"

The old woman laughed in surprise. That was the last thing she expected.

"Why, yes. If you'd really like to."

"Oh yes, I really would."

"Come on then. Don't you want a drink before we start?"

"Maybe later. I'm OK for now."

They climbed the rickety old stairs with their threadbare carpet and their old dog smell, still lingering even though Jed had been gone almost a year. The door to the back bedroom creaked as she pushed it open.

"I really must oil that," she said, half to herself.

"Oh, no! Don't Granny," Rebecca said. "It makes it more creepy when the hinges creak like that."

The woman walked stiffly over to the wardrobe, her legs still complaining after the climb. She pulled an old tin strongbox from the bottom of the hanging space, carried it over to the bed and sat down beside it. Rebecca jumped onto the bed on the other side, threatening to tip the box onto the floor.

"Careful!" the old woman cried. "The things in here are precious!"

Rebecca looked aghast. "Sorry Grandma," she said, staring at the floor.

"Never mind," said the woman. "No harm done." She unlocked the box, the small silver key turning easily in the well-worn lock.

Inside, an eclectic mix of ancient and treasured possessions lay tidily. Some wrapped in old yellowed tissue paper, or pages of The Times from years gone by. Others were uncovered, but each had been placed with care so as not to rub against a neighbour or crush something more fragile beneath. Rebecca picked up a small, gold framed mirror from the top of the assortment.

"What's this?"

"Oh, that was my grandmother's!" the old woman exclaimed. "I used to call her Mammy, because that's what my mother called her and when I was young I didn't know any better. Later it kind of stuck. It's a dressing table mirror."

"What's a dressing table?"

"You call them lowboys," the woman replied, "and these days they usually have big mirrors standing up at the back. Like a little table with drawers in the front. You have them in bedrooms for keeping your toiletries and make-up, that kind of thing."

"I know. Mum's got one. But this is so small."

"Mirrors were expensive in those days. Only rich people

could afford mirrors the size of tables."

Rebecca stared at herself in the mirror. "I'm going to be rich one day."

"Me too," said her grandmother.

"What's this?" asked Rebecca, setting down the mirror and retrieving a small green glass jug from the corner of the strongbox.

"It's a green glass jug," replied the woman, smiling.

"I know that, silly," Rebecca giggled. "I mean where's it from? Whose is it?"

"It's mine, and I've had it since my very first holiday in 1947."

"Wow! That's ages ago!"

"It doesn't seem so long ago to me," the old woman said, taking the jug from the girl and holding it up to the light. "It's hand-painted look, all these flowers and fronds. The war hadn't been over long and my Father had only been back from overseas for a little while. We all went to the sea-side. It was the first time I'd ever seen the sea. First time I'd ever been anywhere except our town."

"How old were you?"

"Eight."

"Wow. When I was eight I'd already been to France and Spain and Disneyland AND Mexico."

"Yes, well travel wasn't as common back then. Ordinary people didn't fly much. We were lucky to be able to take a train to the coast. Rationing was still going in 1947."

"What's rationing?"

"I'll tell you later."

Rebecca started rummaging in the box.

"Careful!" her grandmother reminded her.

"WOW!" Rebecca exclaimed as she unearthed a tooled brass and enamelled incense burner. "What's THIS?"

"That's something my Father brought back with him from the war," the woman said. "It's from Turkey."

"What's it for?"

"You use it to burn incense – special oils or blocks that give off a nice smell."

"Can we light it?"

Author's Notes

Another piece that took me on a journey. I set off with the single idea of a memory box and headed for who knew where? I didn't even know, when I started writing, what was in the box.

I don't have grandchildren, but I do have children that I've left, in the past, in the care of their grandparents. Those grandparents did own a "family chest" containing heirlooms (a grand term for the kind of old tat people hang onto for sentimental reasons). Moreover, as a boy, the right-hand drawer at the top of my chest of drawers was reserved for "treasures". An eclectic collection of tea cards; foreign coins; a shell case (cartridge case) that had been crafted into a miniature telescope; a cannonball made into a piggy bank; a useful piece of string; an ocarina; a paper bag full of embroidered badges I'd collected during a lifetime's family holidays and which I intended to sew onto a sleeping bag, until I discovered I hated camping so I never actually owned one and the badges stayed in their bag; you get the idea.

Rereading this today I did wonder whether I would, if I were to edit it, add something about Rebecca misinterpreting "Turkey". I decided against it immediately.

She seems a pretty clued-up little girl, has quite extensive experience of foreign travel for someone of her age, and has almost certainly heard her parents talking about Turkey even if she hasn't learned about it in school. So the price of contradicting these already apparent characteristics isn't worth the weak humour such an exchange would add.

Notes from an Editor's perspective

We have a problem here right from the outset: "The old woman stood bedside Rebecca…"

BEDSIDE? That one has survived for ten years without anyone commenting on it, including me. I've only noticed it now, while scanning the piece with my editor's eye. Even the 2022-version grammar checker doesn't spot it.

Beyond that, there are a few of the usual small issues with punctuation and the occasional clunky phrasing, but mostly this piece stands as it is, I think.

Day 78: Change in the Weather

Ian stood on the balcony, a cold glass of sangria in his hand. The ice had already melted, in both glass and jug. Ice didn't stand a chance in this heat. They'd said it would be short-lived, but this was the end of the second week and still no end in sight. Thunderheads hung overhead a few miles distant, but there was no wind to move them. For now at least, they held their water.

Below him, Clara climbed out of the pool. Sunlight glinted on her lithe, dripping body as she walked over to the lounger where she'd left a towel. She wouldn't need it, Ian thought. A few minutes drip-drying in this heat and she'd need another dip. She didn't look up. He couldn't tell if she was deliberately ignoring him or simply hadn't spotted him. With the sun at his back, she had an excuse not to look in his direction. As if she needed one.

He stared out over the trees to the distant sea. How long had he hankered after a place like this? All his life, give or take. Be careful what you wish for, the old saying went. He should have been more careful. He sipped his drink, which had already begun to warm up. Of the many things in life that could be enjoyed warm, to Ian's mind sangria was not one of them.

"Ian."

Clara's voice surprised him. He hadn't heard her come in, or enter the room behind him. She stood at the balcony doorway, the bedroom dark behind her. She was naked. The last few drops of pool water stood out on her body, already being replaced with sweat. He could smell her perfume.

He walked toward the door. She backed away, lay down on the bed, her full, firm breasts falling onto her arms, her nipples standing up from her dark brown areolae.

"Ian," she said again, huskily, lifting her arms above her head and looking into his eyes. Challenging.

He entered the room and took off his shirt. As he neared the bed, Clara sat up and pulled down his shorts. His cock sprang up as they fell and she took it into her mouth in one fluid movement. Her mouth, surprisingly, excitingly hotter than the day, moved urgently over him.

They made love, but Ian could not think of it like that. It was sex. Beautiful sex, yes. Erotic in a way that only Clara, in his experience, could have it. But there was no love there. Only passion. Lust. Desire. As they fucked their sweat pooled on their bodies, slippery movements adding to the eroticism and the pools. Their flesh slid and rocked, their hands groped and kneaded, their mouths met in angry battle – a battle in which their eyes did not engage.

Outside a thunderclap cracked. A sudden wind whipped the branches of the trees, sending leaves flying onto the deck. The sky flashed with another bolt of lightning and the roar of thunder followed immediately. Like a celestial faucet being turned on, the rain came. Lashing down in a grey curtain, flooding the deck within minutes, the drops bouncing up over the rail, carrying sand and grit onto the balcony windows.

Ian looked down at Clara. She was crying. Tears welled in her eyes and rolled down the sides of her face into her ears.

"What...?" Ian began. She turned her face away from him, twisted out from under his body. "Clara!" he called, but she didn't hesitate. Picking up a robe from the chair she left the room. The door, blown by the wind or pulled by her hand he couldn't tell, slammed shut behind her.

Ian lay on the bed, on his back, staring at the ceiling. His still-hard member deflated slowly against his thigh. Rain lashed against the glass, drowning out any other sound.

Dashing his conflicted thoughts. Then, as quickly as it had started, the rain stopped. The sun breached the thunderclouds and shone hotly down on the sodden scene. The balcony steamed.

He lifted himself up on his elbow and stared through the open balcony door. Autumn colours had already begun to tinge the leaves, many of which now littered the deck. Another gust of wind released a further handful, which fluttered down in front of him, their transient flaming beauty only a symbol of their death and the death of another year.

Author's Notes

Here again I chose to weave a story around two interpretations of the topic – meteorological and emotional. The parallel between the sudden thunderstorm after days of heat, and Clara's sudden tears, is not accidental. Neither is that between the death of the leaves, the year, and the implicit death of their relationship.

I have third-hand experience of how the early stages of a marriage break-up can result in mind-blowing sex. Almost as if the "guilty" partner is trying to fuck the shame away, or desperately seek the lost passion of the relationship's early days to discover whether – in their eyes – it is worth saving. If that experience was in my mind when I drafted this, I can't say, but I think it's likely that it was my intent for the piece to have that implication. Much of the motivation here, for both parties, is not only unspoken but completely hidden. Only hinted at. But it's not necessarily a bad thing to leave the reader guessing.

Notes from an Editor's perspective

I must have been totally immersed in "the zone" with this one, because there's a huge amount of tightening/redrafting needed.

Drafter's Repetition: "...the end of the second week and still no end in sight." An editing pass would replace one "end" or the other. "...but it had already lasted two weeks with still no end in sight", or "...the end of the second week and it still showed no sign of letting up."

Blatant Thinking: "to Ian's mind" would be excised from a final version.

Accidental Tautology: "He hadn't heard her come in, or enter the room behind him." Entering the room is the same as coming in, but in this case my original intent (although it's not at all clear from the text) was "come into the house from the pool". I would cut this in half for clarity and flow – if she's entered the room it's implicit that she'd entered the house before that.

Use of areolae. Although I never took the Latin class at school, it did at least still exist. So either directly, or indirectly through friends, we were all exposed to "the correct form" of Latin plurals. But however much pedants might insist on that correctness, here in the real world the living language of English moves on, and while dictionaries may lag a few years behind popular usage, they do all now give "areolas" as a valid alternative plural. So when drafting, my experience of Latin – almost as old as the language itself – is uppermost in my mind. But when editing, I would have a decision to make. Which form will my readers be more familiar with? It's an unknown quantity. Some will not recognise "areolae" and its use may pop them out of the story. Some will see "areolas" and scoff at the writer's use of the modern plural. But most won't give a toss either way. I think on balance I'd rather let the scoffers scoff than give any reader a reason to stop reading and start wondering about the word choice.

Awful Adverbs: "Ian," she said again, huskily, lifting her arms…

My daughters are always telling me to cut my adverbs. There's usually a better way. Here, I would split the sentence. Shorter sentences lend urgency, and faced with his naked wife, Ian would be thinking in staccato bursts (assuming he is thinking at all :o)), so:

"Ian," she said again, lowering her voice to a husky whisper. She lifted her arms above her head, stretching, staring into his eyes. Challenging.

"He entered the room and took off his shirt." – unless it's been edited out by now, we already have an "entered" in the piece, so I'd probably replace this one with "crossed." Also, having made much of how hot the day is, would it be realistic for Ian to wear a shirt? The action is helpful to the scene, but at the very least I'd switch it up for "vest."

Drafting Flow: "...and rolled down the sides of her face into her ears." When in full flow, I don't hunt for the right word. I simply document the scene as it's playing out in my mind. So I could see Clara still lying on her back in the aftermath of their sex, and in that position tears would roll as described. But as it stands the sentence is both clunky and mildly amusing. Amusing is not the reaction I'm looking for with this scene, so while editing I'd employ a more accurate description. "...and rolled past her temples, into her ears."

And finally, either the original or one of the changes mentioned above has already used "lifted," so in the last paragraph I'd change "He lifted himself up on his elbow…" to "raised himself".

Day 79: Illogical

Zadi held a cut glass vase in her trembling hand.

"I mean it Ralf!"

"Calm down!"

"Calm down? Damn you!" She cocked her arm, ready to throw. Her cheeks glistened with new tears. "How can I be calm?"

"Just put the glass down. Please. It's your favourite. You don't want to smash it."

"I want to smash something!" she sobbed.

"That's just your emotions talking. Remember you said–"

"Oh God! It doesn't matter what I said! It's how I felt. How I still feel."

"Look, I'm sorry I was late, I couldn't help it."

"You never put me first. Never! You knew it was a special night."

"And I've said I'm sorry."

"What good's that? The dinner's ruined. It's all... so..."

"Can you just put the vase down Zee?"

Zadi looked at the glass, as if she couldn't remember picking it up. She turned it over in her hand, hardly recognising it. It was her favourite, Ralf had said. She wondered why.

"We'll only have to clean the mess up," Ralf prompted.

"There's a lot more mess to clean up than a bit of broken glass," Zadi replied, sniffing back more tears. She set the vase down and rounded on him again. "Don't think this means I've forgiven you! You still haven't explained why you were late."

"It was a work thing."

"Oh, yes. A work thing. Well then, that's all I need to know isn't it? A work thing. That'll keep her quiet. She knows I never say much about work."

"You know I can't."

"No! I don't know that! You say that, but I don't know it!"

"Why would I lie about it?"

"Ha! That's the question isn't it?"

"Zade. This doesn't make sense."

"For Christ's sake Ralf! None of it makes any sense! This isn't one of your puzzles. You can't tidily tick the boxes until it's solved. This is real life! Real feelings. It's about people, not things. Not logic."

"I–"

"Oh, don't bother. I know you don't really understand."

"No, I do–"

"No you don't! Have you ever really felt anything?"

"Don't get yourself all worked up again."

"Argh!" she screamed, moving back toward the vase and then thinking better of it. "No. I don't want to break anything. Except maybe your stupid stubborn neck."

"How can my neck be–"

"Tell me why you were late!"

"I told you, it was a–"

"The real reason. Not some vague work thing."

"You know I'm not allowed to talk about work."

"Who do you think I'm going to tell? You think I'm some kind of spy?"

"No of course not."

"Well then?"

"It doesn't matter whether you tell anyone or not."

"So you think I might?" she bristled again.

"No! That's not the point."

"I think it's exactly the point."

"Well the Government doesn't see it that way."

"Who's 'the Government'? You talk about them like it's one man. Watching every move you make."

"What I mean is, once you've signed the Official Secrets Act, then just telling anyone about anything, when they don't need to know, is an offence."

"I find that offensive, if you must know. If you can't trust your own wife, who can you trust?"

"It's not a question of trust."

"Yes it is. Because if you don't tell me what you were really doing that was so important you had to miss one of the most special nights of our year, how can I trust you?"

"No, you don't understand. I meant–"

"I know exactly what you meant."

"No, I don't think you do."

"Oh, so I'm stupid now too, am I? Stupid and untrustworthy. What the hell are you doing still married to me then? Thick and loose-lipped. Hardly much of a catch is it? You could do so much better for yourself."

"Zade, please. You know I don't want anyone else."

"You've a funny way of showing it."

"I can't win this can I?"

"Oh! So it IS about winning and losing then?"

"No! I meant–"

"Yes, please do explain what you meant. Because you're good at saying one thing and meaning another. You say 'a work thing' when you mean 'I can't be bothered to come home'. You say 'it's your favourite' when you mean 'I don't want to spend the next half an hour sweeping up broken glass'. I can't believe anything you say. It's all like something out of Orwell. Double-speak, or–"

"Double think."

"Why am I not surprised you knew that. You work in the fucking Ministry of Truth as it is."

"It's the Ministry of Defence."

"It was a JOKE Ralf! Christ have things got that bad you can't even recognise a joke now?"

[this is a companion piece to "Only Human" which appears next in the writing challenge – on Day 80]

Author's Notes

My starting point here, when thinking about the topic, was arguments. How they can arise from nowhere, perhaps as a result of an ill-considered comment or look, especially when tensions are already running high for whatever reason. The "last straw" that starts a fight often has little connection with the main issue, hence – in my mind – the leap from "illogical" to verbal jousting.

From that tentative beginning, I let the piece rip. I only had the vaguest hint of where the story would go, or why, but the characters seemed to do alright on their own. Their argument is informed by historical readings of how men and women approach relationships in general and arguments in particular, including but not limited to Men

Are From Mars; Women Are From Venus (now, of course, at least partially discredited).

Ralf perpetually tries to find a solution (a common male trait), and makes the mistake of referring to things that have been said in the past. Zadi really only wants him to understand and empathise with her frustrations, and to see as important the things she believes are.

Day 80: Only Human

[this is a companion piece to "Illogical" which immediately precedes it in the writing challenge – on Day 79]

Ralf set his cutlery carefully down on his empty plate. It still irritated her, that way he had of being so precise with everything. So damned prissy all the time. First the knife, then the fork. Always in that order. Always in exactly the same position on the plate. He was more of a robot than–

"Well. I don't think that was 'ruined' at all. It was delicious darling."

She bristled again, remembering their quarrel earlier. These emotions were just too close to the surface, almost out of control. She let the turmoil subside. Avoided a snappy retort.

"I'm glad you enjoyed it. I like cooking for you. Especially when it's–"

"Special. Yes, I know. And you know I would have been here earlier if I could have. Anyway, let's not start all that again. It was a lovely meal. Did you make a dessert?"

"Crème Caramel."

Ralf smiled a little boy smile. One, Zadi thought, that he must have assumed would melt her defences. It probably would have stood a good chance of working on an ordinary woman.

"My favourite," he said, smiling even wider.

"Why do you think I made it?" she asked coyly.

She fetched the chilled dessert through and set it in front of him.

"Are you not having any?"

She patted her stomach. "Watching my figure."

"Nonsense," he laughed. "You're exactly the same shape and size as you were when we first met. Exactly the same. You never look a day older, and you never put on a kilogram or a single centimetre."

"Flatterer."

"It's true. I don't know how you do it. You never normally miss dessert though. You sure you're alright?"

"Of course. Don't worry. It's not my favourite. Anyway don't complain. It means all the more for you!"

Ralf picked up his spoon and took a huge mouthful of the gelatinous mound.

"I'm sorry we had that little misunderstanding earlier Zee," he said, swallowing and spooning up another mouthful. "If I could tell you what was really going on with work you wouldn't believe it."

"Try me."

He paused, spoon poised halfway to his mouth, considering. Zadi didn't say anything. Didn't want to break the spell. She hoped the crème caramel would work its magic.

"Well, perhaps I could sketch out the basics. Give you enough to understand what I'm faced with."

"It would help me Ralf. Maybe avoid a repeat of earlier?"

"You know I don't like arguing."

"Me neither. But sometimes it all just gets on top of me."

"I know. It must be hard. After all, you're only human." He finished his dessert. Placed his spoon delicately and accurately down on the empty plate. "I think I'll have a nice hot bath before we get comfy in front of the fire," he said.

"Take a brandy up with you. It'll help you relax."

"What a wonderful idea. You do look after me." He paused. "Scrub my back?"

"You go up. I'll be up soon when I've tidied these dinner things away."

Zadi waited until she could hear Ralf's footsteps on the stairs. Confident she could no longer be overheard, she tongued on her bottom left wisdom tooth and sub-vocalised:

"Zee-Alpha-zero-one-five progress report. Subject about to begin reveal. Stand by for further report in approximately two days."

"Received," said a small, tinny voice in her ear. "What's your power status?"

Zadi called up her retina display, scrolled through the status information displayed invisibly inside her eyes.

"I have 57% power," she reported.

"Commander Quantrell suggests recharging before your next report," said the voice.

"Understood. Zee-Alpha-zero-one-five out."

Author's Notes

Seeing this topic following on the heels of "Illogical" brought me back to thinking about AI. Having already had an argument, I pondered how far a sophisticated AI could take a fight without giving itself away, and if the story is set somewhere in the near future, what use would be made of these AIs, especially if they were installed in human-like bodies.

Notes from an Editor's perspective

Although it's only a short piece, I enjoyed scattering the

breadcrumbs of the final reveal in the early paragraphs. Probably the only editing I'd apply here would be to make them less obvious. And remove the instance of overt thinking: "One, Zadi thought, …"

Day 81: A Place to Belong

[this post is a continuation of the story begun in "Lost and Found" earlier in the writing challenge – on Day 27]

The expensive leather-upholstered 4x4 turned into a driveway and Carl suppressed a gasp. The snowstorm, which had begun as soon as Roger had fetched the SUV to the kerb, had highlighted the roof and sills of the house with crisp whiteness to match the bare branches of the enormous aspen tree that grew in a roundel in the centre of the driveway.

Vince, who had spent the entire journey on the back seat with his head in Carl's lap, seemed to sense that he'd arrived home. He lifted his head to stare through the window and gave a muted "Ruff!" that stayed in his throat in much the same way Carl's gasp had.

The house was enormous. 4,000 square feet at least, Carl guessed. His streetwise assessment of the couple's wealth had been, well, on the money. Roger twisted around from behind the wheel.

"Looks nice, huh?"

"It's beautiful," replied Carl. "Like a picture book home."

"Wait 'til you see the inside," Roger went on. "We've done quite a bit to it, haven't we Cyn?"

Cyn of the expensive jeans and lifesaver jacket turned around and gave Carl one of her megawatt smiles. "Please ignore my husband's bad manners Carl," she teased. "I'm sure you're more interested in a hot bath and a change of clothes, whaddaya say?"

Carl, who had been thinking that while he was absolutely not interested in rogering Roger, he wouldn't mind sinning with Cyn, was caught off-guard. "Umm, yeah. Yeah, that would be great, thanks."

Vince replaced his head in Carl's lap as Roger pulled up in front of the house.

"Come on," he urged. "Let's get out of this weather and into the warm."

Inside, the house was as impressive as Roger had implied. A carved oak staircase curled up to the first floor, carpeted with expensive white shag. The hall was floored with an intricate mosaic pattern that appeared to be Moroccan in origin, as far as Carl could tell. Massive panelled doors, also in oak, opened onto six rooms from the hallway. The house, though vast, was warm and smelt faintly of orange blossom.

"I'll show you to your room," Cyn offered.

"Thanks. Umm... should I take my shoes off?"

"If you like. It doesn't matter."

"Fancy some lunch?" Roger enquired as Carl made his way upstairs. "Soup? Got some fresh bread just out of the maker?"

Carl smiled, fighting back sudden tears of gratitude. "Yeah, I mean, yes, please, if you're having some," he replied past the lump in his throat.

Vince barked and ran past Carl up the stairs.

"Vince!" Cyn shouted after him, laughing. "Calm down boy!" She turned to Carl. "It's like he knows he might never have made it back here if it wasn't for you."

"Like I said, I didn't really do anything."

"In here," Cyn opened a bedroom door. The room beyond was painted a cornflower blue. Inside, a double bed was made up with a matching candlewick spread. Through a door in the opposite wall Carl could see an en-suite bathroom with a deep tub which Cyn was already filling.

"Make yourself at home," she said, smiling again, "I'll get you some fresh clothes. I think Roger has something that will fit you."

Carl took off his shoes, checking to see whether they had left a mark on the pristine carpet in the hall or bedroom. He was checking out the bewildering array of toiletries on the bathroom shelves when Cyn returned with an armful of clothes.

"Try some," she said, noticing his perusal of the assorted bath salts, crystals and pearls.

"Whose room is this?" he asked.

"No-one's," she replied airily. "We keep it up as a guest room, but you're our only guest at the moment. I'll leave you to it. When you're done, come down to the kitchen – that's the door Roger was standing in – and the soup should be ready by then."

"Thank you. I can't tell you–"

"Don't mention it. It's the least we can do after you rescued Vince from the madding crowd! Here," she added, reaching a couple of bath pearls from a blue crystal holder, "try these. I really like their smell on a man."

She dropped the pearls into the water and left, closing the bedroom door behind her. Within a few seconds, Carl had discarded his filthy tattered rags and immersed himself in the hot water.

[this story is continued later in the writing challenge – on Day 97 in "Enthusiasm"]

Author's Notes

It's strange to discover which stories have legs and which don't. At the outset I would never have guessed that a simple story of a street person befriending a lost dog would find echoes in so many later topics, presenting an opportunity to flesh out each of the characters and their interactions in a location completely outside the MC's experience. If I were ever to be turned to "the dark side of pantsing", a story like this might do it.

Notes from an Editor's perspective

Minor examples of repetition (e.g. "checking" on his shoes and his bathroom supplies), and on reflection I may have made his internal dialogue about the posh couple slightly less "on the nose".

Day 82: Advantage

[this post is a continuation of "Heart Song" from earlier in the writing challenge – on Day 45]

The little old man looked directly at Tani as she entered the clearing. His eyes were almost as bright green as his tunic, she noticed. She took another step. He stopped playing. Released from the spell of the music, Tani slumped to the ground, the soft carpet of leaf litter breaking her fall. She had not realised she was so tired, but now that the music was gone a terrible fatigue overwhelmed her. The old man stood up and slung his pipes around his shoulder.

"The effect will quickly pass," he reassured her. His voice too had a melodic quality. A faint reminder of the beautiful strain he had been playing. "Come," he continued, "sit."

Tani struggled to her feet. "The Hunt. I have to–"

"They will not find you here," the elf replied.

"How–?"

"This part of the forest is shielded from mortal eyes," he said. At her questioning glance he held up his hand. "Unless they have heard my heart song."

"Heart song?"

"Some call it soul music," he said with a wry smile. "But among my kind we call it heart song. The melody one plays with one's heart. The one no other can play."

"It was beautiful."

He smiled.

"But I can't stay here," Tani said, looking around the clearing nervously, unwilling to believe that it was somehow protected from the Pack. From The Hunt. "I must find my way out, without being caught."

The old man reached inside his tunic. "I have something here that will help you in that regard," he said enigmatically. He opened his hand. A fine gold chain fell from between his fingers, dangling almost to the forest floor. It held a pendant of some kind but in the dim light Tani could not make it out.

"What–?"

The elf wound the gold chain around his fingers and let the pendant drop. It was an amulet of clear amber, held in an intricate clasp of elder wood. He beckoned to Tani. She stepped closer and bent down to allow the elf to slip the chain over her head.

"We call it The Advantage," he murmured. "Only one of your kind has ever worn it before."

A shock of recognition tore through Tani's mind. "Riki!" she exclaimed.

The elf smiled his gentle smile again and nodded.

"What does it do?" Tani asked.

"Its function begins and ends with its name," said the elf, whose circumlocution was beginning to irritate Tani. "When you need an advantage, the amulet will provide one."

"So how do I work it? What do I need to do?"

"You must do what you must," the elf replied infuriatingly. Tani bit down on her anger. This was a gift beyond price. The object that had allowed Riki to defeat The Hunt! It wouldn't do to lose her temper with the giver. "Follow the path you have decided upon. Fear not. Behave as you always have, as you know you should. The Advantage is now yours. You will see."

Tani grasped the amulet, staring into its smoky depths. Unlike most of the amber pieces she had seen in the past it held no fossilised insect or creature of any kind. It absorbed what little light there was in the clearing and reflected only a dusky remnant.

"But–" Tani began, looking up. The old man was gone. She stood alone in the clearing. Through the darkness, back in the direction from which she had entered, several wolves howled. A shiver passed through her. It was time to leave. She looked around the clearing, intending to select the best exit. All but one of the gaps between the ancient oaks were now blocked with thick briars. Almost directly opposite her, a single path was her only option.

"Guess that's the way to go," Tani thought, wondering at the same time whether this was The Advantage's doing or the elf's. Or if there was any difference. She tucked the amulet inside her shirt, surprised at its sudden warmth against her skin, and left the clearing at a run.

[this story is continued later in the writing challenge – on Day 98 in "Game"]

Author's Notes

This was the second story to have sufficient scope to straddle several topics. In this case, a total of four. I'll reserve further comment for the last of those four entries – #98.

Day 83: Breakfast

John examined the invitation for the fifteenth time.

EXECUTIVE BRIEFING CENTER
START TIME: 07:30AM
BREAKFAST WILL BE SERVED

It was his first time at the EBC. The start time had been a surprise. He'd heard of breakfast meetings, of course, but had always assumed they were one of those things whose myth had grown in the telling and that in reality they were neither as early nor as intense as the legend would have it. In this case, at least, the early aspect seemed to have been proven.

He wasn't sure, either, what kind of "breakfast" to expect. His inner trencherman had been nagging him for days to preload with a bowl of cereal and some toast. Then at least he'd have guarded against mid-morning munchies, should the breakfast prove to be nothing more than a croissant and a cup of coffee.

In the end, he'd decided to go with it. Risk an attack of the shakes around 11am for the sake of appearances. The entire complex was a minefield of snack machines anyway, so if push came to shove he could always pop out during one of the smokers' breaks and grab a candy bar or a carton of drinking yoghurt.

Start time, breakfast spread. The third thing he had no hint about was the content of the briefing. His entire management team had been flown over with barely 24 hours' notice and no warning of what all the fuss was about. Even with the remainder of his travel day to acclimatise he still felt jet-lagged. He could only hope it wouldn't affect his appetite.

The early morning sun was already hot as he made his way to the squat anonymous building at the Northern edge of the campus. He still thought 'campus' was a bit bogus. There was no research undertaken here. No learning. The corporation was not connected with education in any way. Just because the three young entrepreneurs who'd started it five years before still thought of themselves as college students shouldn't mean the rest of the company had to behave as if they were 19. His approach triggered the automatic doors. He gave his name at the desk and followed the directions to the first of four double doors in a wide but featureless corridor. One of the doors had been propped open; the other read "EBC". It was all about the acronyms. Or, he mentally corrected himself, the TLAs. Acronyms was more rightly restricted to abbreviations that made a real word. The smell of hot coffee and warmed pastries drifted out into the corridor. The sympathetic rumbling of his stomach confirmed that jet-lag had not suppressed his appetite.

Three of his colleagues had arrived ahead of him and were already filling their plates from the breakfast buffet. John stopped just inside the door, surveying the scene, then reminded himself to act as though everything was "just normal." Don't be impressed; don't be intimidated. Act as if you expected everything to be just like this.

An entire wall – the long wall – of the rectangular briefing room was filled with tables, and the tables were filled with food. A wry smile briefly flickered around John's mouth as he noticed that there were indeed croissants present. And the coffee he had smelled outside in the corridor. But that's where the similarity with his pessimistic prediction ended. Croissants, yes. But eight different varieties. Chocolate, almond, plain, cheese, fruit, raisins, and a couple of others he didn't recognise. There was a toasting machine nestling among a pile of fresh breads. Pumpkin bread, crumpet bread, spicy bun loaf, pancakes, waffles, white and brown bloomer, cobs and tiger bread. There were jams and conserves, marmalades and syrups. An assortment of cold meats, chorizo, salami (peppered and plain), ham, braun, mortadella and, once again, at least half-a-dozen meats he didn't recognise. Large open tubs of cereal revealed their contents next to jugs of milk (1%, 2% and whole), cream, custard and plain yoghurt. Flakes of many shades, granola, bran, muesli, rice krispies, coco pops, oatmeal. Then came the cheeses. John had been led to believe Americans were not especially adventurous when it came to cheese. The impressive array in front of him put the lie to that. Blue cheeses, hard, soft, round, square, triangular, cheese in foil, cheese rolled in herbs, cheese with embedded fruit – and talking of fruit! The biggest bowl he had ever seen sat in the far corner. Bananas, apples (red, green and russet), oranges, grapes, kiwi, pineapple (peeled and sliced), melon (sliced), papaya, star fruit, passion fruit and – yet again – several kinds he was not familiar with.

He reached for a plate and walked up behind Ade Brundrett, who had only just started picking.

"Morning."

"Morning. Sleep alright?"

"At first yeah. Woke up around three. You?"

"Same."

"This is–"

"Don't. Not impressed. Not intimidated. Remember?"

"Umm... yeah. I am though."

"Which?"

"Both"

Ade laughed. "Yeah, me too."

John picked up a mug. "All this food, and only one kind of coffee?"

"I think it's a franchise thing."

"Oh. Don't suppose there's any tea?"

"Joking, right? And even if there was, you wouldn't want to drink it."

Author's Notes

This piece is heavily influenced by my recollection of a real breakfast at the real Executive Briefing Center in a very well-known Seattle Headquarters. "Write what you know", right? I'm pretty sure even my senior colleagues were a little intimidated by the cornucopia on display that morning. It was my first exposure to the catering this global company provided, but over the next ten years or so I came to wonder how on earth their employees stayed so fit. To shift the calories delivered several times a day to their office buildings, in the shape of cakes, pastries, snack bars, and other high-impact, small form-factor food, they must've spent most of their non-working hours in the gym.

I smile now at my side-swipe at American-made tea. It's not that I've never had a decent cup of tea in the USA, but it's a well-worn trope that such a thing is a rare beast indeed. The most recent example that comes to mind is a scene from early in the movie The Second Best Marigold Hotel, but there are many other references to teabags being waved in the general direction of lukewarm water, which is pretty much guaranteed to make an Englishman shudder.

Notes from an Editor's perspective

I stuck strictly to the rules with my documentation of available breakfasting foods, and did no research at all, relying entirely on memory. So if I were to subject this piece to an editing pass, it may well involve extensions to one or more lists of foodstuffs, and a consequent reduction in the number of "unrecognised" items, although I'd certainly also want to retain some of these, for effect.

Day 84: Echoes

Emma, Phoebe and Danielle exited the bus down the steep steps. At the last moment, Danielle missed her footing and collided heavily with the two girls in front.

"Careful!"

"Sorry! These steps–"

"Use the handrail can't you? That's what it's there for."

Emma gave Phoebe a knowing look. They had been looking forward to this school trip for months. She didn't want to be stuck with the class dork. The other girls were already clustered around Miss James who stood on the kerb looking for them.

"Come on you three, hurry up!" she called. They joined the group. "Each of you will have enough time to visit two of the famous landmarks on your list," said their teacher loudly, fighting to be heard over the traffic noise. "You'll need to be back at the restaurant by SIX at the very latest if we're all to get served before the show, then we will all proceed to the theatre together. That's very important. Six o'clock. Don't be late! If you have anything you can set a reminder on – like your mobile phones – I suggest you do it now. We won't wait for stragglers."

Several of the girls began fishing in their bags, purses and pockets for their phones.

"Now do all of you know where you're going," Miss James continued, "or do any of you need any help?"

Three or four hands went up, but Emma knew exactly what she wanted to see. Her plans had been firmed up the day they got their lists of tourist places. She linked arms with Phoebe.

"Come on," she said, "we don't need any help."

As they walked away from the group, Miss James called after them. "Phoebe! Emma! Where are you going?"

"It's alright miss," said Emma, "we know where we're going."

"Yes, but there are only two of you," Miss James said, walking quickly towards them. "I was quite clear that everyone should stay in groups of three or more."

"I'll come with you," said Danielle.

Emma rolled her eyes, but it was too late. Miss James had heard.

"Very good, Danielle, thank you. Well, get along with you, since you're so certain you don't need anything more from me."

She shooed them away and turned back to the group.

The girls didn't move. Danielle blushed. "I know you don't really want me tagging along," she said quietly, "but you need a third, and everyone else is already in a group."

Phoebe sighed. "Come on, Emma. Looks like we don't have a choice."

The coach had pulled up at the other side of the square from Emma's first port of call. They set off across the tarmac, attracting annoyed honks from a couple of drivers.

"God," said Emma, "it's true what they told us about drivers here."

"Bit different from home," agreed Danielle.

"Well it is the capital, dummy," Emma replied.

"Emma," Phoebe said, holding her friend's arm, "calm down. If we have to spend the entire day with her let's at least try to keep it civil."

Emma didn't say another word until they entered the

enormous, ancient, distinctive building.

"I want to go right to the top," she proclaimed, her voice echoing from the smooth stone walls.

They climbed the stairs in silence, needing all their breath for the long ascent. At the top, Danielle turned left. Emma pulled Phoebe to the right.

"We're supposed to stick together," Danielle reminded her.

"We can't possibly come to any harm in here," Emma retorted. "We're not chained together. You go that way, we'll go this way. We can meet in the middle on the other side."

Danielle shrugged and walked off.

"Thank God," said Emma, "I thought we were going to have to babysit her all day."

"She's not that bad."

"Yes she is. She's a mardy cow at the best of times, and always sucking up to the teachers. Especially Miss James. Wouldn't surprise me if she didn't have a thing for her."

"What do you mean, a thing?"

"You know. A dyke thing."

"Emma!"

"Well, she looks the type. All plain trousers and white shirts. And she's such a swot too. Always has her hand up."

"You a bit jealous, maybe?"

"Of her? You must be joking. Mousey little lezzer. She should think herself lucky to be around cool ladies like us. Let's hope our cool rubs off on her, and not the other way round."

By now they had walked almost half-way around the dome and Danielle appeared from the other direction. She was crying.

"What's up?" asked Phoebe. "What's happened."

"Thought you knew everything about this place," Danielle mumbled, sniffing back her tears and wiping her eyes.

"Only what I've read in the handout," said Emma defensively. "Why?"

"Doesn't it say that it's called the Whispering Gallery?" asked Danielle hotly.

Author's Notes

Memories of schoolday cliques are far behind me, but I know it's a lucrative market. One that a friend of mine has exploited to great effect in her YA stories of teenage crushes and angst, in common with hundreds of other writers.

My stories never stray into that territory, so it was quite refreshing to dip my toe in those waters for a change, and imagine this exchange between an outsider and the friends who don't want her around.

It's informed by a similar story I read as a youth (which may explain its familiarity if you recognised the setting), but the details of its author and title are long gone from my memory.

Notes from an Editor's perspective

The differences between British and American English is a subject that's been much on my mind recently. Without intending any offence, I know that US readers can often be very parochial about "correct" English (i.e. theirs), and have little experience of other forms. Obviously that's a blanket statement – there are thousands of US readers with wider experience and who don't care whether the book they're reading uses single or double quotes for dialogue, or spells colour with a U. But while my books sell well in the UK and Canada, they've never made much of an impact in America, and I'm pretty sure that's a big part of the reason.

The appearance of "kerb" in the piece above is what spurred me to make this comment. The word doesn't exist in the US. Over there, "curb" is used to mean both "restrict or curtail" and "the edge of the sidewalk or roadway". In the UK, we spell each of those differently, sticking with curb for the former but using kerb for the latter. One of dozens of instances of being "divided by a common language" that I'm aware of, and which constantly exercise the indie author.

Traditional publishers have the luxury of printing separate stock for each marketplace, and ensuring local spelling and punctuation is used in each. That's a lot of extra work for an indie author that most of us can't cope with.

Day 85: Falling

The party was already a-buzz with conversation when Connor arrived. It was an informal affair, but nevertheless the host – Brian – was his usual effusive self as he noticed Connor across the crowded hall.

"Connor! My dear fellow! SO lovely to see you again. Are you on your own? Oh my word, I did so hope you'd bring that precious little thing I saw you with last time. How is she? You've not parted company have you? I do hope not. What can I get you old chap? Nothing's too much trouble tonight, I'm the host with the most!"

He paused, for breath Connor thought, but it was only to turn and address the throng of guests.

"Everyone, this is Connor – a very dear friend of mine from way back."

Connor made his way into the room. After that fulsome introduction, the crowd seemed to part in front of him without actually moving. The faces of the other guests gradually resolved and he began to recognise a few. Over by the immense gilt-framed mirror mounted under the stairs, Faith Miller was adjusting her hair, releasing it from its elaborate but severe style by the judicious removal of a few clips and ties. Her thick blonde locks cascaded onto her shoulders. There had been a time, Connor reflected ruefully, that he had fancied his chances with Faith. It didn't take long for her to let him know in very clear terms that he didn't come up to the mark as far as she was concerned. Far from it.

He had believed himself in love with her at the time, could distinctly remember the feeling of it overtaking him in their first few days together. Now she was just another might-have-been.

"Connor!"

He turned at the sound of his name. Bunny Hargreaves was making a beeline for him from out of the dining room.

"You'll never guess!"

"What's that Bunny?"

"Miles just proposed! Got on his knees and everything!"

"Wonderful. Happy for you."

"And with the new law we can have a proper wedding and everything!"

"Lovely. Make sure you invite me."

"Of course. I knew he would you know. Knew he couldn't resist me. Who could, be honest."

Connor turned away. Bunny's pride was renowned, but he happened to know Miles had also been seeing Brian – their host – on the quiet. He'd never say anything of course. What happened in people's private lives was their own business as far as Connor was concerned, but Brian was not out. If even the slightest whiff of scandal were to land at his feet there would be a very rapid thinning of the party crowd at Highton Place.

Another guest nudged his elbow as they squeezed past. Their eyes met. It was Trevor. Years before Trevor had found himself on the wrong side of the law. Trapped in a complicated scam that he had not seen coming, he had lost a lot of money after a sudden crash of the markets. A lot of the money he'd invested was his own, but he had also been tricked into investing others' funds and had been manoeuvred into taking all the blame for it by the organised criminals who had originally thought up the scheme.

"Trevor!" Connor exclaimed quickly, masking his mental turmoil at the still painful memories. "How are you?"

"Absolutely marvellous, thanks. Good to see you. It's been

a long time."

"It has indeed. What ever happened with that investment thing?" Connor asked, deciding it was best to be up front about it.

"Oh that!" Trevor grinned. "Turned out to be the best thing I ever did."

Connor was nonplussed. Trevor laughed. "Yeah. Bet you never expected that. I managed to convince all the investors to hang on in there. Some even trusted me so much they put MORE money in, while the market was at its lowest. When the turnround came, I made seven million. Either through my own investment, or through grateful contributions from those who'd made even more money!"

He raised his glass. "Here's to the capitalist system!"

A gust of wind blew through the enormous hall, bringing a distinct chill to the air. Someone had opened the French windows. Slowly, the party moved out onto the patio. In the short time since Connor's arrival the weather had changed for the worse and there had been a brief but intense snow storm. The patio was white over and all the trees painted to match.

Trevor and Connor stepped out together onto the slick crazy paving.

"Whoop– ow!" cried Trevor as he lost his footing on the slippery fresh snow and landed on his backside with a plosive exhalation. Connor noted with respect that he had managed to keep his glass intact and not spilled a drop.

Faith walked up to the slightly embarrassed Trevor and offered him her hand.

"If there's one thing that impresses me it's a man who can hold his drink," she smiled. "I think I should get to know you better."

Author's Notes

My recollection of this piece is so vague and fragmented that all I can do is infer that I intended to cover as many different kinds of "falling" as I could in the allotted time. Falling in love, falling in with the wrong crowd, falling locks of hair, falling markets, and actual falling down, are the ones I can spot at a glance. For once, I didn't keep notes. Tsk, tsk.

Interestingly "of its time" – the "new law" referred to (legalisation of gay marriage) has in the interim ten years become so commonplace as to now be almost unremarked upon, at least in the enlightened circles I'm fortunate enough to move in. I know some of my gay friends still meet with homophobia on a regular basis, but it's nowhere near as prevalent as it once was.

Day 86: Picking up the Pieces

"I'll be back in an hour."

"OK. Bye."

Josh took hold of his daughter's hand, balancing her awkwardly on his other arm. "Wave to Mummy! Bye Mummy!"

Jessica squirmed in her uncomfortable perch. "Down!" she instructed.

Josh let her down gently into the hall. She wobbled slightly, testing her balance, and began to toddle to the kitchen.

"Juice!"

"Juice time!" agreed Josh, removing her coat as she walked and then stepping gingerly around her. He dropped her coat on a chair and opened the fridge. "Orange or pineapple?" he asked.

Jessica thought about it for a moment. "JoJinge," she decided.

"OK. Good choice."

Josh poured half a beaker's worth. It was the smooth kind, but only because the bits got stuck in the mouthpiece. He figured there'd be time to educate his daughter in the finer points of orange juice connoisseurship when she was old enough to use a glass. He fitted the lid onto the beaker and returned the carton to the fridge.

"Take it through," he told her, handing over the beaker.

"Froo," agreed Jessica, grabbing the beaker, plugging it into her mouth, and tottering through to the living room.

The living room floor was littered with wooden blocks in primary colours. Jessica had already passed the "tower of two" milestone in block building, a full six months ahead of the average age. Josh wanted to see how far she'd come on in a couple of weeks. He kicked off his slippers and joined her on the carpet.

"Which block shall we put on the bottom?" he asked, picking up a green one and a yellow one.

"Yed one!" said Jessica, pointing.

"Just like your mother," Josh laughed. He selected the nearest red block and set it in front of Jessica. "Green next?" he offered.

She shook her head. "Boo."

The nearest blue block was over by the skirting board. Josh leant left and rolled over to it. Jessica giggled.

He handed the block to her.

"You do it."

She took the block, dropping the beaker onto the floor where it started to drip juice slowly onto the carpet. Josh ignored it. What was StainGuard for? His attention was focussed on his daughter as she carefully set the blue block atop the red one. She sat back.

"Nuvver one," she said.

"Which colour?" Josh asked.

"Gyeen."

He handed over the green one he'd been holding. Jessica shook her head. "Nuvver gyeen."

He smiled. She was definitely her mother's daughter. He retrieved a different green block and passed it to her.

After ten minutes, Josh was satisfied that Jessica had advanced to tower of three, but a fourth block still eluded her even though she'd come close a couple of times. Her patience with building towers was now wearing thin, so he'd started to build a ziggurat with all of the blocks in the pack. Jessica watched as he placed the last block on the apex of the triangular structure. At the moment he sat back to admire his construction, she rolled forward and gave the pile a whack with her hand. It collapsed with a satisfying woody rumble.

She giggled again. "'gain," she demanded.

Josh built his pyramid three more times, each time it was reduced to rubble in seconds by his resident demolition expert. "Shall we tidy up now?" he asked, standing up and wheeling over the wooden walker that they used to store the blocks. He grabbed two handfuls and lobbed them into the walker. They clattered onto the base. Jessica put her hands over her ears and frowned.

Josh turned to retrieve more blocks. When he looked back, Jessica had thrown the first five blocks out of the trolley across the living room. One landed in the planter.

"Oi!" he said, smiling. "I thought we were tidying up?"

He dropped his blocks into the walker and fetched back the others. Jessica threw two more blocks after him, laughing. "I'd better hurry up," he said, grabbing the handle of the walker and wheeling it around the room.

A car horn sounded in the road outside. Josh's smile faded. "Sounds like Mummy's back," he said.

"Mummy!" shouted Jessica gleefully, running toward the front door.

Josh picked her coat up off the kitchen chair and followed.

Author's Notes

An amalgam of memories in this one. When my elder daughter was at the "tower of two" stage, I was still with her mother, so my fond (and poignant) memories of those times are tempered here by Josh's obvious separation from Jessica's mother. Something that was still nine years in the future with my own daughter, and her sister who came along a little later. I can never resist the temptation to have a sideways dig at my ex when the chance arises, as it did here.

The real tug on the heartstrings is, naturally, the limited activities available to an estranged Dad. An hour snatched at "her" convenience (to enable a shopping trip, in this example), during which there is only time for a few simple games with building blocks. My daughters and I spent quite a few years in that strange hinterland of not-quite-family life before things gradually returned to something more recognisable as "normal".

Day 87: Gunshot

Nal refolded the jacket and pressed it again to the wound in Chang's side.

"Nearly there," he said. "How you doing?"

"How the hell do you think I'm doing?" Chang gasped. His pallor was turning an ash grey and his face and neck were slick with sweat. The autocab's air conditioning had kicked in to try and cope with the increased humidity.

"Can you speed it up any?" Nal said into the intercom.

"Maximum speed is regulated by statute," the cab intoned. "Arrival at Central Medical in 27 seconds."

*

They stood on the sidewalk outside Central Medical. Chang was breathing with difficulty and leaning heavily on Nal. They crabbed their way to the automatic doors. As they entered, blue sensor panels on either side of the corridor scanned them. Ahead, on a suspended monitor, their details were instantly displayed.

GERSHWIN, NAL. : 07-27-2096 : BMI 27 : H 2.02m : BP 119/82 : A+ : ALC 0mg/100ml : NAD.

NG, CHANG : 03-03-2097 : BMI 21 : H 1.98m : BP 130/75 : O- : ALC 0mg/100ml : OPEN WOUND TO ABDOMEN - CAUSE UNKNOWN. CRITICAL BLOOD LOSS DETECTED.

Chang's entry was flashing red and a robot auxiliary was already approaching to administer a saline drip. Nal led him to a bench and sat beside him while the drip was attached. He had no idea what was going to happen next. He had never been to a hospital. At least, not since he was born in one.

Chang's condition appeared to have confused the

hospital's system. Nal suspected that "cause unknown" was an extremely rare occurrence. He wondered if they would have called the police. A man in green scrubs rounded the corner in front of them.

"Which one is Mr. Ng?" he asked.

Nal thought the question a little superfluous in view of Chang's obvious discomfort but even so he kept his temper.

"This is Chang," he said. "I'm Nal."

The doctor tapped out a command on his wristcom. "Come with me please," he said, as a motorised wheelchair emerged from a set of double doors further down the corridor and sped across to position itself in front of Chang. Nal helped him in, and the chair took off after the doctor. Nal followed it into an examination room.

"Are you a relative?" asked the doctor as Nal entered.

"No, but he's my friend," Nal replied.

The doctor frowned. "Well, if Mr. Ng has no objections I suppose it'll be all right."

Chang nodded, his pain a beacon on his face.

The doctor pressed a button on the side of the chair and it morphed swiftly with a hydraulic sigh into an examination table. He selected a pair of surgical scissors from a receptacle in the side of the table and proceeded to cut away Chang's shirt.

"You've lost a lot of blood," he said, peeling back the tattered ends of cloth. He reached for a swab and cleaned away the clotted mass. His eyes widened.

"How did you do this?"

Chang turned his head away. The doctor looked at Nal.

"Do you know anything about this?"

"I didn't see it happen, if that's what you mean," Nal replied.

"This is a gunshot wound."

"A what?"

"I'm not surprised you've never heard of it. What are you – 21? 22?"

"I'm 24. He's 23."

"Well I haven't seen a wound like this in almost 40 years," said the doctor. "Almost 20 years before you were born. And that was the first one my registrar had seen since he took up his post. There haven't been any guns in this city for almost half a century."

"What do you mean? My dad has a gun."

"You mean a zapper? That won't cause damage like this. This is a bullet wound. From a projectile weapon. The bullet is still inside him. How the hell did he get shot?"

Author's Notes

So far, in my writing career, the work has mainly been fantasy with a bit of SF thrown in around the edges. Reading this back now, gives me a small thrill of excitement and anticipation. This would make a great opener. The action takes off immediately, as is the modern norm. No more pages and pages of angsting over Mr. Darcy for today's readers. If writers took as long now to get to the point as Austen did in her day, they would never find readers.

The best of today's writers also know how to introduce their fictional science. They just use it, without any clunky exposition, and trust the reader to infer what it means, or at least read on until they can, or until it becomes obvious by how the tech is being used. China Mieville is a past master at this. His worlds are often bizarre to the point of obscurity, but once the reader plows on, they become natural and understandable, and often breathtaking.

We've recently been re-watching Star Trek: Voyager, where exactly the opposite is true. To the point of annoyance. The number of times Captain Janeway makes a "helpful suggestion" to the helmsman, science officer, or chief of security, to tell them to try something they should have been trying already if they'd had any sense, is beyond count. "Evasive manoeuvres" she will shout, when the ship is about to be overtaken by "some kind of*" shock wave which is so vast in all three dimensions as to be totally incapable of being evaded. And there's always "some kind of*" auxiliary power to switch to, when the main power is on its way out.

*Beware of this if you ever find yourself watching Voyager, although now that I've told you, it will be impossible to unhear. Everything the crew encounters is some kind of something:

Some kind of gravity well
Some kind of thermion pulse
Some kind of gravometric interference in the plasma conduit

Etc, etc

Notes from an Editor's perspective

Looking at this now, two things leap out at me when I apply my editing brain. The first and most obvious one is a touch of Drafter's Repetition. "…haven't seen a wound like this in almost 40 years," said the doctor. "Almost 20 years before…" One of those would have to go.

The second is perhaps less obvious. The futuristic hospital systems recognise our two protags on their arrival at the hospital – names, ages, and various medical conditions. All this information would be immediately available to the doctor, so his comment about their ages – "What are you – 21? 22?" – is entirely unrealistic.

Day 88: Possession

"He is dying, my friend. He does not have long. But... in a moment of clarity... he asked me to show you this."

The rag-clothed old man pulled a stained oil cloth from inside his shirt. Unwrapped it. I couldn't believe my eyes. I had found it at last.

"He cannot tell me from whence he acquired it," the old man continued. His breath reeked of methylated spirit. I turned my head away. "He has not had it long, I know that. He showed it to me not a month before the sickness started in him."

"How much does he want for it?" I asked. It occurred to me that the man lying on his death bed would not see a penny of the price, whatever it was, but I didn't care. I had been looking for this prize for fourteen years. I wasn't about to give up on it now. He would be dead anyway inside the day.

The tramp looked furtive. "Five thousand," he said. Before I had chance to object, he went on, "but personally I think that is... shall we say... a little steep."

He gave no clue what he considered a more realistic price, but it was immaterial. I would gladly have paid ten times that amount.

"If it will make him comfortable in his final hours," I lied, "I will agree to five thousand."

"You are a good man my friend. Cash?"

"Of course."

I handed over an envelope. He handed over the amulet. It shone a deep red in the light from the brazier. From the filthy cot by the wall, the dying man coughed weakly. I took hold of the chain, avoiding any touch of the gem itself. Its legend was infamous in certain circles – the circles I had sought out over the years – and although naturally I was sceptical, I did not want to tempt fate. For a man less certain of how the world worked, the sight of the amulet's previous owner coughing up his lungs in a beggar's bolt hole might have given cause for concern.

I reached a velvet purse from my coat pocket and slipped the jewel into it. A shock of pleasure coursed through me as I drew the cords tight. It was mine!

"Is there anything I can do for him? Drink? Food?"

"Leave him to me, sir. I will tend to his final moments."

"Very well. Make sure he knows I am grateful to him."

The derelict smiled, exposing his rotted teeth. "That I will sir. That I will."

I left. There was no more to be done for the man, or his friend, and I was expected elsewhere. My excitement at the discovery of the precious stone had tightened my stomach. It almost felt as if I was going to vomit. Or perhaps I'd caught a chill in this fell place. For a moment I lost my bearings among the ruins and empty houses, but then I caught sight of a familiar neon sign and remembered I had parked close by. The familiar leather smell inside my car replaced the unpleasant odours of the last hour and as the door closed with a satisfying clunk, shutting out the memory of that awful place, I began to feel human again.

The freeway lights flashed past faster once I'd cleared the edge of town. It was unusually hot inside the car and I wondered for a second whether the heating had developed a fault. Even at its lowest setting the air was still stiflingly hot. I lowered a window to clear the air and my head. I needed to be on my best form for the meeting ahead. Sir Patrick had been waiting for this day even longer than I. Had worked his way through several finders before me. He had no notion that his life-long dream was about to be fulfilled.

I was wracked with a sudden fit of painful coughing. A trickle of saliva had found its way into my lungs, as occasionally happens to me. I pulled onto the verge until the attack passed. The dashboard clock shone its green nine-oh-five pm at me. Plenty of time. My client was not expecting me until ten. I pulled a bottle of water from the glove box and took a deep drink to ease the tightness in my throat. The pain in my chest subsided a little. I could feel the weight of the ruby amulet in my jacket pocket. It pressed against my ribs, held in place by the seatbelt. I adjusted my position and patted it. Mine. If only briefly. And soon I would be, once more, a very wealthy man.

Author's Notes

There are dozens of examples in the world of fiction where a much-sought and highly prized artefact brings doom along with its delight. Where the promised riches are paid for in the most precious currency. The one that pops immediately to mind is "The Monkey's Paw", but if I took a moment I'm sure I could think of many others. It's such a common trope that it's been given its own name: The Artefact of Doom. Tolkien's One Ring can be thought of as an example. Jordan's The Wheel of Time has an entire city that behaves like one.

So that idea forms the heart of this short piece. Of course the doom is barely more than hinted at here, to add to the tension. How long will the sufferer live? How will they die? Can they avoid it? What benefit does the amulet bring, along with its… disbenefit?

Notes from an Editor's perspective

I must have switched to autopilot in the paragraph where the narrator leaves the two men to their doom. He speculates that he may have "caught a chill" and moments later has "caught sight…" The thing he sees is a "familiar neon sign" but once in his car he notices the "familiar leather smell…" As you know by now, such close repetition of a word is something I abhor, and each of these would have been summarily dealt with on the first editing pass.

Day 89: Twilight

The honks of a late skein of geese overflying his garden echoed through the trees. A haunting sound, at once distant and immediate. Graham stood on the new deck, a fresh glass of whisky in his hand, and surveyed the newly completed garden. A short shower earlier in the evening had freshened the grass and released the deep smells of the dark brown loam and bark chippings which had been laid only the day before. Now, in the deepening evening, the first scents of jasmine and stock filled the still air.

This was his favourite time of day. Neither day nor night. A comfortable resting space between the two when the day's work was done and the night's not yet begun. Animals active in daylight hours were winding down. Those who were nocturnal had yet to get started. Being neither one thing nor the other suited Graham. Unusually among all his friends he was at ease with uncertainty and ambivalence.

He sat down in one of the new recliners, sipped his drink and let the smoky sharpness of the whisky roll around his mouth before slipping down his throat. The warmth of it spread through his belly. He set his glass on the arm of the chair and stared out into the grey gloom. Amusement at the thought of the greyness bubbled up in his chest. He sat there, in the grey, wearing a grey T-shirt and grey sweat pants with grey socks and, he laughed out loud at this point, most of his friends called him Gray. He loved greyness so much that if his parents hadn't called him Graham they would probably have chosen Ash.

A bird whickered in one of the old trees the landscapers had left at the bottom of his plot. Good windbreak, they had said. Protection from being overlooked. Graham had just been glad to keep them there for the dark shadows they cast at this time of day.

The evening was still warm. In that gentle way that late summer, or early autumn evenings had. Like they trusted themselves to be warm without really trying, or worrying about how cold it was going to get later. Even in his thin cotton shirt Graham wasn't cold. The whisky didn't hurt though. He took another mouthful, and thought about changes. Day changed into night, and summer into autumn. And what was Graham changing into? He was definitely in transition, he knew that much. Yet in a strange way, he felt as comfortable with it as he did with the twilight. No longer day but not quite night. He laughed again quietly, because he could just as easily say he was no longer Gray but not quite... what? What was he going to call himself? He shook his head at the thought that he might choose something to rhyme with night. And then his fertile mind went off down that rabbit hole, trying to think of things that did. Rhyme with night that is. The whisky had given his imagination wings but he wasn't sure of the direction of flight. That rhymed with night! And so did fright. Was he frightened? Not right now. Here at the start of everything it felt – well – daunting maybe, but not frightening. Exciting? Yes, that.

A toad croaked. It sounded unnaturally loud in the quiet of the evening. So the nature pond idea had worked. Marvellous. The old pond had been ripped out years before but Graham had still, occasionally, unearthed a sleeping frog when moving a large boulder or a length of rotting timber. Now with the new shallow pond and its animal-friendly landing area beside the water, both he and the garden designer had hoped to attract a new generation of assorted amphibians. And Mr Toad was his first new tenant. He reached to pick up the remote control, flicked on the path lights and the spikes, and was just in time to catch a flash of Mr Toad as he jumped for cover. "That's right," he thought, "head for cover. You don't like the bright lights either, do you fella?"

Author's Notes

Another thing I loved about writing these pieces was the opportunity for ambiguity. I think it makes for a more interesting read, but from a writer's perspective it also has the advantage that I don't have to resolve that ambiguity. And in a way, that's a good thing for you too. You can fill in the blanks for yourself. Why does Graham really like the twilight? What is he changing into? Why does he feel as though he is somehow… between?

The piece is hugely influenced by the garden works that had recently completed at what I laughingly refer to as "Beresford Towers" (it's nothing grand, believe me – a turn-of-the-century semi-detached house with four bedrooms – but I do feel very lucky to live here). We did have a new deck. We had installed patio lights, path lights, and spike lights to illuminate one or two specimen trees and bushes. We did have a new pond, replacing the old one we'd ripped up five years before. And the frogs did return.

Notes from an Editor's perspective

There's not a lot I would change in this one, but two things did leap out at me.

Where Graham ponders what may have been his other potential name, it might think about making it clearer. "He loved greyness so much that if his parents hadn't called him Graham they would probably have chosen Ashley, and all his friends would then have shortened it to Ash."

On the other hand, perhaps it works better as it is, trusting the reader to make the short, simple leap of intuition for themselves, rather than beating them about the head with the more obvious version. I've written earlier about my aversion to doing that, so may well choose to leave the original.

The second thing is the thought tag "he thought" in the final sentence. Something else I've mentioned before – when you're writing from a character's POV you're already inside their head. Everything on the page is a thought, or a reaction, or an interpretation. So tags like this are superfluous. The italics are sufficient.

On the other hand (again), used sparingly they work OK (he thought).

Day 90: Nowhere and Nothing

George had never known it this dark. A blackness so complete he couldn't tell whether his eyes were open or closed. Even the usual hint – the occasional spark that would scintillate behind his closed eyelids at night before he fell asleep – didn't work. With eyes open, and he knew they were open because he'd blinked hard and opened them wide, he still saw those phantom flashes.

Silent too. The only sounds he was aware of the rushing of blood in his ears, the pumping of his heart and the inevitable tinnitus. It now seemed even louder than usual, the harsh high-pitched screaming in his ears. But there was nothing else. No distant animal calls, no mechanical grinding, no traffic rumble reaching him from the nearby motorway, no planes overhead. An absence of sound that was almost tangible.

George moved his arms in front of his eyes. There was not even enough light to see them when he held his hands right up close. He couldn't feel their movement. No cool draft of air moving gently over the hairs on his arms as he waved them to and fro. No warmth emanating from any nearby heat source rendered invisible by the blackness. Wherever he was must be exactly the same temperature as his blood.

With no sensory input except what his own body provided, George's mind spun freely. At first his conscious thoughts were taken up entirely with the strangeness of his environment, but after a few minutes (or what felt like a few minutes to him – there was no way to mark the passage of time externally, and he didn't want to spend all his time counting heartbeats) he slipped into a more philosophical frame of mind. The emptiness around him put him in mind of the vastness of the cosmos and he began to imagine his insignificance when compared to the galactic and universal whole. One man, riding in total darkness, on a speck of dust circling a tiny point of light that was one of billions of similar points in a galaxy of billions of other galaxies. Before today that kind of thinking boggled his mind. Somehow, here, now, he found it comforting. The neutral temperature and absence of stimulation made his infinitesimal smallness bearable in some visceral, inexplicable way.

He imagined himself hovering in space, gazing down at the Milky Way from a vantage point directly above its core. The spiral arms stretching out left and right and the whole turning majestically beneath him. Countless lives of untold creatures being lived out on worlds orbiting those billions of tiny lights, each lonely collection utterly unaware of every other lonely collection and separated from them by vast physical distances and even larger conceptual ones.

George began to imagine what those alien worlds might look like. Or sound like. With nothing to distract his senses, his mind started conjuring inputs to replace the usual frenetic melee of sensory evidence. Now acutely aware of the functioning of his body – exactly how full his bladder was; whether or not he would be hungry any time soon; how fast his heart was pumping – George experienced a sudden feeling of panic. If he was bleeding, or heading for an abyss, or about to be crushed under some huge falling weight, how would he know? His previous feelings of safety and calm were supplanted with nervousness and disquiet. All his natural defences, reactions and instincts were blinded along with his sight and hearing. If he couldn't see danger approaching, or hear it, how would he be able to react in time?

His heart rate increased. The blood rushed in his ears. All thoughts of universal serenity or galactic harmony were replaced by his worrying suspicion that he could be in mortal danger and would never know. His life was about to be snuffed out by something dangerous but trivial, and he was powerless to avoid it.

A blinding white knife edge of light scored across the velvety darkness to his right, like a scimitar slicing the heavens in half. This was it! He was doomed! The sky was falling! He was lying on his back directly beneath the cosmic blade that had cleaved his world in two!

With a metallic click the left-hand half of the sky peeled back to reveal a man standing next to what had become a hatchway to another world. A world of light, and warmth, and noise. The man smiled.

"Strange experience isn't it? Revealing. I like to use the Isolation Chamber two or three times a year. It's amazing what insight it can bring."

He fastened back the lid with a clip. "Well, get your bearings George, for a minute or two, and then when you're ready you can step out onto the platform here."

Author's Notes

Informed by several science fiction stories I remember reading as a boy, this piece also includes some more personal insights. A few years ago I was invited to take part in a research project, which involved spending roughly thirty minutes in an MRI scanner, watching a TV screen reflected in a mirror while they scanned my brain. I was provided with a 4-key electronic pad (A, B, C, D) with which I responded to the questions on-screen and the boffins analysed what my thoughts and responses did to my brain activity.

Part of the process involved the insertion of a cannula so they could monitor my blood chemistry at the same time. I've never suffered from claustrophobia, or anything like it, but towards the end of that thirty minutes I distinctly remember developing an irrational certainty that the cannula had somehow become dislodged, and I was bleeding profusely from my arm. I was alone in the MRI room, no-one would see it. How much blood would I lose before someone came in and discovered my predicament? A little of that bizarrely aberrant thinking found its way into this story.

Notes from an Editor's perspective

One pure drafting error – a missing word from "The only sounds he was aware of the rushing of blood…" but beyond that, there's significant evidence of overwriting here. A redraft would definitely tighten things up, add power to the imagery, and reorder some of the text to improve the flow.

Day 91: Answers

Will took a deep drag on his cigarette, squinting against the wisp of smoke that curled up into his eyes. He blew the lungful out over the city that stretched below him in a million points of glowing sodium and neon. There was no kick left in tobacco he decided, grinding the glowing nub into a misshapen remnant on the rock beside him.

Normally, he liked to come up here to the bluff to think. Years before – how many? – he had discovered this spot where the weather had worn the soft rock into a seat that looked out over the urban sprawl several hundred feet below. Protected by an overhang from the path above, the seat was his secret place. At least, in all the years he'd been coming here, he'd never found anyone else sitting in it, or any evidence that it had been occupied since his previous visit.

From this distance the clamour of the city was muted – a little, at least – adding some clarity to his thinking. Or reducing the distraction of everyday life anyway. He came up here when he needed to search for answers, but tonight all he was finding were more questions. His mind kept reminding him how the answer to Life, the Universe and Everything had led the characters from one of his favourite novels to spend millennia in a further search for the real question. A quest for a question. It sounded mad. And of course, in the novel, that had been exactly the point.

But Will didn't need more questions. He needed answers. Specifically, he needed answers to questions like 'Are you sleeping with someone?' and 'Do you still love me?' At least, part of him did. Another part – and which part was in the majority varied by the minute – was scared to hear the answers. Didn't want resolution or clarity. Wasn't prepared for the possible – probable? – pain that answers might bring.

Below him, somewhere in the city hidden from view at this distance, an ambulance siren echoed around the wide streets. Someone, somewhere, would soon be asking the question 'Is he, or she, going to be OK doctor?' or perhaps, if the siren didn't quite perform well enough in the crowded streets and the ambulance was delayed for crucial seconds, they would be hearing the question 'Would you like some time alone?'

Will didn't want to be alone. That was a question he never needed to answer. It was built into him like his height, the colour of his eyes, his smoking habit. He didn't do alone. Never had. The prospect gave him the shivers, right through his gut, like he had a permanent attack of the shits. Up here, in the relative quiet, with every glimmer of starlight blotted out by heavy clouds, surrounded by darkness only relieved by the carpet of city lights under his feet, he could see that more clearly. Could see also that his fear of loneliness had driven him to stay where he was no longer wanted, or needed. Loneliness is a crowded room, said the old song. And with the new clarity that his secret seat granted him, Will could see that it was also a crowded house, or a crowded life. There was nothing lonelier than being surrounded by people you didn't know, didn't like, didn't want to be with. Endless hours and days spent in pointless, circular conversations about nothing important. Everyone trying to hide the fact that they'd rather be somewhere else, with someone else.

The craving for another cigarette surfaced in his chest. He reached unconsciously for the pack and then paused. What was the real answer to the question 'Do you want a light?' Only minutes before he had stubbed out his last smoke. He hadn't enjoyed it. Why didn't he make it, literally, his last smoke? There was another question. A question similar to the one about being alone that, with his new-found clarity, he discovered he already knew the answer to. The light he wanted to let into his life was not the light of a match. Not that of a lighter. He needed sunlight and warmth. He needed moonlight and romance. Not the hollow, cold, empty light that shone in the eyes of people who no longer cared about him. He threw the pack of cigarettes over the edge of the bluff and watched it bounce and spin down the rock face until it disappeared from view.

Author's Notes

This is such a broad topic. From a distance of ten years, I can't recall what made me choose this interpretation of it, but clearly any discussion of answers is likely to involve questions too.

I've never been a smoker, but I do have a lifetime of experience being around them. Parents, friends, wives. Them, and their efforts to quit; occasionally successful. In common with Will, though, I don't really "do" alone either, and I too know all about the loneliness in a crowded room. So I indulged in a little "writer's catharsis" here, even if only at a tangent. Nothing so overt as killing off a wife, although yes, I've done that at least once (in fiction :o)).

Notes from an Editor's perspective

Annoyingly, while drafting, my mind throws out many examples of phrases like "tonight all he was finding were more questions…".

Was finding – a verb conjugation known as "past continuous" apparently. If I ever learned the proper names for these things the knowledge has long evaporated. Even using them (the terms) is a turn-off for most people. But anyway, they are longer and more verbose than the alternatives, and bring a sense of overwriting to the work, even if only subliminally. An editing pass would probably replace that example with "tonight all he found were…"

At the end of the fourth paragraph, the phrase "pain that answers might bring" is ambiguous. I intended to refer to the answers Will feared as a singular entity, which may bring pain. To clarify this, I should have put quotes around "answers". Otherwise, it appears that the original should more properly be written as "– pain those answers might bring."

Day 92: Innocence

"There it is again, see?"

"This one? The one after AMG-1?"

"Yep."

"You're sure?"

"I think the evidence is pretty conclusive."

Gene Richards – a man who regularly caused a great deal of mirth once people discovered what he did for a living – sat back from the gel electrophoresis readout and smiled. Gene was a gene detective, and he had just hunted down his most important find yet. His colleague, Randy Martenson, scratched his head.

"It's going to need a name," he said.

"Yeah. I know. Ordinarily I'd agree with you, and the name would be obvious. But this is different."

"How so?"

"Think about it. If we publish this, and someone develops a test for it, as they certainly will, it could lead to massive exploitation of just about everyone on the planet."

"Why can't we just call it INN-1?"

"You haven't thought it through Randy. I've had this on my mind since we ran the first tests. What if I was right? What if we could track down this trait to a single gene? How would society at large – and politicians and crooks in particular – react? Look how much controversy there was when Daibell said he'd unearthed the gay gene. And that only affects around ten percent of the population. This is much more widespread."

"Any idea how much more?"

"Not at this stage. We'd have to perfect this test and then

run a stat-sig trial. But I'd be willing to bet it'll be at least fifty percent. Maybe higher."

Randy whistled. "I had no idea it would be that much."

"Well, you know what they say," Gene took a swig of coffee. "You can fool all of the people some of the time. I'm guessing there's a nugget of truth behind that old saying. A hunk of genetic lore. We'll probably find there are some modifiers affecting INN-1 – we might as well call it that for now, at least between the two of us – so that it is expressed at some point in everyone's life. Maybe some of the other factors are environmental or developmental, things that turn INN-1 off, or suppress its worst effects, but every test we've done so far supports the results."

"I wouldn't have believed it if we hadn't demonstrated it in the Rhesus batch."

"I know. Those monkeys acted as if they were having a permanent blonde moment. Incredible. Incidentally we must look after them. They'll be ideal candidates to trial some of those environmental factors we should start looking for. But until we know more about how INN-1 expresses itself I think we should keep a lid on it."

"Shame. It's Nobel material this is, you know."

"I know. Hold that thought. We'll get there in the end. Both of us. But if the press get wind that we've discovered a genetic trigger for innocence, they'll make a mountain out of a molehill, and then we'll have hundreds of crooks looking to steal our research so they can MOVE that mountain for their own ends."

"I'm still not sure I–"

"You only have to think about it for a few minutes Rand! Adding a GM component to something as innocuous as cow's milk, or wheat flour – one that causes INN-1 to express at its full potential? Well, we'd end up with a world full of sheeple."

"I hate that word."

"Well what else would you call them? You've seen what INN-1 did to the Rhesus monkeys. Imagine that, multiplied by a thousand, and distributed among the population in their daily bread. That would definitely be a case of 'give us our daily bread and we forgive those who trespass against us'. And what trespasses they would be. All the sales and marketing people would be able to sell anything to anyone. If they ever even noticed they were being sold crap they wouldn't be able to summon up the enthusiasm to do anything about it, even if they realised it was within their grasp to do anything at all! Con artists would be out there taking everyone's wallets in exchange for a 'wallet cleaning certificate'! Politicians would, well, they'd be even worse than they are now and they'd get away with it!"

"When you put it like that, it makes me think we should burn these notes altogether."

"On the one hand, I think you might be right. But on the other... If we can attack it the other way, before anyone else gets wind of it, we can find out how to turn INN-1 off for good."

"Are you sure that's a good idea?"

"Better than the alternative, I reckon. A world full of people who it's impossible to con. Who won't believe anything at all without rock solid proof, cast-iron guarantees and copper-bottomed promises."

"Won't there be side-effects?"

"That's got to be on our research list too. Babies and bathwater and all that. What else does INN-1 influence? What were the evolutionary drivers to it coming into existence in the first place? What are the survival benefits of innocence? I must admit that from a standing start I can't think of any, but there must be some or INN-1 wouldn't exist."

"Procreation?"

"How do you mean?"

"Well – look at ugly guys, to take a simple case. They, or should I say," Randy grinned, "we, have a lot going for us. Good genes in some respects even if they're not in the looks department. If we couldn't persuade a lady into bed, we'd never have a chance to pass those good genes on, would we? Maybe innocence gives us a head start in that respect?"

"You might have a point there Rand. That could be another research avenue. Find a bunch of fuglies and test their wives (and husbands). Find out if they've got unusually high levels of INN-1 activity. Nice one buddy! You just earned your October pay check!"

Author's Notes

Genes cop for a lot of blame in science fiction and fantasy stories. X-Men and Heroes, to name but two, and I include a brief reference to a genetic basis for the Elemental magic in my own stories.

This is hardly surprising. We've only recently completed the sequencing of the whole human genome, but even now, after decades of research, we're still a long way from understanding how all 20,000 of our genes work. And that's before we start looking at the 98% of our genetic material classed as "non-coding." This gives huge scope for fictional genetic effects, hence the subject of this story.

Notes from an Editor's perspective

I often find that when I'm drafting dialogue, punctuation tends to go out of the window. In full flow, I react to every thought – every idea – like that, with em-dashes. Or I split speeches in inappropriate places, which can obfuscate the meaning, or interrupt the flow, forcing the reader out of the moment to ponder what I really meant to say. Much if not all of that is tidied up in the first or second editing pass.

I should also add that in the draft, unless it's a character with a strong personality that I'm thoroughly familiar with, they can all end up "sounding" (i.e. speaking) like me. That's another aspect that has to be addressed during editing, to give each person their own unique – and obvious – voice.

Day 93: Simplicity

The noise of a hundred different conversations struck me like a physical blow as I entered the ballroom. I had no idea Elaine had invited so many guests. There had been no dress code in the invitation, so most of the ladies had taken the opportunity to go to town on their outfits. I say 'go to town' but in the majority of cases they appeared to have chartered a private jet and flown it to Rio, rather than catching the bus to Oldham.

Lights from the two gargantuan chandeliers bounced and coruscated off half a ton of diamanté, sequins, paste and lamé in gold, silver and copper. Hair had been coiffed within an inch of its life, in such a variety of hues and shades as nature had never dreamt of. Short hair, long hair, tall hair, flat hair. Bobs, buns, curls, bangs, and a dozen other styles that I couldn't even begin to tell you the names of.

And flesh! Oh, God, the flesh on display was... well, it was distracting is what it was. And not always in a good way. I'm a firm believer in displaying a well-turned thigh as long as it's... well... firm. Before you get started I'm not being ageist. There's plenty of... older... meat that can be put on display without causing one to lose one's breakfast, but I think we can all agree that we don't need to see anything white and flabby, and blue veins should be restricted to the Stilton, thank you very much. The problem is you can't always avoid seeing it. Fair enough if it's one of those dresses that doesn't reach the shoulders, or something backless. But when it's a long flowing skirt that just happens to be gashed to the... waist, and you don't notice that until it opens up right in front of you revealing half a yard of cellulite. I don't know what they're thinking, some of them. Keep it covered up, for goodness' sake.

Although, having said that, even covering it up isn't all that. Not when the covering is... how shall I put it? A little scant in the yardage department. Somehow the word 'tight' doesn't quite cover it. And not quite covering it is also, by some strange coincidence, the effect of these wannabe corsets. Looking as if they are going to burst at any minute and spill out that which we have already all agreed should remain covered at all times. It's not surprising that their partners look as if they are on tenterhooks. Probably all poised with their capes, or hats, or napkins ready to cover up any offending split as soon as it happens. If it does.

And so, since we have mentioned them, let us turn our attention to these partners. While their lady-folk have quite clearly spent the majority of the weekend, if not the entirety of the preceding week, in their sartorial preparations for this evening, the men folk fall into one of two categories. Can't be arsed, and arseholes. Those that can't be arsed can be further subdivided into through a hedge backwards, through a hedge forwards, directly resembling of a hedge, and hedging their bets (by which last category I mean, of course, that they look as if they've dressed for every possibly eventuality both socially and meteorologically).

The arseholes, in contrast to those who can't be arsed, have made an effort. They have, visibly, tried to smarten themselves up. Unfortunately, none of them have a clue. Mismatched colours and styles abound. Dickie bows with tweed jackets. Cravats with... well, come to think of it, cravats at all. Either they don't have a mirror to their name, or they've never asked their wives' or partners' opinion, or both. Or perhaps they have asked for an opinion, and they're deaf. Because no-one in their senses would come out dressed like that, especially to an occasion such as this. Elaine's annual dinner-dance, the highlight of the Droitwich social calendar.

An expectant hush fell over the assembled throng, in all their sartorial confusion, as Elaine appeared on the balcony. Whether by accident or design, she appeared to have understood implicitly that her invitation would have led all her guests to compete for ascendancy of apparel. And in a single leap of intuition she had sought to outdo them by travelling the opposite path, and succeeded. Oh, my word, how she had succeeded!

She wore a simple, one-piece, flowing satin dress all in black. It shimmered and sparkled as she paraded down the wide staircase. Her hair was simply but beautifully cut, dyed black for the occasion to match her dress. She wore the barest touch of makeup and the lightest whiff of her perfume came to me across the still air of the room, utterly and compellingly different from any other.

She stepped onto the granite tiles and swept toward me with hardly a sound save the gentle swishing of that incredibly elegant dress. A playful smile lit her face and her eyes glittered, reflecting a dozen flashes from a dozen different cameras dotted around the hallway. She reached out to take my outstretched hand and looked up into my eyes. I could hardly breathe.

"You look stunning," I said.

Author's Notes

I'm not known for my sartorial tastes. Unless it's a reputation for having a complete lack of such. Strange, perhaps, for someone whose father spent a lifetime working in gentleman's outfitting, and was hardly ever seen in public unless immaculately suited-and-booted. I don't think the dear old guy ever wore a pair of jeans until he was well into his sixties.

So perhaps stranger still that my first thought on reading today's topic was that famous "little black dress" that renders its wearer stunning through its simplicity. It was a good thought though. It set me off on a fertile vein of writing that led to this longer than average piece, which I still think works really well.

One of the most enjoyable parts of being a writer is being able to let rip with all those non-PC thoughts to which one is never otherwise allowed to give voice. Whether or not one actually thinks them, or believes them, oneself, nevertheless it's inevitable to at least encounter them in daily life. And in that regular daily life, it's incumbent on every right-minded person to purse their lips, draw in their breath, and express the expected amount of distaste at such appalling views.

Not when you're writing. There, you can imbue any of your characters with dreadful beliefs and behaviours, and see where that takes them. There is of course a slight risk of being associated with such views in your readers' minds, and there are many anecdotes of famous writers and their pithy put-downs when accused of that very thing. Of course, the writer of murder mysteries does not need to have committed murder to be able to write about it. Similarly with repugnant antisemitism, homophobia, racism, etc, etc.

Day 94: Reality

The rain bucketed down like an impenetrable curtain, bouncing thigh-high off the saturated pavements. Jez had never seen rain like it. He stood under a railway arch and waited, without much hope that it would let up any time soon.

Any ordinary guy would never venture out in weather like this. A few inches further forward and he would be drenched to the skin in seconds. But Jez was no ordinary guy. He had a need.

He'd known it was coming, of course. He always knew. The first few hints of the gnawing had started in his gut earlier that afternoon. If he'd had more sense he would have come out then, when the last rays of afternoon sun glinted red and gold off the dust-grimed windows of the derelict warehouse district. The only time they ever really looked beautiful. At least, when he had his straight head on. With his smashed head, pretty much everything looked beautiful, even his dingy, rat-infested squat with its mould-stained mattress.

But as usual, he hadn't had more sense. He'd stayed in front of his blurry old portable TV until the red had bled out of the windows and the black had come. And with it, the rain. From inside the squat the rain had been welcome. It freshened the stale air, washed his window, and took away some of the heat. Its familiar sound against the sill was comforting. By the time it started beating a heavier rhythm on the roof, the complaints from his gut had also become louder, driving him out into the night in search of a fix.

Luckily his usual dealer Max was a man of habit. Tuesday was his railway arch day. Jez knew he might have to hang around for an hour or so, but Max would be there. Sooner or later. Jez didn't need to brave the weather. Max would do that part. Max the bringer of light. The seller of dreams. The owner of his soul.

He checked his pockets. His pitiful wad of cash was still there. A handful of greasy notes gleaned from begging, or borrowed from the few friends he had left. Well, the friend, singular. Everyone else had given up on him and left him to spin down the downward spiral they all believed he was on. Like rainwater gurgling down the drain beside him, only not as clean.

From the corner of his eye he caught a movement through the downpour. Collar turned up against the drenching rain and an old oilskin hat pulled down low over his eyes, Max crossed the road in front of him. It had to be Max, even though Jex could not make out the man's face. No-one else would be here in this and besides, no-one ran quite like Max, with that half-loping jog that he had to use on account of an old wound from Iraq.

"Max!" Jez called. "Over here!"

"I see you, you mad bastard," Max replied over the deafening clatter of the rain. "Wasn't sure if you'd be here today. You're lucky I decided you were worth a soaking."

"Yeah, thanks man. I really need it today."

"You really need it every day buddy," Max grinned, pulling off his hat once he attained the shelter of the arch. Raindrops covered his beard, standing out like jewels. They flashed with reflected colours from the few neon shop signs still working.

"Well? What have you got?" Jez asked, holding his arms folded across his aching guts. "Better be something good. I've got the aches real bad."

"Got the usual stuff," Max said flippantly. "But I got my hands on something new too. One or two of my regulars have tried it. Reckon it's the bomb."

"Oh yeah? What's that?"

Max took a small brown drug bottle from the pocket of his raincoat and held it up in front of Jez's face. The contents remained anonymous behind the dark ochre plastic.

"They call it Reality," he said. "Wanna try some?"

"How much?"

"Well, you know, it's a bit steeper than your regular stuff. It's new, what can I say? Gotta cover my overheads?"

"How much!?"

"To you, seein' as you're a regular an' all... fifty bucks."

"Fifty? You have to be kidding. It would need to be a fuckin' big hit for fifty. And anyway," Jez went on, fingering the small wad in his pocket, "I ain't got fifty."

"How much you got?"

"Twenty. Twenty five maybe, in change."

"Look, this stuff is real good. I'll stand you the other twenty-five for now. Like I said, you're a regular. I know you're good for it."

He flipped the lid off the bottle and shook a red capsule into the palm of his hand.

"This little red pill will blow your mind," he said, smiling.

"Looks like something out of The Matrix," Jez joked nervously.

"Well buddy, they don't call it Reality for nothing."

Author's Notes

Leaving aside the famous Red Pill from the Matrix, which I mentioned in this story, drugs play a large part in many SF stories. E.E "Doc" Smith's Lensman series was awash with them: bentlam, nitrolabe and thionite. Minority Report had Clarity and neuroin. Drugs to increase lifespan, loosen tongues, confer temporary superpowers (often with life-threatening side-effects), the list goes on. So ubiquitous are they, I almost felt compelled to introduce an addictive substance in later volumes of my Berikatanyan Chronicles.

So my strange mind made the connection between the topic and the red pill with frightening speed. And the rest was only a matter of setting the stage and deciding which characters would play on it.

Day 95: Acceptance

Roger had always loved moonlight. Legend had it that the light of a full moon could send a man mad. Howling at the moon, or baying at the moon, would be the result of too much exposure. So they said. That had never been more true than on this night. Yet perhaps because of his life-long love of Earth's only celestial partner, tonight Roger felt saner than he ever had. Looking around him at the dozen or so other occupants of Glastonbury Tor, none of whom he knew but all of whom apparently shared, if not his passion then at least his attitude, he also felt saner than the overwhelming mass of humanity.

When he'd left home to take up his position for what he assumed would be a lonely vigil, the television news bulletins had been full of mayhem. Rioting, looting, drunken naked folk running through the streets, fornication everywhere the cameras pointed. Like some crazy hyped-up carnival, the greatest show on Earth. Anything goes, roll up, roll up. Get your last fix before the final curtain. Fulfil your life's dreams. Act out your darkest fantasies. No police, no courts, no charges. In either sense. No criminal prosecutions and no fees. A free-for-all in the widest possible sense. All pretence at government or crowd control finally removed. Mankind at its most bestial. Faced with the ultimate peril, the end of all things, with no hope of survival, the very instinct for that survival was ripped from every soul on the planet. What else was left then, but to revel in the basest of pleasures? Take it while you could. Everything was on offer, no-one had anything left to lose. A few hours of sexual fulfilment, or culinary delight, or alcohol-fuelled mayhem, was all that remained.

Unless you were like Roger. He, and his handful of compatriots, sat quietly on the Tor, watching the moon. He could have chosen a higher spot. Some of the major roads were blocked by those making a desperate last-minute attempt to connect with distant family or friends. To see loved ones one last time, if only for a few brief moments. But he could have made it to Snowdonia, or Striding Edge or any one of a number of taller mountains he had visited in his 35 years on Earth. But Glastonbury, and the Tor, had always had a special place in his heart. Its quietness and spirituality brought a calmness to his soul like no other place he knew. And he needed that now. Needed to be close to what he always considered the centre of things. Whether it was ley lines or magnetic forces or plain Celtic magic was immaterial now. It felt good, that was what mattered. It felt better than swilling down a couple of pints of single malt and welcoming oblivion before the final impact. Better than fighting past hordes of looters to get his hands on long-cherished stuff that would be vapour scant minutes after the grasping. Better than the most experienced whore or the most beautiful virgin.

He grimaced at the thought that there probably weren't any virgins left, at least above a certain, previously illegal, age. No. None of that appealed to him. He wanted to be fully conscious at the end, with his spirit and his integrity intact.

Roger stared up at the moon. Already bigger than the biggest supermoon in history, its silver glow filled at least twice its normal space in the night sky. It had blotted out all but the brightest stars. A fresh October wind picked up some early autumn leaves from the trees at the base of the Tor and set them spinning up to reach him. Was this the start of the freak weather that had been predicted? He pushed his hair out of his eyes. He thought he could detect the moon growing even larger. Even now, with still several hours to go, its disc expanded noticeably by the minute. Scientists had predicted impact at 1:37am GMT. Somewhere south of Glastonbury, he couldn't remember exactly where. Not that it mattered. When the moon was finally reunited with the Earth after their countless millennia of separation, the exact place – where a notional umbilicus of fatal gravity connected the two bodies – would be just as terminal as any other spot on their world.

He had reached a state of calm acceptance of this fact surprisingly quickly, even for him. Where was there to run? Where could provide any protection or hiding place from the gargantuan impact. There was nowhere. All he could do was sit, and watch.

Author's Notes

Glastonbury Tor has the same effect on me as it does on Roger in this story. If you've never visited, and you have the chance to, I would strongly recommend it. It truly is a magical place and I give full rein to my feelings about it in Roger's description here.

"The End of Times" is a common trope in fiction, whether it be through cometary impact, war, alien invasion, mad scientists, or whatever, it crops up again and again. And of course stories of the days after the end – the post-apocalyptic genre – have never been so popular. Maybe people need to read about something that's even worse than what we've all already lived through?

Another well-worn and often expressed feeling, this time in real life, is that "if the bomb drops, I want to be right underneath it." The acceptance of the inevitability of the end, and the desire to avoid surviving, only to live in a world unrecognisable from what went before.

So today's topic brought those three threads together in my mind, to spin the skein of this story.

Notes from an Editor's perspective

I may have mentioned before that "just" is one of my

drafting tic words. I'm always writing about just this, or just that. So one of the few changes I would make to this text is to redraft "..would be just as terminal…" into something stronger. Something along the lines of "...would be no more terminal than…"

Day 96: Lesson

The heavy iron door clanged shut behind him. Felix was on his own for the first time in twenty-six years. He knew he was supposed to be walking away, but somehow he couldn't bring himself to move. Not yet. This close to the prison he could still smell it. Or was the smell merely lodged in his nostrils? How long would it take to clear out? He had no idea, but one look at the sky – all that fresh air just there for the breathing – told him that the reek of a life sentence behind bars would soon be gone.

A small shiver of incipient agoraphobia ran through him, finally urging him into a slow amble away from the prison gates. Too much out in the open would probably be bad for him, at least in the early stages. He should find a bolt hole for a spell. Sit, ponder, decide on his next steps.

It was a strange feeling, the concept of next steps. For twenty-six years his every step had been programmed for him by prison routine. Get up, slop out, breakfast, pool, lock-up, exercise yard, lock-up, dinner, lock-up, bed. Same every day. He'd never been any good at mental arithmetic, but that must have added up to thousands of days. All gone. Shut away behind the clang of that door, out of reach. An uncertain future stretched out ahead of him. He needed a jolt of familiarity to bring him some concrete reality.

He'd been walking for about an hour when he spotted the Starbucks sign. Just the kind of 'familiarity' he'd been seeking. With a pang of regret, he remembered that Starbucks had been Margaret's favourite. They'd always stopped off for a latte and a muffin on trips into town. That was before... well... just before. He wondered briefly where Margaret was now. If she was doing OK. Then he pinched his thigh hard, through his pocket, brought himself back to the moment. The barista was asking him what he wanted. He stopped, open-mouthed, on the point of ordering a latte. Surely there'd be something new on the menu after a quarter of a century? He scanned the board quickly.

"I'll have a venti caramel macchiato."

"Drink in or take out?"

"In. Thanks."

"That'll be £2.95 please."

Felix almost choked. Right enough, the price was on the board in front of his eyes. Maybe this hadn't been such a good idea after all. That was almost a quarter of the funds he'd left the slammer with. He handed over a five pound note and collected his change.

Seated in the window, Felix watched the pedestrian traffic while he sucked on his drink. Busy. It was a cold November day with a light breeze and a clear blue sky. The smell of Christmas in the air. Must be a street market somewhere close, he decided. Well, that was one thing he didn't need to worry about. No presents to buy. No cards. No-one to celebrate with. No money either. But at least there should be some seasonal work going. He was still physically strong, could do regular lifting and carrying, and he'd always been a hard worker. Just so long as he could keep his temper. So long as no-one crossed him. Twenty-six years was a long time to spend thinking about that. To learn the lesson that his sentence was designed to teach him. It had been hard, staying out of that kind of trouble inside. Screws winding him up all the time, and the inmates worse. Taking a pop at him almost every day for something or other. It was a fine line, staying away from a spell in solitary but still managing to stick up for himself so's he didn't get a rep as a soft touch. An easy target. He'd seen it so many times. Regular people who just couldn't cut it on the inside. The slightest show of weakness was all it took. Then the vultures would start circling and pretty soon your life wouldn't be worth living.

Took him a few years to learn to tread that path. It wasn't exactly the lesson he'd gone in for. No, that one was to stay out of trouble altogether. Inside he just had to avoid being seen defending himself.

"Hey!"

A man's voice from behind him gave him a jolt. He turned around, bristling, ready for trouble.

"What?"

"You done with that sugar?"

The innocuous question hung in the air for several seconds while Felix processed the fact that this wasn't an unexpected attack. He looked at the sugar dispenser on the table beside him; back at the man.

"Sure. Help yourself," he said, passing the container across.

"Thanks mate."

Author's Notes

We watch a lot of movies at Beresford Towers. The sight of some guy walking out of prison, – onto an empty street, or across the road to a waiting car, with a friend, or lover, stood beside it ready to throw their unfinished cigarette to the ground and open the door – is a common one. I'm happy to admit that the character of Felix is strongly influenced by Brooks Hatlen from one of my favourite movies: Shawshank Redemption. Thankfully, Felix's first tentative steps back into normal life are a little more positive than Brooksy's.

Notes from an Editor's perspective

In the ten years since I wrote this, electronic, or contactless, payments have become the norm. When we restarted "curry club" for the first time after the pandemic (a hiatus of twenty-one months) I was surprised to find four of my friends (out of six on that occasion) paying their chunk of the bill with Google Pay. Prior to that, we had all left a pile of cash on the table. I felt almost as out of touch with the zeitgeist as Felix! A year later, none of us use cash now, not even at the pub.

I suspect any "pocket money" doled out to long-term inmates leaving prison is still cash though, at least for now. Ex-cons are unlikely to have phones, and may not even have bank accounts, so it's the only alternative. But with e-payment becoming so ubiquitous, I'd almost certainly mention it in a piece like this. The barista's surprise at being handed a fiver, or passing over a payment terminal in expectation of a card, or phone, being presented. One more way to make Felix feel like a man out of time.

Day 97: Enthusiasm

[this post is a continuation of the story "A Place to Belong" from earlier in the writing challenge – on Day 81]

Vince came lolloping toward Carl across the springy green turf. He was wearing a lop-sided grin, made even more lop-sided by the tennis ball he carried in his mouth. He dropped the ball at Carl's feet.

"Woof!" he barked.

Carl grinned at the dog and ruffled his neck. "Again boy?"

He picked up the ball, slimy with Vince's slobber, and threw it high and hard across the garden. Cyn and Roger's garden was as impressive as their house. Even a Yankees baseball star would never have been able to pitch the ball over the tall copper beech hedge that separated it from the next plot. Vince gave another excited bark and took off after the ball, his ears flopping wildly about his head and his tail wagging as he ran.

Cyn watched the scene from the relative warmth of the morning room. A cup of coffee sat steaming on a table beside her, unnoticed. She turned to Roger.

"Vince has really taken to him," she said.

"I know."

"Can't he stay just a little longer?"

"He's been here six weeks already. I offered to give him a hand up, not a permanent residence."

"Just a little longer?"

Roger set his coffee down beside hers. The steam from the two cups mingled, painting the bulls-eye panes of the morning room with vaporous circles.

"How many more weeks? One? Two? Ten? I'm sorry.

Sorry for him, and for us in a funny kind of way. I've felt good having him around. But you know how it is. Before much longer he'll start to feel settled. He must have wondered how long he could stay here. Has he said anything to you?"

"No."

"Well he must have thought about it."

"I don't think he's the kind of person to think about the future. He's just happy to be here. Look at him. Playing with Vince. He's out there every day you know. You don't always see him. Vince loves him."

"I'm sorry, but Vince doesn't get a vote here. Vince loves the postman too. I don't see you offering him a room and board!"

"Hold on just a minute Roger. Don't put this on me. It was you offered him a place."

"Right. And it's me withdrawing the offer."

"It won't be easy. Sending him back onto the streets. Have you thought about where he'll go? Where he'll end up?"

"It won't be any worse than it was before. Spring's only just around the corner."

"It's the middle of February for Christ's sake! It'll be at least another six weeks before it gets any warmer out there."

"Yeah, well, like I said. He's used to it. He'll be no worse off than he was before."

"Of course he will."

"How's that?"

"He's been here, hasn't he? Living in the warm and dry. Sleeping in a soft bed. Three meals a day. Walks with the dog, down by the river. You've dangled that life in front of him, let him have a taste of it. You've done that Roger. Now you're going to whip it all away again and kick him back down the road."

"Well what else can we do? He doesn't belong here. He's nothing to us."

"Isn't he? So why did you bring him here?"

"I felt sorry for him. And he found Vince. We'd have lost–"

"You felt sorry for him then. Why not now?"

"Look, he's had nearly two months to get better. He's healthier, he's put on some weight. All his sores are cleaned up. We'll give him some clothes, shoes. A coat. We can even get him a sleeping roll if you like. I'm not talking about sending him back out there in the rags we found him in."

"And that's it, is it? A few clothes and a pair of shoes. Now run along Carl, there's a good man. Don't want you making the place look untidy."

"What else do you suggest? I don't know why you're making me out to be the bad guy. We've helped him for God's sake. We haven't done anything wrong. We've helped him, and now it's time to move on."

Cyn sighed and reached for her coffee. It was no longer steaming. The fog had cleared from the window panes. "I know you're right," she sighed again. "It's just... well... I've got to like having him around. The house will feel–"

"Don't say it'll feel empty."

"Well it will! Just the two of us."

"That's how it was before."

"I know. It's probably silly. But didn't you ever feel there was something missing? I never really got fired up about anything before. Maybe it was all too easy. Having Carl around, somehow it's given me more energy."

"Anyone would think you were screwing the guy!"

"Roger! How could you even think that!"

"Take it easy. I was just joking."

"Well don't. None of this is a joke, and especially not that."

"Sorry. I'm feeling like the evil twin here."

"I'm sorry too. I guess I'm just not ready to throw Carl out yet."

"Can we at least broach the subject with him?"

Cyn bristled, but Roger waved her objection aside. "I don't mean in a threatening way. I'm not going to give him an ultimatum. But we could ask if he has any plans, or where he sees himself ending up, couldn't we?"

"I guess."

"Like I said, he might already have been thinking about moving on. Or he might have an Aunt Jemima in Oregon he wants to go visit."

"Aunt Jemima!" She slapped his arm playfully. "Where did that come from?"

The tennis ball thumped loudly against the window, rattling a pane. They both jumped.

"Sorry!" called Carl from the garden. "The ball slipped. My bad!"

"Woof!" agreed Vince, running to retrieve the ball from a flower pot on the terrace.

Author's Notes

Another example of a story that has enough material to span several topics – in this case 3 – this entire thread is one of my favourite outputs from this whole process. Though the tale of Tani stretches over one more topic than this one (finishing in the next entry), there's something about each of these characters – rather than those in the longer thread – that resonates with me. This probably explains why each of their entries is so much longer, on average, than others. The dialogue flowed very easily during the draft, and the end result (in my opinion) requires almost no editing.

If I were to proceed and select some of these story fragments to take forward into a longer work, this would be at the top of the list. Whether or not Carl leaves, where he goes if he does, how he might cross paths with Cyn & Roger again in the future. Perhaps with a dramatic reversal of fortunes? Carl catches a break, and his future takes off, while Roger loses his fancy job (whatever it is) and their big house is repossessed.

Day 98: Game

[this post is a continuation of the story in "Advantage" from earlier in the writing challenge – on Day 82]

The darkness closed in again as Tani left the clearing, as black as before and yet somehow not. By some trick of nature the canopy was thinner above the path that had presented itself to her. Light from the twin moons, which had risen during her meeting with the old elf, filtered down through the leaves and guided her steps. Behind her, the baying of The Pack was more muted. Either they had taken a wrong turn, or her more certain feet were carrying her away from them faster.

Without any warning she emerged from the forest onto a clifftop. Below her the river Mizar wound its sluggish way through the valley, a gossamer thin thread of life from this height. At first glance she thought the path had turned into a dead end. There was no way to cross the gorge. After a few seconds her eyes adjusted to the moonlight, brighter now without the leafy barrier of the forest. Directly in front of her, a ropeweed strand hung down from the branches of an enormous ancient yalloak tree. It was a perilous leap, but Tani knew she could make it. She had The Advantage.

She retraced her steps into the edge of the forest, turned, and with a deep breath ran as fast as she could to the edge. She judged her pace and the length of her stride perfectly, taking off from very lip of the escarpment and catching the ropeweed with both hands. Securing her feet in the weed's knotted tendrils she swung out across the gorge. Her swing did not have enough momentum to make the crossing at the first attempt, but she rocked the weed strand backwards and forwards until she felt it would go no higher, and leapt free at the opposite perigee.

The landing knocked the breath from her lungs but she

rolled through it and continued running. This territory was completely unfamiliar to her, but The Hunt could never cross the gorge at that point. She had gained at least two hours on her pursuers. Even so, Tani didn't rest. On this side of the river the high ground was covered in short grass, cropped by the local population of herbivores. She wanted to make good time while the going was easy. In other few hours the alpha sun would be rising and she needed to make cover before then. Even with The Advantage on her side, there was no time to lose.

An hour later, Tani reached the bank of the river, which looped back around the bluff, picking up speed as it fell towards the sea. The moons had reached their zenith and the sky was a clear black. She filled a flask and sat on a rock to catch her breath, cooling her feet in the rushing water which sparkled silver in the moonlight. As it passed over the rocks the river burbled, almost as if it spoke to her. She cocked her head and listened intently to the sound. "Caradh mich," it said. "Caradh mich." With a sudden thrill Tani recognised the language of the elders. "Follow me," the river was saying.

She had no better notion of the right direction to take, and conscious that The Advantage was almost certainly behind this water-imparted knowledge Tani got to her feet and set off along the riverbank, keeping pace with the flow as it bobbed and gurgled over the rocks. Before long the water deepened and slowed, entering a wide sweeping bend to the left. As she rounded the bend Tani gasped as a small coracle came into view, moored at the water's edge. Looking around she could see no sign of its owner and figured in any case her need was greater. She stepped gingerly into the craft and cast off. Instantly the current caught her and set the boat spinning wildly. She caught hold of the gunwale just in time to stop herself being thrown into the water.

Before seasickness had chance to kick in, the coracle

settled into midstream and stopped spinning. Tani had time to look around, watching the bank zip past. Surely The Hunt would never find her now? With no scent trail and so much distance between them?

A sudden roaring noise caught her attention. The small craft rounded another bend and Tani's eyes widened. The river pitched over a waterfall only a few hundred metres ahead and from her position in the boat she had no idea how far the drop was on the other side. She lay down in the boat and wedged herself against the sides, hanging on as tightly as she could as the waves increased in strength and the boat heaved and tossed to and fro. And then it was on her. With a sickening lurch the coracle flew out over the falls into the darkness. Her stomach flipped as the craft fell down, down into an abyss.

Tani sat up into bright white light. For a few seconds she was completely disorientated. She was lying on a couch in a warm, dry room, and someone was standing by her side removing an apparatus from her head.

"How was it Tan?"

Memory flooded back. The game. The most popular game on board IPC Prima Donna. The only way, according to her friends, to while away the long hours between sleeps as they crossed hyperspace to their new home on Cygnus Alpha 4.

Author's Notes

Many elements of this story found their way into the Berikatanyan Chronicles.

I mentioned in one of the earlier entries in this 4-topic thread that I had been influenced by the SF Master Brian Aldiss, and his work Hothouse. I learned very early, from that novel, how to name something in a way that (hopefully) requires no explanation. I first read Hothouse in my very early teens. His naming of the strange and esoteric plants and animals that had evolved by the time the Earth stopped rotating remains a strong influence in my writing to this day.

I thought "ropeweed", a name that flew into my mind without the slightest pause during the draft, was an excellent way to capture the idea of a plant it would be possible to swing from. It also avoids the common misconception of a liana. Since they are anchored at the bottom of trees, they are in truth impossible to swing on, no matter what Tarzan thinks. I always endeavour to avoid being tripped up by facts like that.

Casual mention of "the alpha sun" brings the implication that there is at least a beta sun, and that this planet therefore orbits a binary star. Such an arrangement could potentially lead to a very eccentric orbit, with consequent implications for the seasons on that world. Something that isn't explored in this short piece, but which could bring an added dimension to the story, were it to be extended.

Notes from an Editor's perspective

"In other few hours the alpha sun…" should clearly be "in another few…" – something which a simple edit pass would pick up, aided by the tell-tale underlining of the error by both Word and GoogleDocs.

Day 99: Friendship

This post has a lot of tags. It started off with more but I blew Blogger's limit. I didn't even know there was a limit! See, friendship touches so many areas of my life that Blogger can't cope. I'm half expecting it to seize up in the middle of this post. Let's see how we get on...

With the last post of my 100-day (aka 100-theme) writing challenge in sight, friendship has been much on my mind. I've had some really nice comments and feedback on here, but what's been even better, and more surprising, is the feedback I've had in real life. Whenever I've met up with friends at least one of them has commented on each occasion how much they've been enjoying the writing. I've been enjoying it too, of course, in fact that's one of the things I'll be including in the "lessons learned" follow-up post I'll be writing over the weekend. But it's one thing to gain enjoyment from something yourself, and totally another thing to find out that you've been giving enjoyment to others. Writing can be a solitary experience (all writers say this, at least those who speak/write/email to me) with – often – not much in the way of validation or appreciation, so it's really cool to hear the opinions of readers, which posts they liked best and why, etc.

I'd also be really interested to hear which ones folk thought didn't work out so well. To see how this matches my own feelings, for one thing, but also because it's all part of the learning experience. Just doing this stuff has helped me improve enormously, but really good feedback that mentions the bad as well as the good, is also a huge help.

I appear to have drifted off topic somewhat, so to drag it back to friendship: I've been lucky. When I talk about the times we have with mates – the trips to the Lakes, weekends away, meals out (and in) – the single most common response is how unusual it is for a bunch of guys to have kept a communal friendship going for so long. I'm not sure how rare it is in the great scheme of things, but those who comment on it seem to think it's pretty rare. Much more common for women to have a "girly group of friends"; less so for guys to have a "blokey group", apparently.

I've known for many years that social groups depend on key individuals to hold them together. I had an old colleagues network at one time – around two dozen people who all used to work together in the same part of the organisation until one dark day a reorganisation came along and scattered us all across the company. Some left for other jobs, some took the opportunity for early retirement, most split up into three or four units, separated by geography, department and skill set. For several years after the split, we would get together two or three times a year (Christmas, obviously, and then one or two other meals or social events like bowling, walking, pub crawls). These were all marvellous events, well attended and very popular, but they all had a single individual – the same guy in every case – as the instigator. And then one day he stopped doing it. And none of us have ever met up again since that day.

The small group of friends I always refer to as my "Nottingham" mates (even though only two of them live there now) have strength in depth when it comes to organising get-togethers. It's not driven by just one of us. Once a few weeks, or months, have gone by since our last meet, one or other of us will get in touch to set something else up. Often we don't need to do this, as we arrange it in advance at the previous one. It's a source of infinite variety, pleasure, amusement and fun to Nikki and I to be able to be part of this, as I'm sure anyone who is lucky enough to have their own strong ties of friendship will understand. Friends, they say, are the family you choose, and I would tag that with "lines I wish I'd written" if there was any space left in the tag list :0)

As I've discovered (and blogged about before), friends come at you from all parts of life, and another group that I've been blessed to reconnect with – a few years back now – has been the curry crew. We may only meet once a month, but I find myself looking forward to those evenings immensely. The conversation always flows, it's always stimulating and amusing, and the food is only the icing on the cake (if curry can be said to be any kind of icing).

I have a small number of friends that fall into another different category. All of the aforementioned might be classed as "regular" friends, and if such a term fits then this small number I'm talking about now might correspondingly be referred to as "irregular" friends. People who, over the years, have meandered in and out of my life seemingly at random, but who whenever we meet will pick up the threads of friendship (and even conversation!) and knit them back into something recognisable within a few hours. I met one such person outside a hotel once, a few years back. Having not seen him for more than five years, suddenly there he was, leaving a hotel at which I had arrived to meet someone else. We only had chance for twenty minutes frantic catching up and exchanging of current contact details, but it rekindled some long-buried memories and the spark of yet another friendship stretching back to the mid 1970s. We originally met at university and the names of other uni friends crop up regularly in the strangest places. Naturally the Internet is the perfect medium for this and over the years I've had the occasional email from old friends who've read this blog, or seen my profile on LinkedIn, or Friends Reunited, or found my website through Google.

There is a downside to this though. The reality of how easy it is to lose touch with people was brought home to me when I attended a school reunion about 15 years ago. It was such a strange experience I vowed never to attend one again (although I was tempted a couple of years back when they held a 25th – or was it 30th? – reunion). Not only the experience – spending 3 or 4 hours in a function room with 50 people who at one time I saw on a daily basis but who, with one exception, I hadn't seen for 15 years – but the aftermath. The impact of the realisation that I had completely lost touch with all of them, even those I'd thought of as close friends, really hit me surprisingly hard. I guess it just shows that friends are more than simply people you spend time with. Just as it's easy to be lonely in a crowded room, rubbing shoulders with a bunch of people every day for six years doesn't necessarily make them your friends. It knocked me for six a bit, did that.

Author's Notes

Friends Reunited? Good grief, that alone dates this post, doesn't it? And to mention that in favour of Facebook? Weird. Even at the time of writing, I'd been on Facebook for 5 years. Still, ten years on, everything about this piece of personal insight remains true. The curry crew are still meeting, as are the "Nottingham" mates (coincidentally we are, in fact, meeting up for lunch with two of them on the very day I'm writing this). My website contact form has recently been the source of renewed acquaintance with someone I worked with fifteen years ago, and who has now read, enjoyed, and more importantly (for me) reviewed, all of my books. Life, eh? Always finds a new way to surprise you. And a constant source of new, or possibly rekindled, friendship.

Day 100: Endings

[this post is a continuation of the story begun in "Introductions" on Day 1 of the writing challenge]

"Steven? It is Steven, isn't it?"

"Yes."

Steven looked puzzled, in that way people have when trying to put a name to a face. Like their brain is so occupied with the task it forgets to hold any kind of expression in the facial muscles and they adopt a default position which usually looks either vague or cross.

"Gerald, is it?"

"Nigel."

"Ah yes, of course. Nigel. And we met...?"

"At her book launch. Seems impossible to believe it was only nine months ago, give or take. And now–"

He stared at the coffin lying under a scarlet velvet blanket at the other end of the chapel. His eyes widened.

"Scarlet? Hardly appropriate, is it?"

"Appropriate? What could be more appropriate! You did read her book did you? Or are you just another one of those hangers-on?"

"Oh, I see. Scarlet as in Scarlette. Scarlette Mendellsohn. Well, I suppose that clears up any debate about whether her heroine had an autobiographical element."

"Good grief," exclaimed Steven, tossing his head. "It does nothing of the sort. Look here, what are you doing here? Are you related, or something? I find it hard to believe she would have anyone so... obtuse... as a friend."

"No, not related. I did mention it when we last met, but I could hardly expect you to remember. We worked together on a magazine once. Fellow writers. Kept in touch. Occasionally."

"So you just thought you'd come along to see off a rival, did you?"

Nigel took a step back.

"I don't know why you're being so aggressive. This is a funeral, for God's sake. I remember you now. You were the same at the launch. I thought at first it was nerves, or you didn't like crowds, or something like that. But you're just an obnoxious twerp really aren't you?"

"Yes, it is a funeral. So you might take your own advice and relax a bit. I'm sorry if my attempt at humour fell on stony ground. It does get me into trouble more often that not. To my mind a funeral's exactly the right place for black comedy."

"Well, really!"

"Oh don't get all upset. She wouldn't want that. What do you think that scarlet blanket is all about. It's not just an homage to her heroine, who she invested with every strength she aspired to in life. It's a statement. A declaration that today is not about mourning, it's about celebrating."

"Celebrating her life? How predictable."

"Not just her life. Ours. The fact that life goes on."

"In the midst of life we are in death?"

"It's more the other way round. Even though we're surrounded by death, we're all still alive. Yes, we'll all miss her, of course we will. Some more than others," Steven said, looking sharply at Nigel, "but we shouldn't get lost in grief when there's so much to be grateful for."

"Like what?"

"Are you serious? Look around! To take one obvious example: her book. She's left that for us. It's full of life lessons you know, if you could but read between the lines."

"I haven't."

"I didn't think you had."

"No, read the book I meant. You asked me earlier if I'd read it. I haven't."

"Well you should."

"It's a bit late now."

"What for? You wouldn't be reading it to tell her what you thought."

"I probably wouldn't have done that anyway if I'm honest. I never really liked her writing when we worked together. I always found it a bit twee."

"Twee? Twee!?"

"Sorry, maybe it's just me."

"I'm pretty sure it is just you. Everyone we know loved her writing and took every opportunity to tell her so."

"That's nice."

"You don't sound convinced."

"Don't mind me. I have a particular sensitivity to sycophancy."

"Now who's being aggressive?"

"I'm not being aggressive, just stating a fact. I can smell it. Makes my nose itch to tell you the truth. Did you really like her writing?"

"Yes!"

"Really?"

"Well, not all of it maybe. But most of it was good."

"Most?"

"Well, some."

"How much?"

"Oh, all right. I hated it. But she was one of my best friends. I could hardly tell her the truth now, could I?"

"And exactly what gives you the right to call yourself one of her best friends if you couldn't tell her the plain truth?"

"It's only my opinion. Everyone else loves it!"

"Or they're all in the same boat as you. They hate it really, but they think you love it."

"Hardly matters now anyway, does it?"

"That depends very much on what you believe. Because if there's an after-life then she'll be up there right now, seething about the fact that you hated her writing and you never had the guts to tell her."

"I'm an atheist."

"And yet here you are, in church."

"It's expected."

"What is?"

"Coming to the funeral. Singing a few songs."

"Saying a few prayers."

"I mumble through that bit."

"I expect you mime to the songs too, do you?"

Steven blushed.

"Thought so. So you pretended you liked her book, pretend to sing and pray at her funeral. And you reckon you were her best friend. God help her, she's better off dead.

Author's Notes

I'd planned this post from quite a long way out. I thought it was a great idea to "bookend" the whole 100 days with the same two characters, drawn together in the first instance by the book launch, and then later the writer's funeral. As I mentioned in the Author's Notes to Day 1, I did (do) know a writer who fits the description, so I should quickly add – because there's a slim but finite chance that she will read this and perhaps even recognise the connection – that (a) she's not dead, and (b) I always loved her writing. At least those small parts of her quite extensive oeuvre that I read.

So with that out of the way, the second thing I loved about this piece was the opportunity it gave to peer beneath the blanket of sycophancy and bogus bootlicking that infects so much of our society. The story only took that direction when it was halfway through. I spotted the chance, and snatched it. I remember reading a science fiction short many years ago where the population wore implants in the middle of their foreheads that glowed different colours to indicate their mood. It was impossible to get away with lying – the implant would give you away – and as a result all dissembling, or prevarication, or equivocation, was absent. Everyone told the truth, all the time.

Notes from an Editor's perspective

"It does get me into trouble more often that not." There's that common drafting tic of mine again – mistyping "than" as "that". Fortunately another example of a slip that is now caught by grammar checkers.

100 Themes Writing Challenge – Lessons Learned

So there you have it. 100 days; 100 themes; 100 posts. Some of them linked (quite pleased with the way I managed to do that, and how they've turned out), some of them work better than others (yes, there are a few turkeys) but in a way it's a bit like photography. Professional photographers take hundreds of shots to guarantee capturing the one, or two that really pop. Professional writers write hundreds of pieces (and/or go through hundreds of edits) and only really hit the mark a few times (unless they're geniuses).

And remember none of those 100 pieces I've written in the days since July 28 have been edited. They're all first draft, written off the cuff, with only the vaguest notion of what I was going to write about at the beginning and often including ideas that dropped into my head as I was writing.

So there's the first lesson…

Lesson 1: running out of steam, or full steam ahead?

Without a firm writing plan it's easy to dry up, even in half an hour! You feel as though there's no mileage left in the idea, or maybe you've taken it down a dead end, or it wasn't such a great idea in the first place. But whatever the idea was, it must have felt good enough to write about to start with. So more time spent plotting would (maybe) have uncovered the dead ends and the dross. On the other hand – again maybe – you just have to try writing it out to prove that it doesn't work so well.

And then just occasionally I'd hit on an idea that felt as though I could keep writing much longer than half an hour. It didn't take long for me to get a feel for 30 minutes, which is why some of the early stories stop in mid sentence but later on I was able to bring them to a satisfying (if cliff-hangery) conclusion. On a handful of occasions I reached this point after much less than 30 minutes, and if this happened I didn't force it.

Lesson 2: The more you write, the more you want to write

I had a particular reason for wanting to get in front of my schedule: I was away for the last week of October/first two days of November. This meant I needed at least 5 posts in hand, but because this enforced absence also came right at the end of the challenge, I wanted those tail-end posts done too. I didn't want to come home exhausted from a week in London and have to sit right down and bang out another two posts. So all told, I needed to be ahead of the game by seven days. What I found as I completed those extra posts was how easily I could write two a day rather than one. Some days three in one day. By the time I wrote post #100, I was 21 days ahead. And on (notional) day #101, with no prompt, I quite missed the impetus of "having" to write. Which brings us on to lesson 3...

Lesson 3 (a good one for us procrastinators): JFDI

Having not only a pre-defined theme but also the public declaration, or commitment, to write something every day is a great enabler. Out of the ~80 days I actually spent writing I can remember less than half-a-dozen when I really "didn't feel like it." Ordinarily, on days like that, I wouldn't have bothered. But I felt the need to keep up – with the momentum and my growing stash of scheduled posts – so I made a start with the next theme and after only a few minutes I would usually find myself getting into it. Making a start is the thing.

After writing post #100, I gave myself a break.

Legitimately I feel – we all need some time off even from the things we love doing – but even so, another ten days elapsed before I got around to writing any follow-ups in terms of these "lessons learned". No impetus at that point, see? So I was acutely aware of the danger that I would fall back into my old habits of spending days on end not writing anything. I needed another trick to get me started every day. I had proved how easy it is to write a lot (see Lesson #4) with even only a short commitment of time, now all I needed was a reason – a good enough reason – to do it. I've never had an editor-imposed deadline, or an agent-imposed publication target. It all has to come from me.

Lesson 4: 100 days worth of word count

Quite a revelation, this. I wasn't but a week or so into the challenge when it occurred to me (OK, sometimes I can be a bit slow) that it would be a good idea to keep track of how much I was writing. Regular readers will not be surprised to read that I graphed this up:

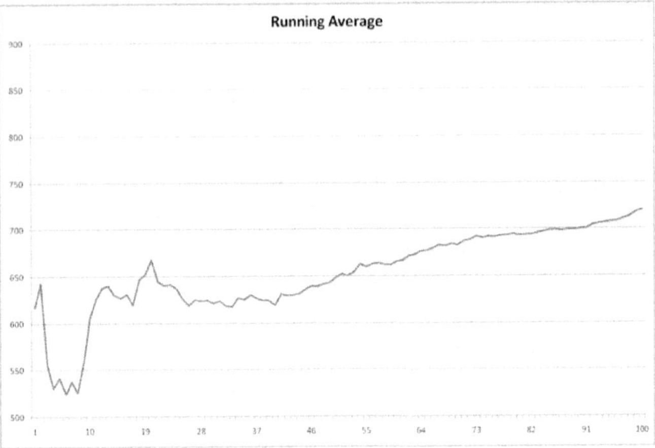

Allowing time for the average to establish itself, it's clear that as I got into my stride, my average word count increased through the challenge, ending up at 720 words for half an hour's writing. That's overall – from all 100 posts.

The fact that I became more prolific, word-wise, over the 100 themes is even more clearly demonstrated by a graph of a sliding 10-day average word count:

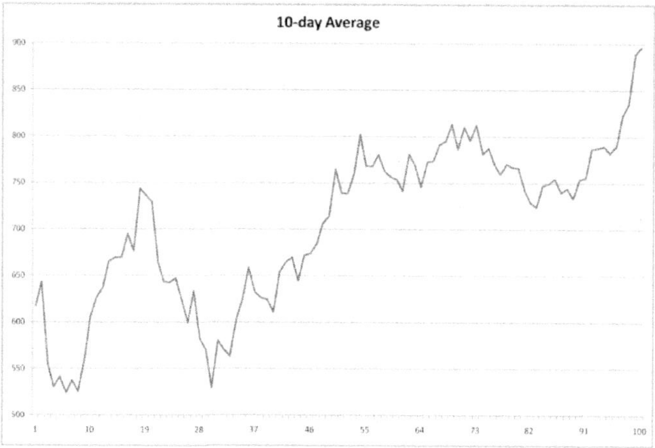

As you would expect this line bounces around a lot more, but shows an even clearer increase in my output in the last quartile, peaking on the last day at an average of 897 words for the previous ten days.

Obviously, it's not all about the numbers. But leaving everything else aside for the moment, the lesson here is that, with only half an hour's effort per day, in 100 days I could have the equivalent of the first draft of a novel. My first novel, War of Nutrition, is about 80,000 words. That's 800 words a day for 100 days – easily what I was achieving in the latter half of my challenge. Bringing back all that stuff I left aside before, it would still need plotting, character development, editing, and all those good things. I'm not pretending anyone, least of all me, could just sit down and write a novel in half an hour a day for 100 days (although, you know, many tens of thousands of people are attempting to do just that this month, if they're taking part in NaNoWriMo). But it certainly shouldn't take anywhere near seven years ;0)

For an update on daily word counts, see "Later Lessons Learned" below.

Lesson 5: You can write something about anything

Finally, although as I mentioned earlier what I wrote for some themes worked better than others, it's obviously possible to write on any given topic. Even those you wouldn't normally consider writing about. Some will be shorter, some not good enough to keep, but there'll be some hidden gems in there too. Among my 100 I had a fair crop of rough diamonds. To be sure, they would need polishing and developing if I were to (for instance) include them in a collection of short stories, but when I started this back in July I didn't have anything. Now I have starting points for at least a dozen strong stories.

Later Lessons Learned

If you've reached this point you'll be thoroughly familiar with the fact that much of the writing in here is ten years old. I've learned a lot in those ten years, published three more books with a fourth currently in the editing phase, and five more planned.

I've made contact with the indie author community, learned how to create and manage advertising (in a small way), and a host of other things, but in the particular context of this work, the biggest surprise to me was the discovery of what is known as "rapid release."

It's a huge topic, way beyond the scope of my little book, and with a wealth of material – both free and paid – available to anyone interested in exploring in depth how to pump books out in quick succession.

But the headline is, my "revelation" that it's possible to write around 800-1000 words in half an hour (i.e. 2,000 words per hour) is not news to a lot of people. They do it on a regular basis. They have ways – call them what you will: "mechanisms"; "processes"; "tricks"; "habits" – that enable them to achieve those levels of output consistently. And when they hit 2,000 words an hour, and write for (for example) five hours a day, then that 80,000 word novel is only going to take them 8 days.

And just in case your mind still isn't blown by that, remember that in some genres, 80,000 is a long book. I write fantasy, so a novel that size is small by comparison. The largest volume of The Berikatanyan Chronicles weighs in at 150,000 words. But in these days of short attention spans, limited reading time, and voracious readers, many genres "expect" shorter work. Anything between 40,000 and 60,000 is perfectly fine. So now we're looking at finishing a book every "working week", with two days off at the weekend (to organise covers, editors, beta-readers, etc). 50 books a year! That is what they mean by rapid release.

Clearly that's an extreme case, but I regularly see authors posting in the online groups on reaching the end of their tenth, twentieth, or occasionally thirtieth book "this year."

For the avoidance of doubt, this approach is not for me. If you are waiting for my next book you know not to expect it this side of Christmas (whenever you're reading this, lol). But there's no doubt it's "do-able" and there is also strong evidence that Amazon and its famous algorithms reward this approach with lots of attention, promotion, and increased presence in things like "also-bought" lists and so on.

And Finally…

I hope you've enjoyed reading this. But more than that, I hope it will inspire you on your own writing journey, whether you're already on it, or yet to take your first step.

"Imposter Syndrome" is a very well known mental hang-up for anyone, but especially for authors. You may be surprised that even long-standing, very successful, and hugely famous writers like Stephen King and Lee Child still suffer from it to some degree. So perhaps even more understandable to suffer from feelings of inadequacy before you've even published your first story.

An exercise such as the one I've described here can help. Most people can find 30 minutes a day somewhere. Lunch time, early morning, late evening. It doesn't matter when. And proving to yourself that Lesson #5 – you can write something about anything – applies just as much to you as it does to me, is a strong weapon to use against that Imposter Syndrome.

Good luck!

John Beresford
November, 2022

Appendix 1

Order of clichés/cultural references in Day 41:

1. It was a hot afternoon, the last day of June, and the sun was a demon;
2. a fork in the road;
3. step up to the plate;
4. the road less travelled;
5. cooking on gas;
6. a watched pot never boils;
7. a lot on his plate;
8. biting off more than he can chew;
9. barking up the wrong tree;
10. driving me up the wall;
11. burn rubber;
12. taking candy from a baby;
13. put that in your pipe and smoke it;
14. kill two birds with one stone;
15. stop and smell the roses;
16. gone in the blink of an eye;
17. it's not the heat, it's the humidity;
18. draw a line in the sand;
19. rearrange the deck chairs (on the Titanic);
20. still waters run deep;
21. it's all water under the bridge;
22. cross that bridge when we come to it;
23. the grass is always greener on the other side;
24. take the high road;
25. preaching to the choir;
26. light at the end of the tunnel

About The Author

Since the first time a story of his made the rest of the English class screw up their faces in horror and disgust, John Beresford wanted nothing more than to write. He was 12. Later that year he came second in a sponsored writing competition with a short story about how the Sphinx is really a quiescent guardian against alien invaders. He won £10. That was big bucks in 1968.

For more than three decades, real life stepped in between him and his writing. During a 38-year career in computing he wrote dozens of design documents, created and delivered presentations to audiences from 1,000 technical experts to a handful of board members, interviewed innumerable technical candidates and taught core skills and development subjects to many younger colleagues through both formal courses and ad-hoc coaching. But all that was really just a way to hone skills that might be useful as a writer. And, of course, to pay the bills and support the family. A man's gotta do...

In 2001 John woke up to the passage of time and decided to get serious about writing before it was too late. His first novel – War of Nutrition – took 7 years of spare time to write and was published for Kindle in 2012.

Since beginning that first novel, John has also created work as a songwriter, screenwriter, freelance TV reviewer and playwright. Now retired from the computing industry, he completed his fantasy trilogy The Berikatanyan Chronicles in 2021 and is now working on a second trilogy set in the same world.

Also by John Beresford:

The Berikatanyan Chronicles Series

Gatekeeper
Water Wizard
Juggler

Other Work

War of Nutrition

Well of Love

Valentine Wine

Connect with John online:

Facebook:	https://www.facebook.com/garretguy
Twitter:	https://twitter.com/#!/garretguy
Web site:	http://www.johnberesford.com/

Printed in Great Britain
by Amazon

49001304R00229